DEMOCRATIC POLITICS
AND SECTIONALISM

The Wilmot Proviso Controversy

DEMOCRATIC
POLITICS
AND
SECTIONALISM

The Wilmot Proviso Controversy

by

CHAPLAIN W. MORRISON

The University of North Carolina Press
Chapel Hill

To my wife, Claudia

Preface

JUDGING BY THE FUROR IT CREATED, THE ISSUE OF SLAVERY IN the territories was one of the most significant in American history. Not only did it give birth to the only major political party to emerge in the United States since the time of Andrew Jackson, the struggles it engendered culminated in southern secession and civil war. While the development of this issue in the 1850's has been subjected to careful scrutiny by historians, relatively little attention has been given to its origin and early progress, which is the subject of this book.

Essentially, the early history of the territorial issue is part of the history of the Democratic party in the late 1840's. Against the background provided by the contest over the annexation of Texas, the issue emerged full-blown when the Wilmot Proviso was generated out of the intraparty struggles. The continued agitation of the Wilmot Proviso question by factions within the party forced the national party leaders to deal with the territorial issue, something that the Whig leadership was able to avoid. In their efforts to avert party disruption, the Democratic leaders advanced every alternative ever suggested to a direct confrontation of the territorial issue, but not even the most **palatable** of these alternatives, the doctrine of popular sovereignty, proved acceptable to the voters in the election of 1848. The failure of the Democratic party to find a solution to the territorial issue in the 1840's clearly presaged the failure in 1860-61. A study of the earlier failure is therefore valuable not simply for its own sake as a study of Democratic politics, but for the light it throws upon the disunion crisis as well.

A considerable portion of the research which went into this work was made possible by a research grant from Washington and Lee University, for which I should like to express my appreciation. I should also like to thank Dr. Edwin Hemphill, editor of the South Caroliniana Library at the University of South Carolina. Dr. Hemphill, who is editing the papers of John C. Calhoun, gave me full access to the enormous number of photostats of letters to and from Calhoun collected at the South Caroliniana Library from various depositories around the country. Finally, I should like to acknowledge permission from the Butler Library at Columbia University to quote from the letters of John A. Dix, and from Prentice-Hall, Inc., to quote from Kenneth M. Stampp (ed.), *The Causes of the Civil War.*

Contents

DEMOCRATIC POLITICS
AND SECTIONALISM
The Wilmot Proviso Controversy

CHAPTER I

The Background
of the
Wilmot Proviso

IN AUGUST OF 1846 THE DEMOCRATIC ADMINISTRATION OF James Knox Polk seemed on its way to becoming one of the most successful in American history. In the year and a half since his inauguration, the President had accomplished three of his four major objectives.[1] He had induced Congress to pass an act establishing an independent Treasury, a measure which had become an article of the Democratic faith since its proposal by President Martin Van Buren in 1837. He had managed to settle the controversy with England over the Oregon territory, if not to the satisfaction of some of his Democratic supporters, at least to the general satisfaction of the nation as a whole. And he had just pushed through Congress a new tariff measure which effectively repudiated the protection principle. At the same time, the prospects appeared favorable for attaining his fourth objective, the acquisition of California and New Mexico.

Polk believed that the time was ripe for reopening peace negotiations with Mexico. He felt that the weak and bankrupt

Mexican government was now prepared to accept a final settlement of the war in which it would cede the desired territory in return for a financial remuneration. But he recognized that such a treaty, which would be very unpopular with the Mexican people, would subject their already tottering government to the danger of a revolution that would probably lead in turn to a repudiation of the treaty. It was therefore necessary to proceed with caution. Polk wanted Congress to appropriate without debate $2,000,000 to allow him to take advantage of the opportunity. The $2,000,000 would be used as the first installment of whatever payment to Mexico might be agreed upon in a treaty. This immediate payment would enable the Mexican government to pay the army, which was the key to power in Mexico, and thus maintain its control of the country.[2] But the effectiveness of the $2,000,000 appropriation as an inducement to the Mexican government to negotiate would depend upon the speed and secrecy with which the appropriation was made. Polk therefore was disappointed when the Whigs in the Senate demanded that he assume official responsibility for the measure by sending a confidential message recommending the appropriation to the House of Representatives as well as to the Senate. Since the President thought that a confidential message to the House would arouse great public attention, and since the contents of the message would soon become public knowledge in any case, he decided instead to submit a message to Congress in open session.[3] In spite of the developing Whig opposition, he still hoped for immediate congressional action. Since the Congress had only two more days to sit before it adjourned, there would be little time in which to debate the measure.

Polk had failed, however, to take into account the growing dissatisfaction with his administration within his own party in Congress. The very triumphs of the administration—the annexation of Texas, the Oregon settlement, and the tariff act of 1846 —as well as Polk's selection of the cabinet, intensified this dissatisfaction, which had originated in his own nomination for the presidency back in the spring of 1844.

The leading Democratic candidate for the nomination in 1844, prior to the meeting of the national convention, had been former President Van Buren; but at the convention southern and western Democrats, led by Robert J. Walker of Mississippi, deserted Van Buren, ostensibly because of his opposition to the immediate annexation of Texas. The convention had finally united on Polk, as an annexationist who was otherwise unobjectionable to the Van Buren supporters. The hard core of Van Buren's Democratic following was centered in his home state of New York, but it also extended into New England, Pennsylvania, and Ohio. It was this faction, in general, which resented southern domination of the party and was most hostile to the South's peculiar institution, slavery.[4] Although the Van Buren Democrats supported Polk in the presidential campaign, the convention's action in setting aside their leader for yet another southerner rankled. The events of the next two years intensified their bad feeling. They objected to the extension of slavery which the proposed admission of Texas into the Union would bring, an objection which had been a decisive factor in Van Buren's decision to oppose immediate annexation.[5]

In the spring of 1844, when Secretary of State John C. Calhoun, the archdefender of the slave system, placed the justification of annexation on the grounds of defense of the "peculiar institution," Van Buren Democrats joined the Whig opposition in overwhelmingly defeating the treaty of annexation submitted to the Senate by the Tyler administration. When Congress reassembled in December, after Polk had been elected, the renewed efforts of the Tyler administration to annex Texas precipitated a sectional clash over the extension of slave territory, a sort of dress rehearsal for the later Wilmot Proviso struggle.[6]

The administration proposed to annex Texas by joint resolution of Congress in order to avoid the treaty requirement for a two-thirds majority in the Senate, rendered virtually unattainable by Whig opposition. Van Buren Democrats objected to the measure as designed to extend slavery and increase the political power of the proslavery interests, headed by Calhoun. On the other hand, they maintained that they were not opposed to annexation per se.[7] As an alternative to the administration bill, Thomas Hart Benton, Van Buren's leading supporter in the Senate and a bitter enemy of Calhoun, proposed that a new treaty be negotiated with Texas, admitting the settled area as a state and dividing the remaining territory into free and slave portions along the 36° 30' line of the Missouri Compromise.[8]

In the House of Representatives, action on the joint resolution was delayed by the antislavery Democrats, under the leadership of Preston King of New York, a short, chubby man whose amiable appearance and manner belied his firmness on matters of principle.[9] Confident they could block the passage of the administration's proposal, the Van Burenites refrained at first for tactical reasons from openly stating these objections in Congress.[10] Nevertheless, early in January, one of the members from New Hampshire, John P. Hale, after conferring with King, issued an address to his constituents in which he undertook to prove "the perpetuation of slavery to be the origin and object" of annexation. King's idea was to have Hale "fire at slavery, being as careful not to hit Texas as possible, under the circumstances."[11] Hale then tried to introduce an amendment to the joint resolutions dividing Texas into equal portions of slave and free territory, but the requisite two-thirds majority to suspend the rules for such a purpose was not available.[12] Finally, after the slavery question had been injected into the debate by a number of southern and northern Whig speakers, Jacob Brinkerhoff of Ohio explicitly stated the objections of the Van Buren Democrats to annexation: "[Annexation] was not a national question. It was a sectional question, hatched and got up as a southern question, for the benefit of the South; for the strengthening of her institutions; for the promotion of her power; for her benefit, for the advancement of her influence."[13] George Rathbun, one of two other Van Burenites who made speeches opposing the acquisition of Texas on antislavery grounds, maintained that a second Missouri crisis was at hand. Rathbun denounced a report that the incoming administration would punish the opponents of annexation through its use of the patronage and reminded his fellow northerners of the political demise of the northern dough-faces who had sold their votes to the South during the first Missouri crisis.[14] In the meantime, Representative Orville Robinson had proposed a measure which defined the terms on which the Van Burenites desired annexation: the prohibition of slavery in *all* of Texas except the area to be admitted as a state.[15]

In order to bypass the antislavery opposition to the joint resolution, Democratic advocates of unqualified annexation agreed to accept a compromise measure sponsored by a group of southern Whigs, which admitted the entire area of Texas as a state but provided that up to four additional states might be formed out of the territory in the future, with slavery permitted in the ones located south of the 36° 30' line and prohibited in the one or more located north of the line. With eight affirmative southern Whig votes, the House passed the bill, although twenty-seven Van Buren Democrats voted against it.[16] Thirteen of these votes were given by members from New York, where antislavery opposition was particularly strong. Preston King wrote to Van Buren that it was his belief that the Democrats would "fall in every free state except Illinois" if the party were "made responsible for legalizing slavery in the whole of Texas."[17] Local Democratic politicians in New York denounced the House measure as "a cheat and a fraud," and only the strenuous efforts of governor-elect Silas Wright on behalf of party harmony prevented the Democratic legislature from passing resolutions condemning the House bill.[18]

In the Senate, where the Whigs had a slight majority and every Democratic vote was needed to pass an annexation measure, strong pressure was brought to bear on the Van Buren men to yield to the compromise.[19] Partly in response to this pressure, Benton proposed a new alternative early in February which called for the immediate admission of the settled part of Texas as a state and a renegotiation with Texas of the terms of annexation for the remainder of the territory.[20] The Van Buren Democrats, who did not wish to be alienated from the incoming administration on the annexation question and who expected the renegotiation of a treaty to produce a reasonable compromise on the slavery question, were willing to accept Benton's new proposal;[21] but Calhoun and his followers, and other friends of annexation as well, objected that the delay and uncertainty which renegotiation would entail would effectively defeat acquisition.[22]

Shortly after Benton's move, Senator Robert J. Walker tried to harmonize the party's efforts by combining the House measure with Benton's bill, giving Texas the choice between them.[23] But John A. Dix, the Van Burenite Senator from New York, continued to hold out for a more satisfactory settlement from an antislavery point of view. Finally, after obtaining assurances from President-elect Polk that he would implement the Benton alternative if the decision were left to him, Dix agreed to the combination bill provided the President and not Texas were given the option.[24] This was done, and the measure passed the Senate by a vote of twenty-seven to twenty-five, three southern Whigs joining the Democrats to provide a majority.[25] When the bill was returned to the House, the Van Burenites, who had already signified their approval of Dix's course, helped to pass it.[26] The question of whether Tyler might not act before Polk's inauguration elicited from George MacDuffie of South Carolina, who it was assumed could speak for the Tyler administration, the assurance that such action was unthinkable.[27]

After failing to block the move to combine the two annexation measures, Calhoun determined that the Tyler administration should opt for the House alternative before Polk was inaugurated, thereby committing its successor to that course of action.[28] Accordingly, Calhoun persuaded Tyler, on the last day of the outgoing administration, to authorize him to send instructions to the American envoy in Mexico to implement the House plan for admitting the entire area of Texas as a state. Tyler insisted upon first consulting Polk, but the President-elect refused to express a preference between the two alternatives.[29] Nevertheless, on March 7, three days after his inauguration, Polk wrote a private letter to the American envoy in Texas, telling him not to act on Calhoun's instructions but to wait for further orders which would probably modify them.[30] New instructions awaited the first meeting of the cabinet on March 10. The unanimous opinion of the cabinet was that the action of the previous administration should be confirmed in order to avoid confusion and delay, which might be fatal to annexation. Despite his previous assurance to Dix, Polk concurred in this opinion and had official instructions sent to the American envoy ordering him to extend to Texas the offer of immediate annexation as a state.[31]

The Van Burenites, evidently recognizing the futility of further opposition, made no mention of Polk's breach of faith. In September, Van Buren himself wrote one of his followers, in a letter which was subsequently published, that annexation was "so far consummated under the constituted authorities of both governments as to render all factional agitation of the question or obstacles to its completion highly inexpedient."[32] When called upon to confirm annexation at the next session of Congress, the entire Democratic delegation from New York, with the exception of Preston King and two others, voted to do so.[33] Notwithstanding this acquiescence, the outcome of the annexation struggle, with slavery legalized throughout Texas, made the Van Burenites more sensitive than ever on the slavery question and inclined them to suspect Polk of bad faith.[34]

These suspicions appeared confirmed by Polk's selection of the cabinet.[35] Van Buren's supporters in his home state of New York expected to be rewarded for their successful efforts in the campaign by the appointment of a New Yorker to either the first or second cabinet post, Secretary of State or Secretary of the Treasury. The President-elect did offer the Treasury position to Silas Wright, Van Buren's closest political associate in New York; but Wright, who had resigned as senator to run for governor at the insistence of the New York Democrats, considered himself honor bound to serve in the state office. After Wright's refusal, Polk wrote to Van Buren asking his advice about a New York appointment. Van Buren suggested the selection of Benjamin F. Butler for the State Department or else Azariah C. Flagg or Churchill C. Cambreleng for the Treasury Department. Wright gave Polk similar advice.

By this time, however, Polk had become aware of the strong anti-Van Buren feeling in the national party which extended into New York itself. Yielding to this pressure, Polk passed over New York and chose James Buchanan and Robert J. Walker for the first two cabinet posts. Walker's appointment was particularly obnoxious to the Van Burenites because of his role in the nominating convention. Van Buren tartly stated these objections in a letter to Polk in which he strongly urged that Polk appoint Butler Secretary of War, and, in order to expedite matters, offered to guarantee Butler's acceptance. Instead of mailing the letter, however, he notified Polk that he would send it to him via his son Smith as soon as he had consulted Wright.[36] In the meantime, Polk, acting on his own initiative, had already offered the War Department to Butler and sent another letter to Van Buren urging him to use his influence to get Butler to accept. But Butler, who had wanted to be Secretary of State, refused the offer.

Considering himself absolved of the obligation to consult Van Buren, Polk then turned to William L. Marcy, who once had been a close ally of Van Buren's, but who was now the leading politician in New York associated with the conservative Democratic faction unfriendly to the former President. This faction had been strongly urging Marcy's claims, suggesting to Polk that his views were more compatible with those of the President-elect, particularly on the Texas question, than those of any appointee that Van Buren and Wright would recommend.[37] Marcy did his part by professing adherence to the principles of the incoming administration in a letter to Daniel S. Dickinson, conservative Democratic Senator from New York, which was shown to Polk.[38] Evidently this consideration, and the pressing need to complete the cabinet immediately, outweighed the strenuous objections the Van Burenites in Washington raised against Marcy. In spite of a promise to wait for Van Buren's letter, Polk went ahead and appointed Marcy. Van Buren's letter of protest, already outdistanced by events, arrived too late to change the situation. Polk's precipitate selection of Marcy, coming on top of his appointments to the State and Treasury Departments, infuriated Van Buren and his followers. They were now convinced that the President had betrayed them, and his attempt to divide the patronage in New York equitably between the two factions only strengthened this belief.[39]

The administration's settlement of the Oregon question also antagonized many Van Burenites, as well as many other northern Democrats. Probably the most significant development in the Oregon dispute was the extent to which the Oregon question, which was apparently totally divorced from the slavery issue, became entangled with the sectional conflict within the Democratic party. The origin of this development was the linkage of the Oregon with the Texas question in the Democratic platform of 1844, which called for the reannexation of Texas and the reoccupation of the entire Oregon territory up to the line of 54° 40'. After the British government rejected Polk's offer for a compromise settlement on Oregon at the 49th parallel, the President adopted the extreme position of the Democratic Platform in his first message to Congress in December of 1845.[40] Northern Democratic advocates of 54° 40', particularly those from the Northwest who had consistently supported the southern move to annex Texas, were pleased at this support for their position from the administration and expected the southern wing of the party to follow the President's lead.[41]

Southern Democrats were extremely reluctant to support the extreme claim in Oregon, however. They responded positively when John C. Calhoun, fearful of a war with England, returned to the Senate from South Carolina to assume the leadership in obtaining a compromise settlement at the 49th parallel.[42] On December 30, 1845, Calhoun proposed to amend resolutions offered by Senator Edward A. Hannegan of Indiana asserting the United States claim to the entire Oregon Territory to approve the President's earlier offer to England to compromise the dispute.[43] Hannegan responded with a protest against the bad faith of the South on the Oregon question: "Texas and Oregon were born in the same instant, nursed and cradled in the same cradle—the Baltimore Convention—and they were at the same instant adopted by the democracy throughout the land. There was not a moment's hesitation, until Texas was admitted; but the moment she was admitted the peculiar friends of Texas turned and were doing all they could to strangle Oregon."[44] In the House of Representatives impediments to action on Oregon raised by southerners caused Stephen A. Douglas to complain that "there seemed to be a game playing to object to the Oregon bill when it came up." "There now appeared to be a great terror in the Oregon question," continued Douglas, "that made gentlemen shrink from it, who had met the Texas question boldly and without shrinking last year."[45]

The Van Burenites were prepared to capitalize on the feeling that the South was acting in bad faith. The day after Douglas' remarks, Preston King offered an explanation of southern action. King used a quotation from the London *Times* to suggest that Calhoun had committed himself to a compromise settlement of the Oregon question in return for British acquiescence in the American annexation of Texas with slavery.[46] King made it clear that he was in favor of the claim to all Oregon and opposed to compromise. John Quincy Adams, Joshua R. Giddings, and other antislavery Whigs were also advocating the extreme claim to Oregon, on the ground that it would weaken the slave power. Calhoun believed that the ultimate purpose of these men was a war with England, "with the avowed intention of abolishing slavery," and he therefore interpreted King's move as a sign that the northern Democrats would follow their lead in an effort to compete with them for the abolitionists' vote.[47] The most noticeable effect of the Van Burenites' support for the 54° 40′ claim, however, was not to gain them the favor of the abolitionists but to place them at an advantage in competing with the southerners for the good will of the western Democrats.

The southerners were very concerned about the alienation

of their western allies on this issue and about the tendency of the westerners to turn to the Northeast for support. William Lowndes Yancey warned western Democrats that if war came the Northeast would fight only to acquire eastern Canada and not to sustain the full Oregon claims, intimating that the Van Burenites were looking after their own peculiar sectional interest.[48] Neither this nor the more familiar southern argument that the South's position was not a sign of hostility or bad faith was very convincing to the westerners.

The Polk administration's treaty with England settling the boundary at the 49th parallel was to many northern and western Democrats an indication of the President's duplicity and his willingness to sacrifice the interests of other sections to those of the South.[49] Moreover, the western conviction that the South had acted in bad faith tended to disrupt the southern-western alliance and undermine Democratic harmony.[50] Polk's veto of the Rivers and Harbors Bill, a special favorite of western Democrats, and the southern Democratic votes sustaining that veto added to this intraparty strain.[51] The result of all this was to give the dissatisfied Van Burenites an opportunity for mischief on the slavery question.

The Mexican War, which began in the spring of 1846, added a strong incentive to the Van Burenites' opportunity. The deepest source of dissatisfaction among the Van Buren faction was resentment over having been deprived of control of the party machinery on the Texas question by the alliance of southern and western politicians. Polk's replacement in the spring of 1845 of the official Democratic organ, Francis P. Blair's Washington *Globe,* with the Washington *Union,* to be edited by Thomas Ritchie, had removed the last vestige of the former Van Burenite dominance.[52] The outbreak of war with Mexico the following year brought the central issue of conflict to the surface again. Northern Whig charges that the war had resulted from the slaveholders' successful annexation policy reopened the Texas question as a political issue.[53] Moreover, the probability of new territorial acquisitions in the Southwest

seemed to foretell a further shift in the balance of power within
the Democratic party at the expense of the Van Burenites, while
at the same time making them more vulnerable than ever to the
charges of their Whig opponents that they were sacrificing northern interests to those of the slaveholding South. Van Buren himself had warned one of the members of the incoming administration of the political dangers of a war with Mexico the previous
spring:

Too much care cannot be taken to save us from a war, in respect to
which the opposition shall be able to charge us with plausibility, if
not truth, that it is waged for the extension of slavery. . . . [In such
a war] the Democracy of the Free States would, I very much fear,
be driven to the sad alternative of turning their backs upon their
friends, or of encountering political suicide with their eyes open.
Whilst therefore we perform to the uttermost the duties of political
fraternity to our southern allies, according to our known principles,
it behooves us as well as them to eschew all counsels which shall
necessarily involve us in such an issue.[54]

The events in New Hampshire in the summer of 1846 indicated the problems raised for northern Democrats by the coming of war. The situation of the party was peculiar there in that
an antislavery faction, under the leadership of John P. Hale,
had already split off on the Texas question and had just helped
to elect a Whig governor.[55] Hale used the state legislature as a
forum for charges that the Polk administration had annexed
Texas for the perpetuation of the institution of slavery and was
now waging war for the same reason.[56] The Democrats were
further embarrassed by resolutions pressed in the legislature by
Hale and his followers which committed the state to action within the limits of the constitution to effect "the suppression and
extermination of that terrible scourge of our race, slavery."[57]
Sensitive to charges of advancing the slaveholding interest, the
regular Democrats felt compelled to vote in favor of the resolutions which the legislature then ordered the governor to forward
to the other states.[58]

Outside of New Hampshire, however, the deep dissatisfaction among northeastern Democrats with the Polk administration generally and with its Mexican policy particularly did not openly manifest itself.[59] Although some Van Buren Democrats in Congress privately agreed with the charges of certain northern Whigs that the Polk government and its southern supporters were trying to acquire territory in the Southwest in order to extend slavery,[60] none chose to undertake the politically suicidal task of opposing the administration's war effort. Instead, John A. Dix, the Van Burenite senator from New York, sought assurances from Polk that he did not intend to annex any Mexican territory.[61]

A small group of Democratic congressmen who were highly suspicious of the President's war aims did attempt to embarrass the administration, however, by means of certain actions they took in connection with the Walker Tariff. These and other Van Buren Democrats had been displeased by the South's rejection in the House of their substitute measure which would have set certain duties somewhat higher than the administration desired.[62] But unlike their fellow Van Burenites, they expressed their hostility towards the South and what they felt was a "southern" administration by voting with the Whigs in several moves which threatened to defeat the administration bill when it came back to the House with minor amendments.[63] Despite these actions, the tariff was ultimately approved unchanged by the House, but not without arousing further resentment against the highhanded methods of the administration and its southern supporters in getting its measures approved.[64]

When Polk requested an appropriation of $2,000,000 on August 8, 1846, therefore, the request went to a House of Representatives full of northern Democrats who were angry with the administration for one reason or another. Among these Democrats was a small group of Van Buren dissidents, deeply suspicious of the President's war aims and prepared to exploit the antiadministration feeling to frustrate these aims. Polk's message asked for "an appropriation to provide for any expenditure which it may be necessary to make in advance for the purpose of settling all our difficulties with Mexico."[65] In this connection the message discussed only the dispute over the boundary between Mexico and Texas. It failed to mention the acquisition of additional territory upon which Polk was determined.[66] This omission was undoubtedly designed to lull the opponents of territorial expansion into approving the appropriation,[67] but the intentions of the administration had become too well known for it to succeed in that. Believing their suspicions of Polk's war aims fully confirmed by the request for an appropriation, the Van Buren dissidents voted with the Whigs to table the measure.[68] The combined strength of these two groups was not sufficient to prevent consideration of the bill, however, and when the House took a two-hour recess for dinner at three o'clock, it was made the next order on the agenda for that evening, with debate limited to two hours.[69]

During dinner, David Wilmot, one of the Van Buren dissidents who had voted to table the bill, conceived the idea of amending it so as to prohibit slavery in any territory which might be acquired from Mexico by virtue of the appropriation.[70] Originally a strong supporter of the administration, Wilmot had become more and more disenchanted with it during the session, gravitating into the hostile Van Buren clique. When Robert Dale Owen, an Indiana Democrat with whom Wilmot was eating, protested that the move would result in the defeat of the appropriation in the Senate, Wilmot replied "that he had rather see the Three [Two] Million Bill defeated, than to see it passed without the Proviso."[71] Wilmot's two other tablemates, Democrats from the Northeast, encouraged him to propose the amendment.[72]

After dinner Wilmot communicated his plan to other Van Burenite opponents of the appropriation, some of whom evidently already had the same idea.[73] The amendment appeared perfectly suited to their situation: it would enable them to fully exploit the northern Democratic resentment against the administration and the South created by the passage of the tariff, the compromise settlement in Oregon, and the veto of the Rivers and Harbors Bill.[74] Under the circumstances, few northern Democrats could be expected to go on record against freedom in the territories merely to avoid embarrassing the administration. These northern Democrats, combined with the northern Whigs, would produce sufficient votes to get the amendment adopted; and the vote on the amended bill would reveal, so the Van Buren dissidents thought, whether the southern Democratic desire for expansion was tainted with the desire to extend the institution of slavery.[75] If, as some of the Van Burenites suspected, it was so tainted and the southern Democrats proved it by voting against the amended bill, they would then identify *themselves* as the opponents of the orthodox Democratic doctrine of territorial expansion and yield to the Van Burenites their role as expansionistic allies of the western Democrats. If this should occur, the southern-western expansionist alliance within the Democratic party would be replaced by an antislavery expansionist alliance between northeastern and western Democrats.

Once Wilmot and his associates had ascertained that the amendment would be generally supported by northern Democrats, they reassembled on the House floor, after the session had been resumed, to put it in writing.[76] The northern Whigs, having learned of the scheme, were very anxious to have the Van Buren dissidents bring forward their amendment, if for no other purpose than to defeat the appropriation and with it territorial expansion.[77] The first speaker on the Two Million Bill, an antislavery Whig from New York, told the House: "I cannot give my sanction to this appropriation unless the bill now upon your table shall be so amended as to forever preclude the possibility of extending the limits of slavery. And I call upon gentlemen on the other side of the House to bring forward such amendments as shall prevent the further acquisition of territory which may be caused by the adoption of that institution."[78] He was not disappointed. Shortly afterward, Wilmot obtained the floor and submitted the amendment his group had agreed upon, which ultimately came to be known as the Wilmot Proviso. The wording of the amendment, modeled on that of the Northwest Ordinance of 1787, was as follows: "Provided, That, as an express and fundamental condition to the acquisition of any territory from the Republic of Mexico by the United States by virtue of any treaty which may be negotiated between them, and to the use by the Executive of the money herein appropriated, neither slavery nor involuntary servitude shall ever exist in any part of said territory except for crime, whereof the party shall first be duly convicted."[79]

In spite of its potential explosiveness, the amendment not only failed to produce an inflammatory debate but was given scant attention by the succeeding speakers. This was owing to the fact that it was treated more as a political maneuver than as an assault on the slavery institution; this being the case, there was still a natural reluctance to agitate the dangerous slavery question.[80] Although several southern congressmen privately registered violent protests against the introduction of the slavery question in this form,[81] they refrained from attacking Wilmot's proposal directly in order to avoid giving prominence to an issue which they wished to keep suppressed. The only southerner to mention the amendment argued only that it was "premature" and designed merely to defeat the appropriation.[82] Northern congressmen were equally circumspect. Speaking for the Van Buren dissidents, Bradford R. Wood expressed his distrust of the administration without specifically referring to slavery and announced that he and his group would oppose the appropriation if the amendment were not adopted.[83] Of the two northern Whigs who noticed the amendment, one took a line similar to Wood's.[84] The other was John Quincy Adams, whose antislavery principles had induced him to oppose the annexation of Texas. Notwithstanding these principles, Adams favored the acquisition of territory in the Southwest, just as he had previously favored the 50° 40' claim in Oregon, presumably because he thought expansion would weaken rather than strengthen the slaveholding interest. Adams said that although he would favor the amendment as a statement of principle, it was entirely unnecessary and he would vote for the appropriation with or without it. According to Adams, slavery was not only totally incompatible with the soil and the climate in the southwestern territory but, being prohibited by Mexican law, it could not be introduced there except by congressional enactment establishing the institution after the territory had been acquired.[85]

Whatever the merits of Adams' argument about the unimportance of the amendment, nearly every representative voted with his respective section on its adoption, and it was passed by the northern majority, in spite of a last-minute effort by the administration to defeat it.[86] With the complexion of the bill thus changed, the southern Democrats and a few of their staunchest allies in the Northwest now joined the southern Whigs in opposing the Two Million Bill. They wanted to defeat the amended bill and try again to get an unencumbered appropriation.[87] But the northern Whigs, whose principal aim was to strike at the administration's expansionistic war effort, voted again with the great bulk of the northern Democrats to pass the amended bill.[88]

The amended appropriation bill passed the House of Representatives on Saturday, August 8; Congress was due to adjourn on the tenth. On Sunday the administration leaders in Congress got together and concocted a scheme for getting the appropriation without the amendment. The House bill was to be defeated in the Senate, and the $2,000,000 appropriation added surreptitiously to the General Appropriation Bill. The opposition learned of this scheme, however, and was prepared to hold up the bill so that the plan had to be discarded.[89]

The administration forces made a final effort to get an unamended bill in the Senate on August 10. Shortly before adjournment, Senator Dixon H. Lewis of Alabama got the Senate to take up the House bill, whereupon he moved to strike out Wilmot's amendment. When John Davis, an antislavery Whig senator from Massachusetts, questioned the move, Lewis replied that there was no time for explanations. The plan was apparently to return the bill to the House with the amendment stricken out so late that the House would have no choice but to accept the unamended bill. Whether the votes were available to strike the amendment is a moot point, since Lewis' motion never came to a vote. Senator Davis, perceiving the strategy and believing a majority in the Senate to be favorably inclined toward it, proceeded to fillibuster. His intention was to postpone the vote long enough so that the Senate would have no choice but to accept the House bill. However, the clock in the Senate was eight minutes slower than that in the House, and by the time Davis was ready to yield the floor for the vote, the House had already adjourned, officially ending the session.[90] The $2,000,000 appropriation had been defeated by Wilmot's antislavery amendment.

CHAPTER II

The Articulation
of the
Wilmot Proviso Issue

ALTHOUGH THE SECTIONAL VOTE IN CONGRESS ON WILMOT'S
proviso prohibiting slavery in the territories reveals its potency
as a divisive issue, the significance of the event was little noted
at the time. The reaction of the administration organ, the Washington *Union,* is indicative of the general lack of awareness of
its sectional implications. The *Union,* obviously interested in
the proviso only as it affected the appropriation, was so slow to
recognize its significance that it somewhat naïvely interpreted
the Whig and Van Burenite votes for the amended bill as a sign
that an overwhelming majority in Congress, including Whigs,
were in favor of giving the President the appropriation. Recognizing that it had delayed action on the bill and had alienated
some of the bill's original supporters, the *Union* merely repeated
John Quincy Adams' contention that the proviso was unnecessary, but did not attack it directly. Ritchie's editorial left the
distinct impression that the paper preferred the amended bill to
no bill at all, an impression which the adherents of the proviso

were to remind the administration of in their later fight for the measure.[1]

Outside of Washington, Wilmot's amendment received little attention. Both Democratic and Whig politicians avoided injecting the issue into party politics. In the election campaigns held in the fall of 1846, the tariff and war questions absorbed most of the public attention, and the proviso went largely unnoticed. Even in Wilmot's own campaign, his amendment was scarcely mentioned.[2] Insofar as they took account of it at all, both parties seem to have recognized and sought to avoid the divisive effect the measure would have in their national organizations. Northern Whigs still attempted to appeal to antislavery sentiment but not, in general, by means of the proviso; instead, they continued to develop this appeal out of the general policy of opposition to the administration's war program, a policy upon which nearly all Whigs could unite regardless of section.[3] On the other hand, the administration's war program received the support of Democrats, even of those Van Burenites who were privately dissatisfied with it, while the issue of slavery in the territories was generally ignored by them, where this was possible. None of the platforms adopted by Democratic state conventions in 1846 specifically mentioned the issue and most avoided the slavery question entirely. In New England states like Massachusetts, where the emphasis which the Whigs gave their antislavery appeal rendered such a course inexpedient, the official Democratic response was to denounce agitation of the slavery question. The Massachusetts convention deprecated "as disunion in its worst form, the attempts of any party or class of men to stigmatize and denounce one portion of the Union for its domestic institutions."[4]

The only northern state in which there was any effort to commit the Democratic party to the principle of the nonextension of slavery was New Hampshire. The reaction of the state convention to the introduction of resolutions embodying nonextension and other antislavery principles reveals how sensitive New England Democrats were on the subject of slavery, and how deeply committed they were to keeping the issue out of politics. The delegates of the convention refused to allow the author of the resolutions a full hearing and would not permit him to speak at all until after they had listened to the party leaders roundly denounce the proposals.[5] The resolutions were almost unanimously rejected for others which deplored the existence of the slavery institution but condemned attacks upon it as likely to excite "the prejudices of the slaveholding communities," and thereby "to fasten rather than unloose the bonds of the enslaved."[6]

Democratic politicians in New York evinced the same unwillingness to face the slavery question. The desire to retain control of the state administration gave the dominant Van Buren faction a vital interest in maintaining party harmony. The Van Buren leaders suppressed the hostility toward the Polk administration and the South which had induced the more radical Van Burenites to introduce the antislavery amendment at the recent session of Congress. The resolutions which John A. Dix prepared for the Democratic state convention not only totally ignored the issue of slavery in the territories, they also promised full support for the administration's war effort.[7] The only hints of the Van Burenite dissatisfaction with Polk's Mexican policies were the resolutions' expression of a desire to see the war brought rapidly to a close and the statement in the convention's address that "no schemes of conquest should be allowed to influence us."[8] Since the Whig convention in New York also ignored the slavery question, except insofar as an antislavery appeal could be deduced from its attack upon the Mexican War, the question received very little attention in the campaign.[9]

In Ohio there were sporadic signs of interest in the issue of slavery in the territories among local Van Buren Democrats,[10] but these were eclipsed in the state campaign by the slavery, or rather the Negro, question in another form. The Whig candidate for governor called for the repeal of the state's "black laws" which discriminated against Negro residents, and antislavery Democrats were disgusted to find their party making retention of the "black laws" the principal issue in the campaign.[11] Elsewhere in the North the slavery question did not become an important issue in any form.

In the South there seems to have been even less awareness of the antislavery amendment and its significance than in the North.[12] The one group that did know something about it, the southern congressmen, evidently regarded it more as a piece of temporary political strategy than as a genuine threat to southern institutions.[13] Even the strong proslavery faction of the Democratic party, which looked to John C. Calhoun for leadership, voiced no special concern about the amendment.[14] The Pendleton, South Carolina, *Messenger,* generally considered Calhoun's personal organ, dismissed it with the comment that it would have failed in the Senate had it been brought to a vote.[15] Perhaps even more significant was the action of the South Carolina legislature returning without comment the incendiary antislavery resolutions passed by the New Hampshire legislature at Hale's insistence the previous summer.[16] Nor did any of the other southern legislatures take exception to the New Hampshire resolutions until after the territorial issue had been again raised in Congress. The southern political leaders gave no evidence of a desire to agitate the question of slavery in the territories in the fall of 1846.

In spite of the people's lack of awareness of the antislavery amendment and the reluctance of politicians to raise the issue publicly, there were forces at work in New York which affected the efforts to keep the question out of national politics. The dominant Van Buren faction in the state, known locally as Barnburners, was engaged in a fierce struggle for control of the state party machinery with their rivals, who were called Hunkers. Although the factional split had originated in disputes over local questions, both factions tried to use national issues to their advantage in the struggle for control. The Hunkers had successfully used the Texas issue to secure Marcy's appointment to the Polk cabinet. Even after the acquisition of Texas, the Hunkers continued to play up the annexation question in order to strengthen their own ties and to weaken further those of the Barnburners with the national administration. The resolutions which they introduced in the legislative session of 1846 endorsing both annexation and expansion in the Southwest were patently designed to embarrass their opponents.[17] For their part, the Barnburners in the state legislature tried to appeal to local resentment against the South for its presumed sectional attitude on such issues as the Oregon dispute.[18]

The most important decision facing the state party in the fall of 1846 was the selection of a candidate for governor. The Barnburners succeeded in obtaining the renomination of the reluctant Wright, in spite of Hunker objections. Efforts to maintain party harmony proved unavailing as the Hunkers began to work covertly to defeat Wright.[19] Some of the federal officeholders not only opposed Wright but claimed that the national administration approved of their opposition.[20] When Polk was informed of this, he tried to demonstrate his good faith by announcing to his cabinet, some of whose members the Barnburners suspected of being behind the Hunker effort, that he intended that Wright should be given the full support of the administration and that disloyal appointees were to be fired.[21] Nevertheless, Hunker federal officeholders continued to work against Wright and helped to bring about his defeat in November.[22] Polk was disgusted with the Hunkers' behavior in the campaign and vowed to give them no further patronage.[23] But the Barnburners blamed the administration for the previous support it had given the Hunkers.[24]

Wright's defeat loosened the restraints which the older, more prudent leaders of the Van Buren faction had exercised on the more radical antislavery men like Preston King. As the radicals saw it, now that control of the state government had been lost and the perfidy of the Hunkers and the national administration finally demonstrated, there was no need to suppress sectional resentment and forego principle on the question of the extension of slavery in the interest of party harmony.[25] Political considerations seemed to them to point in an entirely different direction.

They held the administration's identification of the party with southern slaveholding interests responsible for the Whig victories not only in New York, but elsewhere in the North. Although sectional issues had not been discussed much in the campaigns, it seemed evident that sectional feeling had heavily influenced the outcome of the northern state elections.[26] Furthermore, there were signs that this sectional feeling in the North was rising,[27] tempting the radical Barnburners to exploit it in order to recoup their fallen fortunes. Their ultimate goal was to regain control of the national party and the national administration, and their hopes were centered on Wright as a presidential candidate for 1848. Wright's defeat seemed to eliminate him as a possibility, unless some new issue could be raised which would give him an advantage over his rivals.[28] The evident failure of the policy of the older Barnburner leaders to suppress the slavery question in order to avoid the loss of Hunker and administration support for Wright helped to persuade the radical Barnburners of the necessity for an antislavery appeal to gain support for him from alternative sources.[29] These considerations strengthened their feeling that the time had come to take a decided stand against the further increase in the political power of the slaveholding interest.[30]

When the twenty-ninth Congress reassembled in December, King returned to Washington prepared to lead the fight against the extension of slavery into the Mexican territories, in spite of efforts by the older Barnburner leaders to restrain him.[31] There he found like-minded Van Burenites, and together they began to seek support among northern congressmen for a reintroduction of Wilmot's proviso and the means of reintroducing the measure which offered the best chance of its success.[32] The most promising way seemed to be to append it once more to the appropriation which the President again requested, in his opening message to Congress, for the purpose of negotiating peace with Mexico.[33]

President Polk, in the meantime, was trying to keep the slavery question out of politics. Although a slaveholder himself, Polk was not particularly anxious to extend the institution.

Like most southerners, however, the President thought that its prohibition in the territories was unfair to the South, and, what was even more important at the time, he recognized that the adoption of such a measure would effectively prevent the annexation of new territory in the Southwest by alienating southern congressional support.[34]

On December 19, soon after Congress met, Polk arranged an interview with John C. Calhoun to sound the proslavery leader on the question of a new appropriation to be used to facilitate the making of peace and the annexation of California and New Mexico.[35] Calhoun, who had opposed the war to begin with, was amenable to this project, but he was evidently becoming concerned with the recent progress in the North of sentiment in favor of prohibiting slavery in the territories.[36] He insisted that he must oppose any appropriation or peace treaty to which an antislavery amendment was attached even though he agreed with Polk that slavery would probably never exist in the territories to be acquired, and claimed that he had no desire to see it extended there.[37] According to Calhoun, the safety of the South's peculiar institution, and ultimately of southern rights in general, demanded that the principle of territorial exclusion be defeated.[38]

Three days later, Polk brought up the subject in a cabinet meeting at which it was decided not to insist upon the appropriation unless it was ascertained that it could pass Congress without an amendment prohibiting slavery.[39] The President thereupon called in Wilmot and tried to dissuade him from encumbering a new appropriation with his amendment. Polk evidently convinced Wilmot that he was sincere in his denial of any desire to extend the institution of slavery, and in the course of the conversation the Pennsylvania congressman agreed to introduce his amendment in the form of a joint resolution declaring the principle.[40] With this obstacle to the appropriation thus far removed, Polk consulted with three key Democratic supporters on the Committee of Foreign Affairs in the Senate to see if he could get their approval for an unamended bill.

Among the senators whose approval Polk sought was Lewis

Cass of Michigan. Cass was an old soldier from the War of 1812 who had served for a time as Secretary of War under Andrew Jackson. Although not without talent, Cass had a well-deserved reputation for being a political trimmer. He owed most of his fame and influence to his ability to articulate the chauvinistic impulses of the young American republic, which were particularly strong in the American West. He had first caught the attention of the general public in 1842, when as minister to France he vigorously denounced England's attempt to secure permission to search vessels of other nations suspected of plying the illegal slave trade.[41]

Cass's defiant assertion of American rights pleased the Anglophobe as well as the proslavery elements in the Democratic party and earned him a hero's welcome when he returned from France. Back in the United States, he tried to capitalize further on these opinions in order to gain the Democratic nomination in 1844. Although he was initially indifferent to the fate of Texas, he came out strongly in favor of annexation on the eve of the nominating convention, emphasizing the threat of British influence in Texas and playing upon southern fears of British emancipation schemes.[42] This maneuver almost succeeded in getting him the nomination, but the hostility of the Van Buren forces coupled with Polk's adventitious candidacy kept the prize from him. Elected to the Senate, Cass continued to advocate expansionist policies directed particularly against Great Britain. He strongly urged United States claims to the entire Oregon territory, and he opposed the administration's compromise settlement at the 49th parallel, thereby strengthening his political position in the Northwest.[43] On the Mexican question his belligerent attitude coincided more closely with that of the President and the southern wing of the party. Chairman of the important Committee on Military Affairs as well as a member of the Committee of Foreign Affairs, he was the acknowledged leader of the prowar forces in the Senate.

In spite of his approval of the administration's policy of expansion in the Southwest, Cass had expressed his disappoint-

ment, at the end of the preceding session of Congress, that Davis'
filibuster had prevented him from recording his vote in favor of
the antislavery amendment. He had also claimed that other
northern Democratic senators felt the same way and that if
Davis had allowed the measure to come to a vote immediately
it would have passed with the amendment.[44] Since Cass had a
large following among the Democrats in Congress from the
Northwest, his present attitude toward an appropriation and the
amendment was of particular importance to Polk.

The President explained to Cass and his two colleagues his
objections to the insertion of the slavery issue in the form of
Wilmot's amendment into the question of the war and southwestern expansion. Polk described their response: "They said they
would report the Bill without the restriction, but that if it were
moved in the Senate Gen'l Cass and Mr. [Charles G.] Atherton
[of New Hampshire] would be in great peril with their constituents to vote against it. . . . Gen'l Cass and Mr. Atherton agreed
to consult the Northern Democratic Senators, and if they could
induce them to stand together and vote against the restriction,
if moved in the Senate they would do so."[45] Faced with these
weak commitments, Polk apparently decided not to push the bill.
It was not until nearly a month later, when the administration's
hopes for a settlement with Mexico were temporarily raised, that
the Committees of Foreign Relations in the House and Senate
reported an appropriation bill.[46]

Polk's deferment of the appropriation did not prevent the
introduction of the slavery extension question into the congressional debates for very long, however. The primary difficulty
which King and his associates encountered in trying to get the
question before Congress was the reluctance of most northern
Democrats to reopen the issue. For partisan reasons, the latter
wanted to avoid any move which might strengthen their Whig
opponents by threatening to interfere with the annexation of
territory, the current principal Democratic aim. They preferred,
just as the administration did, to postpone discussion of the
slavery extension question until the territory had been safely

annexed. Presumably they could then insist on the prohibition of slavery there.[47] Opposed as they were to this policy of silence, King and his group did not violate it in speeches of their own but chose instead to work behind the scenes to secure northern Democratic votes to reintroduce Wilmot's amendment.[48] They continued to hold their tongues in spite of their sensitiveness to a northern Whig charge that the administration action establishing civil governments over the conquered territory was designed to permit the establishment of slavery there.[49]

But the Whigs did not exercise the same restraint. They could not refrain from using Wilmot's proposition to try to discredit the administration's policy of annexation. Citing the Wilmot measure as a sign of a united northern determination to keep any territory acquired free soil, Meredith P. Gentry of Tennessee finally openly asserted what had previously been said only privately, that Democratic insistence upon annexation would inevitably produce a devastating sectional conflict over the slavery issue.[50] To drive home his point about the inevitability of conflict, Gentry asked the southerners rhetorically whether they would permit the admission of a cordon of free states in the Southwest.[51]

Gentry's assumption that the South was irrevocably opposed to the annexation of free territory in the Southwest disturbed antislavery Democrats, who expected to prohibit the institution there *after* the territory was annexed,[52] and provoked a reply from one of them, Samuel Gordon of New York. In a strong defense of the annexation policy, Gordon confirmed Gentry's contention that the North was determined to prohibit slavery in the territory to be acquired and announced his own willingness to support Wilmot's proviso whenever the question was raised. Gordon expressed a preference for waiting until Congress was in the process of giving it a territorial government after annexation had taken place, but his speech made it apparent that his concern over the southern attitude toward the annexation of free territory had brought him to the brink of supporting the immediate reintroduction of Wilmot's resolution.[53] In a speech immediately following Gordon's, Joseph R. Root, a Whig from Ohio, tried to push Gordon and other hesitant antislavery Democrats over the brink by taunting them with the suggestion that Polk would take advantage of a delay in the fight for free soil to introduce slavery into the territory.[54] It appears that the taunt not only had some effect on these hesitant antislavery Democrats but also helped to convince Preston King that the attempt to get the antislavery measure before Congress should be delayed no longer.[55]

A few days after the exchange between Gordon and Root, King announced his intention to reintroduce the Two Million Bill as it had passed the House the previous August, i.e., with Wilmot's resolution appended.[56] In spite of an apparent last-minute effort on the part of the older Barnburner leaders in New York to stop him, King carried out his intention on January 4.[57] There were still not quite enough northern Democrats prepared to reopen the issue at this time, and permission was denied to King to introduce the measure. But the following day King broke the long silence of the antislavery Democrats. Receiving permission from the House to make a personal explanation, King launched into a spirited defense of his proposal. "The time has come," he announced, "when the Republic should declare that it will not be made an instrument to the extension of slavery on the continent of America." He maintained that he had offered the bill to disprove the "monstrous" charge that it would "not do to propose a law that any such territory should be free because a southern administration will take no territory unless it shall be arranged that the territory shall be open to slavery."[58] King concluded by announcing his determination to continue the fight for free soil.[59]

King's speech caused a sensation. Many Whigs and Democrats charged that the Barnburner leaders in Albany had planned this move in order to strengthen their political position generally, and more particularly to advance the claims of Silas Wright to the Presidency.[60] It seemed clear, in any case, that the move committed the Barnburners to the fight for free soil, which meant that the question of slavery in the territories could no longer be ignored.[61] Calhoun and his followers, who had previously refrained from making public comments on the issue, now began to stir up discussion in an effort to arouse the South to its danger.[62] In the House of Representatives, James R. Seddon, a Calhoun Democrat from Virginia, denounced King's speech as a "direct attack on the institutions and peace of one half of the States of the Union," and an "insult and injury, outrage and wrong, on them and theirs."[63] The immediate aim of Calhoun and his supporters was a settlement simultaneously repudiating the free-soil principle and removing the slavery question from public controversy. The best opportunity for such a settlement appeared to be in the extension of the Missouri Compromise line into the conquered territory.

A suitable occasion arose for the proposal of their solution one week after King's speech when the House of Representatives took up a bill providing territorial government for Oregon. The bill, with a slavery prohibition appended, had passed the House the previous summer but had died in the Senate. The House had passed the bill a few days before Wilmot offered his proviso, and the southerners, satisfied that the slavery question was an impracticable one in this instance and reluctant to raise the question in any case, did not protest the prohibition at the time, although some of them voted against it.[64] Now Armistead Burt of South Carolina, acting at Calhoun's instigation, offered to amend the slavery prohibition by adding the words: "inasmuch as the whole of the said territory lies north of 36° 30' north latitude, known as the line of the Missouri Compromise."[65] This would vindicate the Missouri Compromise principle and prepare the way for the extension of the 36° 30' line to the conquered Mexican territory. Burt defended his amendment with a constitutional argument which denied to Congress the authority to legislate for the territory on the subject of slavery.[66]

The Barnburners had already determined to oppose Burt's proposal, which they regarded as an effort to extend the slavery institution and the political power of the slaveholders under the guise of a compromise.[67] They were particularly concerned lest the southern threat to oppose annexation or the deeper threat to secede from the Union if the fight for free soil was persisted in would sway wavering northern Democrats to support the proposal.[68] John Pettit, the Indiana Van Burenite who answered Burt, brushed aside the constitutional argument and went to what he considered the heart of the matter. He warned the southerners that if they tried to dissolve the union over the free-soil issue, the southern people themselves would hang them "higher than Haman was hung."[69] Pettit's remark was calculated to influence northern votes in two ways, by deflating the southern threats and by appealing to northern resentment against what appeared to be their use of these threats for the purpose of spreading slavery.[70] At the same time, the counterthreat touched one of the deepest fears of the Calhounites, the fear of southern apathy on the slavery question.[71] The rejection of Burt's proposal, by a nearly unanimous northern vote, seemed to them to confirm Pettit's disdain for their opposition to free soil and strengthened their determination to arouse the South to its supposed danger.[72]

The antislavery Democrats were equally determined to continue the fight for free soil. Even before Burt's proposal, Preston King had written to Albany requesting that the state administration have his position sustained by the New York legislature.[73] Shortly thereafter, resolutions supporting both annexation and congressional prohibition of slavery in the acquired territory were introduced in the state senate where the Democrats commanded a majority.[74] The senate passed the resolutions by an overwhelming margin after having rejected a Hunker substitute deploring agitation which might "impair the harmony of the Union."[75] The lower house also approved the resolutions, making New York the first northern state to go on record in favor of Wilmot's proviso.[76] Pennsylvania and other northern states passed similar resolutions as antislavery Whigs and Democrats vied with each other in expressing opposition to the extension of the institution.[77]

At Washington the Polk administration's belated introduction of its appropriation, now raised from two to three million dollars, presented King and his cohorts with the opportunity to get their antislavery measure directly before Congress. Since the Barnburners apparently wanted to identify the original sponsor, Wilmot, with the measure, rather than one of themselves, they gave it the name by which it commonly came to be known, the Wilmot Proviso.[78] They overcame his reluctance to violate his promise to Polk not to append his proviso to the appropriation by convincing him that a resolution embodying the principle would not receive consideration in the House.[79] Consequently, when the appropriation bill at last reached the House floor, Wilmot moved that his amendment be added to the measure. The opponents of the amendment raised technical objections, but owing in part to Preston King's skill as a parliamentarian, they were unable to prevent House consideration.[80] A solid week of discussion of the Proviso began to impress the issue indelibly on the political consciousness of the nation at large. Although political pressure from the administration induced some northern Democrats to oppose the Proviso, enough continued to support it to pass it together with the appropriation. Of the Democrats from the area northeast of Pennsylvania, only one voted against the Proviso. The delegations from Pennsylvania and the northwestern states were somewhat more evenly divided, but all except Illinois gave more votes for than against the measure.[81]

The House passage of the Wilmot Proviso convinced Calhoun that he must clearly define the fundamental issue between the sections in regard to slavery in the territories. On February 19, four days after the House action on the Proviso, he offered a series of resolutions which described the basic southern rights on the question and warned of the consequences of a northern invasion of these rights. They read in part:

Resolved, That Congress, as the joint agent and representative of the States of the Union, has no right to make any law, or do any act whatever, that shall directly, or by its effects, make any discrimination between the States of this Union by which any of them shall be deprived of its full and equal right in any territory of the United States, acquired or to be acquired.

Resolved, That the enactment of any law, which should directly or by its effects, deprive the citizens of any of the States of this Union from emigrating, with their property, into any of the territories of the United States, will make such discrimination, and therefore would be a violation of the constitution and the rights of the States from which such citizens emigrated, and in derogation of that perfect equality which belongs to them as members of this Union—and would tend directly to subvert the Union itself.[82]

In the speech with which he accompanied the resolutions, Calhoun argued for the absolute necessity that the South unite in fully maintaining these rights and elaborated on the dangers to the union of a northern attempt to violate them.[83] He described the purpose of his resolutions and speech in a letter to his followers the same day. "You will see," he wrote, "that I have made up the issue between North and South. If we flinch we are gone, but if we stand fast on it, we shall triumph either by compelling the North to yield to our terms, or declaring our independence of them."[84] Calhoun's resolutions were never discussed or voted upon, but they did provide a platform for the defense of southern rights. Although most southern politicians were willing and many were anxious to extend the Missouri Compromise line to the new territory, so strong was the feeling in favor of southern rights that virtually all of them ultimately accepted Calhoun's constitutional objections to the Proviso which were legally inconsistent with that solution.

The unyielding positions taken by both the Van Buren and Calhoun factions threatened to paralyze the Democratic party, interfering with the war effort and the annexation of territory.[85] The threat was particularly disturbing to western Democrats who were more interested in western expansion than the slavery question. Cass was the recognized leader of this group in Congress. Since his conversation with Polk, he was becoming more and more impressed with the strength of southern opposition to the Wilmot Proviso. True to Gideon Welles's characterization of him as a politician who "supports measures because others do whose support he desires,"[86] Cass's attitude toward the Proviso was ultimately determined by his desire to gain political support for himself and his expansionist policies. He had little to hope for from the Barnburners, most of whom would remain committed to Silas Wright and hostile to himself whether he continued to adhere to the Wilmot Proviso or not.[87] On the other hand, by repudiating the Proviso he might win southern support for his presidential aspirations while rebuilding the alliance of southern and western Democrats, which would help the administration prosecute the war more effectively. On the day Calhoun introduced his resolutions in the Senate, Cass explained his position to a political associate in Michigan:

The Wilmot Proviso will not pass the Senate. It would be death to the war—death to all hopes of getting an acre of Territory, death to the administration, and death to the Democratic Party. It was not so intended. It no doubt originated with proper feelings; but things have now come to such a pass that its adoption will produce these effects. It is distinctly avowed by the Southern members of Congress that they would not vote for any measures for the prosecution of the war, nor would they ratify any treaty, if this provision becomes a law.[88]

Cass's opposition to the Proviso foretold the result in the Senate, but the Van Burenites, nonetheless, were determined to make it a matter of public record.[89]

On March 1, John A. Dix made the New York legislature's final passage of its Wilmot Proviso resolutions the occasion for introducing the subject into the debate on the Three Million Bill in the Senate.[90] Although Dix did not move the Proviso as an amendment, his speech was characterized by Senator Andrew P. Butler of South Carolina as "the prologue of the Wilmot Proviso," which was "designed to prepare the way for what was to come."[91] Shortly afterward, a northern Whig introduced the Proviso commenting that "he could not well avoid it after the remarks of the honorable Senator from South Carolina, [Mr. Butler]."[92]

Cass was well prepared for the occasion. He immediately rose and announced his opposition to the Proviso, in spite of instructions from the Michigan legislature to the contrary.[93] He argued that its present introduction would merely create sectional controversy and impede a united war effort without accomplishing its avowed purpose, since Congress, when it came to provide a government for any territory which might be acquired, would have to deal with the question all over again, independent of the present decision. The effect of the Proviso, he claimed, would therefore be simply to "bring the war to an untimely issue," and "prevent the acquisition of a foot of territory."[94] As was usual with him, Cass tried to offer evidence of popular support for his position. "The progress of public opinion upon the question of the adoption of the proviso," he maintained, "seems to indicate very clearly, that since its introduction at the past session of Congress, the conviction has been gaining ground that the present is no time for the agitation of this subject."[95] Actually Cass, who admitted having undergone some such change in opinion himself,[96] was speaking more for those northern Democrats concerned with party loyalty and the successful prosecution of the war than for northern public opinion at large. But this did not diminish the effectiveness of the argument in the Senate. In the vote on the Proviso, the Democratic senators from Indiana and Illinois, as well as Daniel S. Dickinson, the Hunker Senator from New York, followed Cass's lead and provided the margin by which the measure was defeated.[97]

When the unamended Three Million Bill which was passed by the Senate came up in the House, the motion to append the Proviso was this time rejected, as seven northern Democrats changed their vote and six more absented themselves from the proceedings.[98] The administration got its appropriation unencumbered by the Wilmot Proviso, but the issue had been injected into national politics, and the full ventilation of the question in Congress had articulated, in one form, the basic division of American society on the institution of slavery.

CHAPTER III

The Southern Rights Movement

WITH THE END OF THE CONGRESSIONAL SESSION, JOHN C. CAL-houn returned to South Carolina determined to arrest the anti-slavery movement which he saw developing in the North. To Calhoun the Wilmot Proviso was but a single incident of this movement which jeopardized the existence of the South as an entity by its threat to southern institutions. He was therefore resolved upon a united southern demand that the North not only surrender the free-soil principle but immediately stop every encroachment upon the rights of southern slaveholders, which included a suppression of the abolitionists. At the same time, he recognized that the Proviso gave him an extremely effective weapon, as well as a splendid opportunity, for uniting the South in defense of southern rights. He explained the situation to one of his followers in the fall of 1847: "I am of the impression that if the South act as it ought, the Wilmot proviso, instead of proving to be the means of successfully assailing us and our peculiar institution, may be made the occasion of [our] successfully asserting our equality and rights *by enabling us to force the issue on the North.*

Something of the kind was indispensable to rouse and unite the South[1] [italics mine]."

Arriving in Charleston early in March, Calhoun addressed a huge meeting, held to welcome him, on the dangers faced by the slavery institution and, by inference, southern rights generally. In his speech Calhoun analyzed the attitudes behind the northern agitation of the slavery issue on questions like the Wilmot Proviso. Discounting the tremendous appeal of the free-soil position to the northern public, he maintained that the agitation originated purely in political considerations and that the fact that the two major parties were so evenly matched in the North had induced both parties to bid for the relatively small number of abolitionist voters who held the balance of power there. In so doing, he claimed, the parties had virtually committed themselves to the abolition program. The remedy, according to Calhoun, was for the South to unite in demanding that the parties forsake the abolition program and in withholding its support in the forthcoming presidential election from whichever party refused to do so. In this way the South and those people in the North who adhered to the southern design would come to hold the balance of political power, and since the parties were solely concerned with maintaining their power rather than their principles, it would mean that the South could dictate its principles to the winning party, which would be the one which had bid for its support.[2]

The first requirement in implementing such a program was to break down existing party loyalties in the South and weld the section into a single unit whose primary political concern would be the slave question. With this object in mind Calhoun ended his speech with the exhortation: "Henceforward let all party distinctions among us cease so long as this aggression on our rights and honor shall continue, on the part of the non-slaveholding states. Let us profit by the example of the abolition party, who, small as they are, have acquired so much influence by the course they have pursued. As they make the destruction of our domestic institution the paramount question, let us regard every man as of our party who stands up with us in its defense; and every one as against us, who does not, until aggression ceases."[3]

Calhoun was encouraged by the immediate response in the South to his movement for southern unity.[4] Several southern journals expressed approval of some of the aims of the movement.[5] Meetings were held in various places in the southeast which denounced the Proviso as an encroachment on southern rights and called upon southerners to submerge their political differences in a common effort to oppose all such encroachments.[6] One meeting in Alabama, under the influence of one of Calhoun's political lieutenants from Charleston, resolved to oppose presidential and vice-presidential candidates committed to the Wilmot Proviso, as well as the Proviso itself. The meeting went on to declare "that on the subject matter of these resolutions, among ourselves we know no party distinctions and never will know any."[7]

Evidence of southern Whig interest in the movement for southern rights was particularly encouraging. One Whig congressman from Alabama confided to Calhoun that he could "not for a moment doubt that your views, so fully expressed upon this question touching slavery, will be the views of the whole South."[8] And from Georgia, Robert Toombs, perhaps the leading Whig congressman from the deep South, wrote him that his Charleston speech had been reprinted in virtually every Whig newspaper in the state and concluded with the statement that "the people of the South are now anxiously waiting to see what direction you give [the question.]"[9] In June a meeting of Whigs in Putnam County, Georgia, passed resolutions approving of Calhoun's movement.[10] In reply he sent them an open letter which was reprinted throughout the South hailing the resolutions as "the precursor to the union of all parties with us to repel an outrageous and unprovoked assault upon us."[11]

The meeting of the state convention of the Whig party in Georgia made it evident, however, that Whig politicians were still very far from subordinating their party loyalty to the movement for southern rights. Aside from a routine repudiation of the Wilmot Proviso, the convention did not mention the slavery question. It commended Calhoun, not for his southern rights movement, but for his opposition to the Mexican War.[12] The outcome of the convention made it clear that the Whigs were primarily interested in Calhoun's movement as a means of discrediting the Democratic party and gaining support for themselves and their presidential candidate, General Zachary Taylor.[13]

Regular Democratic politicians in the South resented Calhoun's movement for the same reason that it appealed to the Whigs—because it tended to disrupt the unity of their party, of which Calhoun was a nominal member and from which his support was largely drawn.[14] While they were strongly enough opposed to the Wilmot Proviso to accept Calhoun's constitutional objections to it, they did not view it as a northern gambit to a full-scale assault on the slavery institution, as Calhoun did. For them the Proviso was but one political question among many, albeit a crucial one. Being anxious to continue their co-operation with northern Democrats on these other questions, they had no desire to surrender their party association and commitments to merge with their Whig opponents in the South on the slavery question alone, as Calhoun demanded. The principal spokesman of the Democratic regulars, Ritchie's Washington *Union,* argued that such a course would merely unify the North in opposition, leaving the South clearly in the minority.[15] Following the *Union* lead, the southern Democratic press, generally, maintained that despite the defection of the Barnburners northern Democrats were still the most reliable allies of the South and, as long as they were not repudiated, would provide the necessary support to protect southern institutions. In proof of this they pointed to the fact that every northern congressman who had voted with the South against the Wilmot Proviso was a Democrat. They therefore rejected Calhoun's attack on the national convention system at Charleston, and endorsed the convention as the most practicable and equitable means of selecting a presidential candidate.[16]

The party regulars were all the more opposed to Calhoun's

drive for southern unity because they suspected him of trying to use the slavery question to realize his own presidential aspirations.[17] Calhoun's presidential ambitions were by no means incompatible with his deep concern, not to say obsession, with the slavery question. One respectful abolitionist opponent pointed out that, given Calhoun's strong positive attitude toward slavery, it was "natural that he should seek continually its perpetuation; and being a man of strong ambitions, seek, through its influence, the highest office in the republic—not alone for his self gratification, but also that he may bring the whole power of the Federal government to bear for the augmentation of its power."[18] Many Democratic regulars in the South, however, questioned the sincerity of Calhoun's motives and considered his southern rights movement no more than a self-seeking effort to rehabilitate his own political fortunes which had been severely impaired by his opposition to the Polk administration's war effort. This opposition gave the party regulars an additional reason for opposing Calhoun as well as the means of limiting his influence in the Democratic party.[19]

Calhoun's conflict with the Polk administration over the conduct of the war had come to a head in the recent session of Congress, just as he was becoming convinced of the necessity for a drive for southern unity on the slavery question. At the same time that the House of Representatives was debating the Wilmot Proviso, the Senate rejected, only temporarily as it turned out, an administration measure for prosecuting the war, because Calhoun and several of his followers united with the Whigs in opposing the bill. Ritchie made this act of party disloyalty the occasion for a strong attack on the Senate rejection in an article in the *Union* by an anonymous author under the title, "Another Mexican Victory."[20] The following day, Calhoun and his group retaliated. Senator David Yulee of Florida, one of Calhoun's adherents, introduced a motion to the effect that the editors of the *Union* having "uttered a public libel upon the character of this body, they be excluded from the privilege of admission to the floor of the Senate."[21]

In the ensuing debates on the motion, the argument became more and more bitter; and the final passage of the measure by Whig and Calhounite votes completed the break between Calhoun and the administration, which now proceeded to try to isolate the South Carolinian from his southern following.[22] Unfortunately for Calhoun, the vast body of the southern Democratic party sided against him on the questions of the war and Ritchie's expulsion.[23] His followers in Virginia were completely routed in the state convention in February which officially approved of the administration's conduct of the war and expressed "regret" that "certain Senators" had voted to expel Ritchie and had opposed a vigorous prosecution of the war.[24] Several of the important Virginia Calhounites felt compelled to desert their leader openly.[25] Others were defeated for renomination. One of the few remaining staunch supporters who was renominated was selected by a convention which specifically disavowed any "approval to the political course of the Hon. J. C. Calhoun."[26] This overwhelming defeat was in striking contrast with the situation a few months before when the Calhounites had been strong enough in the state legislature to dictate the choice of both Virginia's senators, in one case in direct violation of the decision of the party caucus.[27]

In spite of these formidable obstacles, Calhoun and his supporters went ahead with their efforts to effect southern unity. One of Calhoun's first moves, even before he left Washington, had been to write an address to the southern people which he tried to get leading political figures to sign.[28] But the reluctance of southern politicians to desert their parties to follow Calhoun's independent course prevented him from obtaining significant support, and the idea had to be dropped. After the meeting on March 9, Calhoun's Charleston clique concentrated its energies on trying to raise money to establish a proslavery organ in Washington. At the end of March they prepared a prospectus which they proceeded to circulate among potential subscribers.[29]

The campaign for funds was intensified late in the summer after a series of events occurred which Calhoun considered an even more ominous portent than the Wilmot Proviso itself. In March the Pennsylvania legislature passed a law which hindered slaveowners from recovering runaway slaves in the state, as they were legally entitled to do under the federal Fugitive Slave Act of 1793.[30] The slaveholders in Maryland and western Virginia protested that the law rendered their property insecure. Tensions were increased still further when the governor of Maryland asked that all runaway slaves in Pennsylvania be returned as fugitives from justice in Maryland, and the Pennsylvania governor rejected the request.[31] One of the protesting slaveowners informed Calhoun of these events and the latter seized upon them to strengthen his unity campaign.[32] "I doubt whether repeal of the act would do good now," he wrote in answer to his Virginia correspondent. "Now, if ever, in my opinion, is the time to bring the [slavery] question to issue. The longer it is delayed the worse in the end both for us and the Union."[33]

The day after Calhoun's reply, the Charleston clique prepared a new appeal for funds incorporating this and other alleged northern violations of southern rights. The central piece of evidence of northern aggression, however, remained the Wilmot Proviso.[34] This appeal and an "extra" issue of the Charleston *Mercury* of August 11 discussing the Wilmot Proviso were widely distributed throughout the South.[35] Shortly after the intensified drive for funds got under way, Calhoun began to urge the immediate implementation of a suggestion by one of his lieutenants in Charleston, Henry W. Conner, that a southern association be established to supplement the work of the proslavery journal.[36] Connor's idea had been that the Charleston clique should wait for new provocations by the northern advocates of the Wilmot Proviso to galvanize the South into further action.[37] The Charlestonians were very sensitive to charges by southern politicians that South Carolina was much more radical on the slavery question than the rest of the South, and they wanted the association movement to be initiated some place else.[38] At Calhoun's strong insistence, they agreed to hold a meeting in Charleston to launch the association movement, but the meeting was eventually postponed indefinitely to await action in New Orleans which never materialized.[39] The effort to establish the proslavery journal ultimately failed for much the same reasons.

The lack of concrete support outside South Carolina also frustrated another of Calhoun's projects, a convention of the slaveholding states, upon which he concentrated more and more of his attention after the failure of the association plan. He wanted the convention to implement a program of commercial retaliation against the North, which he had come to believe was the only action short of disunion that would halt northern encroachments upon southern rights.[40] In order to avoid recriminations about radical South Carolina leadership, the organ of the Charleston clique, the Charleston *Mercury,* waited until several southern journals had proposed a convention before it endorsed the proposal.[41] Nevertheless, the movement evoked little response outside South Carolina, and Calhoun was unsuccessful in his efforts to get his southern correspondents to initiate action in their own states.[42] Calhoun warned Governor David Johnson that South Carolina must be prepared to take the lead if, as seemed probable, "no other state should move," but for the present he had to content himself with having the governor prepare the South for more decisive action in the future by raising the threat of commercial retaliation against the North in his message to the state legislature.[43] Calhoun and his followers were forced to postpone their efforts to unite the South until after the congressional session which began in December of 1847. They expected and were even hoping for new northern assaults on the slaveholding system which would further arouse southern opinion and give a stronger impetus to their movement.[44]

While Calhoun failed in his primary purpose to create a proslavery movement to replace both major parties in the South, his efforts nonetheless had a considerable influence upon southern politics. He helped to keep the slavery issue before the southern public at a time when many of the regular party politicians would have liked to suppress it. Contrary to his intention, however, his agitation tended to focus attention on the specific issue raised by the Wilmot Proviso rather than the slavery question as a whole. In part this was because Calhoun's general proslavery position was too abstract to appeal to the general public, while the Proviso represented the antislavery threat in a concrete form. Almost all the southern newspapers roundly denounced the Wilmot Proviso, but few commented on Calhoun's proposals and those that did generally opposed them.[45]

The workings of the political system tended to produce the same result. The regular party organizations' survival of Calhoun's assault meant that the politicians who ran them continued to exercise a large degree of control over political discourse. Even the Democrats, who were more directly affected by the southern unity movement than the Whigs, were able to ignore or reject as impractical theorizing Calhoun's general position on the slavery question. On the other hand, Democratic politicians, and the Whigs too to a lesser extent, found it increasingly difficult to avoid taking a strong public stand on the specific issue of slavery in the territories. The problem was more acute for the Democrats because, in the first place, they were committed to the acquisition of territory in the Southwest and could not evade the issue by opposing annexation, as the Whigs could and did. Moreover, they had long claimed that their party was friendlier to the institution of slavery in both the South and the North and they did not wish to forego the political advantage of this claim. The introduction of the Wilmot Proviso by certain northern Democrats rendered this claim vulnerable to Whig criticism, and where the Whigs seized this opportunity Democrats had to engage in a discussion of the issue in order to justify their determination to continue to co-operate with these northern "traitors." At the same time, the unanimous support which the northern Whigs in Congress had given the Proviso gave the Democrats a chance to turn the issue to their own further advantage since they could argue, with plausibility, that it was the Whig party which should bear the onus of abolitionism.

The decisive factor, however, in raising the territorial issue was the existence in every one of the southeastern states except

North Carolina of a sizable Democratic faction which was strongly influenced by Calhoun's proslavery ideas. In the Southwestern states, where there were no such factions, the issue was bypassed. The Democratic state convention in Tennessee which met in April of 1847 avoided any explicit mention of either slavery or the territorial issue, confining itself to going on record in favor of "strict construction" of the Constitution and "a careful abstinence from the exercise of all doubtful powers by the General Government."[46] The Mississippi state convention was only slightly less oblique, resolving that "all legislation not founded upon equality of rights and privileges, irrespective of classes of the people, or geographical divisions of the country is at war with the genius of republican government."[47] But in the southeastern states the regular party politicians were unable to get away with any such evasions. Holding the balance of power in their respective states, particularly in Alabama and Virginia, the proslavery factions, commonly known as the Chivalry, were in a position to force the territorial issue upon the party regulars. The regulars felt compelled to satisfy the expectations of their constituents on this issue; but as they were forced to define their position more and more precisely, they were left with less and less room to maneuver in reaching an accommodation with the northern Democrats, with whom they wished to continue to co-operate in national politics.

The keystone of the Democratic party in the South was the Virginia organization. Prior to his departure for Washington in 1845, Thomas Ritchie had dominated the organization as editor of the Richmond *Enquirer*. Ritchie was the most influential southern Democratic spokesman for full co-operation with the state parties in the North, an important factor in his selection by Polk to edit the party organ in Washington, and Democratic regulars in Virginia still looked to him for leadership.[48] The Chivalry, on the other hand, were seeking to use their political leverage to stiffen the resistance of Ritchie and the party regulars to northern encroachments upon southern rights, at the expense of party harmony.[49] It was in Virginia where the strength of the territorial issue was first revealed, when one of the Chivalry, Lewis E. Harvie, offered resolutions defining the state's position on the Wilmot Proviso.[50] The resolutions, modeled on those Calhoun presented to the United States Senate, declared the Proviso unconstitutional and pledged the state to "determined resistance" against it, "at all hazards and to the last extremity."[51] They received the unanimous vote of both houses of the legislature, no one daring to vote against them, and ultimately became known as the "Platform of the South."[52]

Harvie and his associates were on the defensive, however, at the Virginia Democratic state convention which met shortly after the resolutions passed the senate. There the regulars were able to capitalize on Calhoun's move expelling Ritchie from the U.S. Senate. They brought in a platform which condemned Calhoun and his followers in Congress for their opposition to the administration's war policy as well as for their votes for Ritchie's expulsion. The ensuing debate between the regulars and the Chivalry centered on this condemnation, rather than on participation in a national convention, although the platform also advocated this.[53] Harvie raised the territorial issue in his speech opposing the platform,[54] but he did not try to amend it with his Proviso resolutions. Instead he and a handful of others walked out of the convention when the platform was adopted and refused to campaign for the state ticket.[55] Some of the Chivalry remained and apparently extracted an informal promise from the regulars that the party would not support a Wilmot Proviso man for the presidency.[56] When the Whigs taunted the Democrats for their silence on the territorial issue, the Richmond *Enquirer* made the commitment explicit. "The Southern Democracy," declared the *Enquirer*, "will go into convention with the implied condition that no 'Wilmot proviso' man is to be nominated, for in that event the Southern members will retire and act for themselves."[57]

The *Enquirer* took the offensive on the territorial issue in the state campaign. It accused the Virginia Whigs of being prepared to sacrifice the South on the altar of their alliance with

northern Whiggery and condemned the Whig stand against annexation as a surrender to the antislavery forces.[58] The effort
to use the territorial issue to discredit the Whigs was not successful in preventing a Whig victory in the spring elections for
local office. This result strengthened the hands of the more mili-
tant members of the Chivalry, since it was their disaffection to
which the defeat was attributed.[59]

In Alabama, the proslavery influence was much stronger
than in Virginia, and the territorial issue had an even greater
impact. The central figure in Alabama politics from this time
until the Civil War was the great orator, William Lowndes Yancey. Although Yancey was not closely associated with Calhoun,
he held much the same opinions. He had resigned his seat in
the House of Representatives in August of 1846, even before
the introduction of the Wilmot Proviso, because he had become
convinced that northern and western Democrats were lacking
in good faith. In his letter of resignation Yancey advised his
constituents never again to participate in a national convention.[60]
The events of the year following his resignation confirmed Yancey's distrust of northern Democrats, and, by the spring of 1847,
he was participating in southern unity meetings and urging bipartisan support for candidates of either party who were strongly committed on the territorial issue.[61]

In spite of his participation in the southern unity movement,
however, Yancey was a popular enough figure to exercise considerable influence at the Alabama Democratic state convention
which met in May. Yancey's choice of a candidate, Reuben C.
Chapman, was nominated for governor.[62] The party platform
was silent on the question of a national convention, in spite of
the desire of most Alabama Democrats to be represented there.[63]
On the territorial issue, the convention followed the lead of one
of Calhoun's agents from Charleston, adopting the Virginia
Resolutions (the "Platform of the South") and recommending
to the southern people that they withhold their vote from any
presidential candidate "who shall not, previous to the election,

distinctly, unequivocally, and publicly avow his opposition" to federal interference with the question of slavery in the territory.[64]

The territorial issue played a significant role in the gubernatorial campaign. The Whigs tried to use it to exploit the hostility of the proslavery faction toward the northern Democrats in order to gain the support of the Chivalry for the presidential candidacy of Zachary Taylor.[65] Although the Whigs lost the election, they did make some progress in this direction. Governor-elect Chapman privately confessed his willingness to support Taylor if his principles were sound, and Senator Dixon H. Lewis, one of the leaders of the strong proslavery faction, was interested enough in supporting Taylor to inquire of one of the General's political intimates about his views.[66] The Whigs were able to obtain even more than this from Yancey—a conditional public commitment to support Taylor for the presidency. At a nonpartisan meeting held to endorse a strong proslavery Whig candidate for Congress, Yancey made a speech in which he denounced blind party loyalty and described the circumstances under which he would vote for Taylor. He concluded: "If this foul spirit of party which thus binds and divides and distracts the South can be broken, hail to him who shall do it. If he shall be as I fondly hope, Zachary Taylor, honored be his name. But let not the Whigs think or attempt to appropriate him as a partisan."[67] In spite of its electoral victory, the Alabama Democracy seemed to be floundering on the issues raised by the Wilmot Proviso.

In Georgia, the regular Democratic politicians were firmly in control of the party machinery and were able to commit the party to co-operation with the northern Democrats but only at the cost of an even stronger stand on the territorial issue than in Alabama. In the Georgia state convention which met on June 28, an effort was made by the strong proslavery faction to nominate Zachary Taylor. But after the delegates were assured that the Democrats would not nominate a Wilmot Proviso man, they voted down the proposal and instead adopted a resolution recommending a national convention as the best method of se-

lecting a presidential candidate.[68] Congressman Howell Cobb
and his supporters, party regulars par excellence, tried to go even
further and have the convention give a vote of confidence to
their northern Democratic allies, but this aroused such a spirited
protest from one ardent supporter of Calhoun that the motion
was dropped in the interests of party harmony.[69]

On the territorial issue the convention had endorsed the Virginia resolutions, but to soften this stand it had declared its willingness to accept the extension of the 36° 30′ line of the Missouri Compromise.[70] However, one of Calhoun's friends was
able to exact a further price for the commitment to participate
in a national convention. At his insistence, the convention resolved that the Georgia party would support "no candidate for
the presidency of the United States who does not unconditional-
ly, clearly, and unequivocally declare his opposition to the principles and provisions of the Wilmot Proviso."[71] The official state
Democratic organ hailed the convention's platform of conditional co-operation with northern Democrats as a brilliant solution
to the problems raised by the Wilmot Proviso and as the best
course of action for southern Democrats to take.[72] Moreover,
the strong stand of the convention enabled the party to fully
exploit the territorial issue in its state campaign against the hap-
less Whigs who were not so emphatic in their defense of southern rights.[73] Reversing the situation in Virginia, the Democrats
won their first gubernatorial campaign in six years.

Outside as well as inside Georgia the platform of the state
convention was widely acclaimed as the proper approach of
southern Democrats both to the territorial issue and to the national convention.[74] Under the prodding of Calhoun's movement for southern unity, a significant portion of the southern
Democracy had made a northern Democratic disavowal of the
Wilmot Proviso a *sine qua non* of its continued participation in
the national party.

CHAPTER IV

The Meaning of
the Wilmot Proviso
for the General Public

THE SOUTHERN DEMOCRATIC TREATMENT OF THE WILMOT Proviso question, like the earlier conflict over the question in Congress, indicates that the politicians were faced with an issue which was highly charged emotionally and capable of moving large numbers of people. The problem of the tremendous public appeal of the issue is an extremely vital one in view of the fact that it was this same issue which gave birth to the Republican party and precipitated the final crisis of the Union in 1860. The problem also appears somewhat baffling since the territorial issue seems in retrospect and seemed to many people at the time to be of dubious practical importance. It was widely recognized in the 1840's that the territory to which the Wilmot Proviso was to be applied was not particularly suited to slave labor, and later events were to demonstrate the reluctance of slaveowners to emigrate there with their slaves.[1] As has been pointed out, Calhoun himself initially did not expect slaves to be taken into the territories. And some antislavery men like John Quincy

Adams came to the same conclusion. Throughout the entire struggle the Polk administration and its supporters, as well as a number of other politicians, maintained that the contest was over a meaningless abstraction.

Even a contrary assumption, however, that significant slave-holder emigration to the territories was likely, does not resolve the questions raised by the widespread and intense appeal of the territorial issue. The nonslaveowners in both North and South appear to have had a very deep interest in the issue, all the more puzzling in view of the fact that relatively few of them would go into the territories. Why did the overwhelming majority of northerners demand that the right to take slaves into the territories be denied? And why were the three-quarters of the southern population who had no direct interest in the slavery institution—and who displayed when they themselves did emigrate a notable lack of interest or even an antipathy toward the institution—why were these people virtually unanimous in demanding that the right be upheld?[2] In retrospect, it would appear logical for the people in both sections to have decided that since the existing inhabitants of the territories were opposed to slavery, and since more emigrants would come ultimately from the North than from the South, the territories would eventually be formed into free states regardless of any action taken on the Proviso. It seems obvious, if only from the fact that even those southern politicians who were convinced that slavery could not exist in the territories were unalterably opposed to the Proviso, that the issue had a great deal more meaning for the people than the practical question which was involved, and it was this meaning which gave the Proviso its importance.[3]

It is difficult to apprehend the meaning of any particular political measure to the individuals who comprise the voting public, regardless of how important an issue the measure becomes. This is because public opinion must be inferred from the acts and thoughts of the politicians who mediate between it and political action, in the process by which the measure emerges and is dealt with as a major issue. The prominent journalist,

Walter Lippmann, has described this process as follows: "Since the general opinions of large numbers of persons are almost certain to be a vague and confusing medley, action cannot be taken until these opinions have been factored down, canalized, compressed, and made uniform. The making of one general will out of a multitude of general wishes . . . consists essentially in the use of symbols which assemble emotions after they have been detached from their ideas. . . . The process, therefore, by which general opinions are brought to cooperation consists of an intensification of feelings and a degradation of significance."[4] Although it appears to overestimate the politicians' control over the symbols and their ability to use them to manipulate the public, at least in its application to the Wilmot Proviso, the statement does offer a convenient starting point for an investigation of the meaning of a measure which became a major issue. The first thing to be noted is its suggestion that meaning lies in the emotional rather than in the intellectual content of the issue. If one chooses to follow Lippmann in dividing human experience into these categories, he can scarcely deny the importance of "emotional," as opposed to "rational," factors in the Proviso issue and in the sectional conflict in general.

The writers who have given the most careful attention to these "emotional" factors are those of the so-called revisionist school of American Civil War historians. These historians tend to view the concrete questions which separated North and South, such as slavery in the territories, as superficial issues which were exploited by agitators until they became so emotionally explosive that the election of Lincoln, which appears in retrospect to be a relatively minor provocation, brought on a war.[5] Avery O. Craven, one of the more moderate revisionists, maintains that what happened in the ante-bellum period was that the South became identified (and identified itself) with the institution of slavery, and that this identification made the abstract "emotional" question of the right and wrong of the institution the overriding issue which absorbed all others, reducing them to different forms of itself. Craven thus describes the process:

These larger [ethical] notions of the nature of the sectional struggle had emerged out of the conflicts over concrete issues such as expansion, land, and tariffs. A power struggle had developed which encouraged the glorification of selfish and unselfish attitudes toward positions and lifted them into the defense of principles. Abstractions had become more important than concrete things, and symbols had been substituted for them. The concrete issues had remained but more and more they represented some higher abstraction, some principle which could not be yielded.[6]

Although Craven's statement provides insight into the sectional controversy, there is, both in his work and in that of the other revisionists, a strong tendency to play down the basic moral conflict between the sections over slavery and to deprecate its absorption into the concrete issues of the day as an "irrational" departure from realism. Their attitude is vividly illustrated in the terse phrase which Craven elsewhere uses to sum up the effect of this absorption: "the right to hate had been achieved."[7]

This depreciatory attitude has been singled out by one critic of the revisionists, Arthur Schlesinger, Jr., as their major failing:

By denying themselves insight into the moral dimension of the slavery crisis . . . the revisionists denied themselves a historical understanding of the intensities that caused the crisis. It was the moral issue of slavery, for example, that gave the struggles over slavery in the territory or the enforcement of the fugitive slave laws their significance. These issues as the revisionists have shown with cogency were not in themselves basic. But they were the available issues. They were almost the only points within the constitutional framework where the moral conflict could be faced; as a consequence, they became charged with the moral and political dynamism of the central issue.[8]

It is not necessary to accept Schlesinger's assumption, which accords so well with current opinion, that the North assumed a moral and the South an immoral attitude toward the Negro in order to see that he has uncovered a real defect in revisionist thought. By evaluating actions and thoughts according to the categories of "emotional" and "rational," the revisionists tend to give short shrift to moral attitudes which do not fit exclusively into either. To denigrate the moral aspect of the conflict in this way is to distort the meaning which the historical events had for the people participating in them. The thoughts and actions of men reflect their entire personalities, including their moral attitudes, and are not better understood by being artificially categorized for purposes of historical valuation.[9]

On one point, however, Schlesinger and Craven are agreed. Both maintain that the concrete issues like the Wilmot Proviso came to symbolize the fundamental difference between the sections on the slavery question. This common conclusion suggests a modification of Lippmann's statement about the emergence of a vital public issue by the crystallization of a general will around a symbol. The process may involve an "intensification of feeling," but there is a "degradation of significance" only in the sense that there cannot be assigned to the symbol a single "rational" meaning which can be clearly and precisely defined. Political symbols tend to be open-ended, to convey a variety of meanings at several different levels, but they are the more, not the less, meaningful for that.

While the emergence of a significant political symbol depends much less upon the calculations of politicians than Lippmann and the revisionists suggest, it is not altogether a random process. It seems to occur in accordance with a principle by which the fittest of a number of symbols—i.e., the one which has the maximum potential for expressing the various meanings which come to cluster around it—achieves prominence in the public consciousness. It was not accidental, therefore, that the Wilmot Proviso issue should have become the principal symbolic realm in which the sectional controversy developed. The fundamental conflict appears inextricably linked, as Craven maintains, with the identification of the South with the slaveholding system. Of the other "available" concrete issues, the points, as Schlesinger calls them, "within the existing constitutional framework where the . . . [sectional] conflict could be faced," the tariff and internal improvements questions were less capable of operating symbolically because they were not directly connected with the institution of slavery. And the fugitive slave question, which was directly linked with the institution, was in certain respects a local issue and lacked the comprehensiveness of the territorial question.

Merely to indicate that slavery in the territories was the "fittest" of the "available" issues, however, does not demonstrate its peculiar adequacy as a symbolic vehicle for the conflict. Its own role in focusing the conflict and bringing it ultimately to a head should not be underestimated. Furthermore, Schlesinger's talk of "available issues . . . within the constitutional framework" tends to obscure the fact that a direct attack on the slavery institution never received any considerable support in the North. It is impossible to believe that this was wholly or even principally the result of constitutional delicacy. There was never any effort made in the North to change the constitution, such as occurred on the later questions of women's rights, prohibition, and the direct election of senators.[10] Another critic of the revisionists, Bernard De Voto, suggests that this failure is the vital question to be investigated with respect to the sectional conflict:

It is true that slavery in the territories was a peripheral issue. But for historians . . . *this is the point which must be explained.* It cannot be impatiently shrugged away or dismissed with a denunciation of some agitators whose blindness or willfulness or bigotry is supposed to have dropped it in the path of men of good will and so switched them into the maelstrom. . . . What was there in the nature of the American people, in their institutions, in their development and way of life, or in the sum of all these and more, that prevented them from facing their inescapable problem [slavery] in the nakedest light, with the soberest realism? What was there in the sum of American life that forbade us to go to the fundamentals and forced us to escape through subterfuges into war?[11]

De Voto's questions assume that the people consciously avoided the central issue of sectional conflict, the destruction or preservation of slavery. Thus the need for peripheral issues to "escape through subterfuges into war." It is possible that the Wilmot Proviso represented for some northern people a compromise be-

tween their bad consciences about slavery on the one hand and
their unwillingness to risk disunion as well as other terrifying
consequences of abolition on the other.[12]

The evidence on the Wilmot Proviso, however, suggests that
the answer to De Voto's question is that the "peripheral" issue
of slavery in the territories was a more adequate vehicle for
representing the sectional conflict—was, in fact, closer to the
essence of that conflict—than the more direct and practical question of the existence of slavery itself. Why this was so can be
fully explored through an analysis of the symbolism of the Wilmot Proviso, the prototypic form of the territorial issue, in order
to discover the various meanings the Proviso as symbol con-
veyed. The analysis will be largely, though not wholly, confined
to the period from 1846 to 1848, and since Calhoun and his
followers in the South and the Van Burenites in the North were
the principal political elements trying to make a popular appeal
on this issue, their respective interpretations will be emphasized.[13]

Man creates his social reality through his use of symbols. In
the process of symbolization he frequently exhibits a tendency
to treat unreal issues as if they were real.[14] The point to be made
in connection with the Wilmot Proviso is that most of the politicians of the day treated the issue publicly as if it were a question of the greatest *practical* importance, in spite of considerable
evidence that slavery was incompatible with the geography of
the territories. And this was true even of certain southern politicians who admitted this impracticality.[15] Thus, while Calhoun
told Polk that he did not expect slaves to be taken into the territories, he constantly acted as if there were a real and not just a
theoretical right to be defended. And General Waddy Thompson, the South Carolina Whig who went so far as to maintain
publicly that it was impossible for slavery to take root in the
territories, concluded from this not that the territorial issue was
meaningless but that the South should dissolve the Union if the
Wilmot Proviso passed Congress.[16] In general, however, those
who felt most strongly about the Proviso refused to admit that

the territorial issue might be purely academic. In defending the Proviso in Congress, David Wilmot claimed that not only would slaveholders take their slaves into the territories in the future if the measure was not adopted, but that they were already doing so, even before the territories had been annexed.[17] The report of the census of 1850 that there were only a handful of slaves in the territories would seem to indicate that these fears were groundless,[18] but, needless to say, it did not change the opinion of Wilmot and other advocates of the Proviso.

The politicians' treatment of the territorial issue in public speech and action as real indicates that it had a reality for the people as a whole, the apparent impracticality of the question to the contrary notwithstanding. A recognition of this returns to their proper perspective the intense arguments over the issue, which appear quite fantastic and divorced from reality as long as the debate seems to be no more than a mere academic exercise embittered by an infusion of "emotional" animosity between the sections. The question is not why was the public unrealistic, but what realities were embodied for the public in the territorial issue.

As the South began to identify itself with the slaveholding system and to differentiate itself from the free society in the North, which came to seem antithetical to it, it became more and more afraid of the growing relative strength of the North as evidenced in the census figures. This fear was reflected in the intense hostility of southerners to the Wilmot Proviso, which represented to them the determination of this growing power to appropriate the territories to itself, destroying the sectional balance of power and leaving the slaveholding states in its thrall. It was this fear that Calhoun expressed in his impassioned speech in the Senate opposing the Proviso, in which he said:

If this aggressive policy be followed—if the determination of the non-slaveholding States is to be adhered to hereafter, and we are to be entirely excluded from the territories which we already possess, or may possess . . . what will be our situation hereafter? . . . There will be but fourteen [states] on the part of the South—we are to be fixed, limited, and forever—and twenty-eight on the part of the non-slaveholding States. . . . The Government, sir, will be entirely in the hands of the non-slaveholding States—overwhelmingly. . . . We shall be at the entire mercy of the non-slaveholding States. Can we look to their justice and regard for our interests?

The answer was obviously no. He went on to predict: ". . . the day that the balance between the two sections of the country—the slaveholding States and the non-slaveholding States—is destroyed, is a day that will not be far removed from political revolution, anarchy, civil war, and widespread disaster. . . . If this scheme should be carried out—if we are to be reduced to a mere handful . . . wo, wo, I say to this Union."[19] It need scarcely be pointed out that in view of the geography of the far West it is difficult to see how the South could ever expect to maintain the sectional balance of power indefinitely, nor did Calhoun have any immediate suggestions on this score.[20] The speech was designed to appeal to the deeply rooted southern fear of northern dominance, and the unmentioned inevitability of that "dominance" (according to Calhoun's definition) merely heightened the appeal.

Adherents of the Wilmot Proviso represented their advocacy of the measure in the same way Calhoun and his followers represented their opposition to it, as an effort to stave off the complete subjugation of their section by the other. As the northern people came to identify the South with the alien slaveholding system, they came more and more to resent the disproportionate power that the slaveholders had been wielding in the republic, notwithstanding northern preponderance in numbers. The possible expansion of slavery into the territories in the Southwest threatened to increase that power still further. The Proviso, representing as it did a northern act of determination to prevent the territories from falling into the hands of the "slave power," expressed the northern fear of this threat.

This aspect of the Proviso's appeal to northerners is reflected in a speech defending the Wilmot Proviso given by George Rathbun, one of the leaders of the free-soil movement. In his speech

Rathbun "protested against the North being sacrificed, surrendered, betrayed, given over to the tender mercies of those who had governed them too long already."[21] According to Rathbun, the continued southern political dominance, in the face of northern numerical superiority, was the direct result of the slavery institution, which bound southern slaveholders together "by a cord so strong that no power had ever yet broken it," and invariably allowed them to triumph over a divided North.[22] Since the penetration of slavery into territories in the Southwest meant to Rathbun, as well as to the northern people to whom he appealed, the final triumph of the slaveowners, he argued that the defeat of the Wilmot Proviso would surrender the free states "bound and manacled to the South."[23] In a speech given to the Barnburners' convention at Utica in June of 1848, Martin Grover, another leader of the Proviso movement, reiterated the same theme. "The question is not whether black men are to be made free," said Grover, "but whether we white men are to remain free. (Cheers)" Grover went on to say that he "would as soon live under a monarchy as under the rule of 300,000 slaveholders."[24]

Northerners were all the more concerned about the threat of slaveholder dominance because of their conviction that the presence of slaves inhibited the emigration of nonslaveholders, thereby allowing the territories to become slaveholding states by default. This belief that free and slave labor were incompatible, one of the most frequently expressed ideas in congressional debate on the Proviso,[25] was boldly stated by the leading Barnburner organ, the New York *Evening Post,* in its explanation of the distinction between the abolition and the nonextension of slavery. "We put aside the question how long the slaveowner is to hold his negroes, and how he is to get rid of them if at all," said the *Post,* "and only demand that he shall not take them into the territories to expel the free laborer by the repulsion of their presence."[26] Advocates of free soil maintained that, given this incompatibility, to surrender the Wilmot Proviso would be to play directly into the hands of the slaveholders. "They want it [the new territory] for slaves," said Rathbun, "because where slavery exists the slave power prevails."[27] Precisely because they viewed the "slave power" through their own fears, as a political ruling class which could be expected to try to extend its power under any circumstances, the free-soilers tended to discount the economic impracticality of slavery in the territories, even when they recognized it.[28]

The claim of the slaveholders that they could speak for the entire South on the slavery question intensified the northern fear of national political dominance by the slavery interest. Since northern free-soilers believed that the real interests of nonslaveholders in the South were antithetical to the institution, the fact that these supposed interests did not produce any effective southern dissent from the slaveholders' policy of unmitigated opposition to the Proviso seemed to demonstrate the proof of Rathbun's dictum that "where slavery exists the slave power prevails." One antislavery journal,. the Washington *National Era,* examined in detail the slaveholders' claim to speak for the whole South. Unable to understand how southern nonslaveowners could be "anxious to fasten it [slavery] upon the new territory," the *Era* concluded: "We cannot believe the People of the South are represented fairly by the press. That powerful organ has fallen under the control of the ruling caste, the Slave Power, which recognizes no interest in the slave States but Slavery, no citizens there but slaveholders. We do not believe that even all the slaveholders are justly represented by this crusade in the Press in behalf of Slavery. But the iron despotism of the caste is too strong for individual independence."[29]

The "slave power's" apparent control over the South seemed to confirm the common northern belief that the institution of Negro slavery made it an aristocratic rather than a democratic society.[30] "Slavery converts society into two classes," claimed John Van Buren in a speech at a Barnburner meeting, "negroes and nabobs."[31] This oversimplified conception of southern society grossly underestimated the political, economic, and social significance of the nonslaveholding whites in the South, whom northerners tended to think of as poor white trash.[32] "We wish not to sneer at the South," editorialized Walt Whitman in his Barnburner journal, the Brooklyn *Eagle,* "but leaving out the educated and refined gentry, and coming to the common people of the whites, everybody knows what a miserable, ignorant, and shiftless set of beings they are."[33] Southern politicians tried to correct this distortion, but their protest appears to have been muted by their fear that an undue emphasis on the place of the nonslaveholding whites in southern society might impair their vaunted southern unity on the slavery question.[34]

The common northern image of an aristocratic South was an image of a backward and degraded society. Aside from violating the basic American democratic traditions, this kind of society was felt to be incapable of the "natural" progress characteristic of a free society. One of the favorite rhetorical devices of the adherents of the Wilmot Proviso in the congressional debates was to make invidious comparisons of the relative progress in free and slave states.[35] The advocates of the Proviso claimed that the presence of Negro slaves in a community degraded labor itself, an idea which fortified their belief that the presence of slaves in the territories would automatically exclude free labor.[36] This concept of "degradation" is fully developed in the "Address of the Democratic Members of the Legislature of the State of New York":

Where labor is to a considerable extent committed to slaves, to labor becomes a badge of inferiority. The wealthy capitalists who own slaves disdain manual labor; and the whites who are compelled to submit to it are regarded as having fallen below their natural condition in society. They cannot act on terms of equality with the masters for those social objects which in a community of equals educate, improve and refine all its members. In a word society, as it is known in communities of freemen, with its schools and its various forms of voluntary association for common benefit and mutual improvement, can be scarcely said to exist for them or their families.[37]

A later Barnburner manifesto summarized the unhappy results of this situation in the slaveholding states. According to one of the resolutions of the Utica Convention of June, 1848: "One of the great evils of slavery is the false degradation of labor, whereby, in slave countries the free laborer is, in effect, excluded from all those branches of industry usually carried on by slaves. Thus the accumulation of national wealth, and the progress of civilization are greatly retarded for the want of that energy, intelligence, and inventive skill which results from the competition of freemen."[38] The threat of slaveholder dominance, therefore, meant not only the perversion of the normal democratic institution of majority rule, but the triumph of a degraded society and a retrogression from civilization. As one of the leaders of the Proviso movement put it:

This is a national question. . . . It is one in which the North has a higher and deeper stake than the South possibly can have. It is a question whether in the government of the country she shall be borne down by the influence of your slaveholding aristocratic institution that have not in them the first element of Democracy. It is a question whether this Republic shall be weakened, cramped and degraded by an institution doomed of God and man. We know something of the curse of slavery and we have seen more; and had we not got rid of it we should be in as bad a condition as your more northern slave states now are. Hug this institution to your own bosom if you choose, until it eats out your very vitals, but let it not blast, and blight, and curse, with the mildew of heaven, any other portion of God's heritage, save where, by leave of the Constitution, it now exists.[39]

As evil an influence as they found the slavery institution, however, most advocates of the Proviso preemptorily dismissed the idea that their ultimate aim was abolition.[40] As long as the supposed threat of the triumph of the "aristocratic" slaveholding system could be met by excluding slavery from the territories, the South could be allowed to work out the problem of slavery on its own.[41]

Despite the apparent incompatibility of slavery with the geography of the territories, southerners deeply resented this attempt to isolate the South. "We are not advocating slavery," said the Washington *Union* in protest against the Wilmot Proviso, but "we deny the justice and fairness of making, by act of Congress, the new territory all northern in its social system."[42] One of the most galling aspects of the Proviso for southerners was its implicit assumption that southern society with its slave-holding system was inferior to that of the North. This concept is clearly illuminated in the following objection to the Wilmot Proviso by an Associate Justice of the United States Supreme Court, Peter V. Daniel of Virginia:

There is another aspect of this pretension which exhibits it as fraught with dangers far greater than any that can flow from mere calcula-tion of political influence, or of profit arising from a distribution of territory. It is that view of the case which pretends to an insulting exclusiveness or superiority on the one hand, and denounces a de-grading inequality or inferiority on the other; which says in effect to the Southern man, Avaunt! you are not my equal, and hence are to be excluded as carrying a moral taint with you. Here is at once the extinction of all fraternity, of all sympathy, of all endurance even; the creation of animosity fierce, implacable, undying. It is the unmitigated outrage which I venture to say, there is no true Southron from the schoolboy to the octogenarian, who is not prepared for any extremity in order to repel it.[43]

The deep resentment at being discriminated against manifested itself in early southern protests against the Proviso as depriving the South of its equal rights in the territories. One meeting in Alabama in the fall of 1846 resolved:

We hold this principle [of excluding slavery from the territories] to be unjust and upon it set our mark of disapprobation. We maintain that the territory when acquired should be open to the settlement of all citizens without restrictions; and assert that it is unjust to tax the slave states to pay for the country and to summon them to the battlefield to maintain our nation's rights and our nation's honor; and when the war-worn soldier returns to his home, with victory on his standard, is he to be told that he cannot carry his property to the country won by his blood, or purchased by his money?[44]

These protests, with their underlying resentment, were ab-sorbed in the southern constitutional arguments against the Pro-viso.[45] The southern penchant for constitutionalism was only in part responsible for this development. The real strength of the appeal of the constitutional argument was rooted in its denial of southern inferiority which the Proviso appeared to assert.[46] This explains why the South hastened to clothe the right to take slaves into the territories with the protection of the Constitution and made *it* the test of southern constitutional rights in general.[47] The Proviso represented to the South a denial of the very southern equality upon which Calhoun and the other southern politicians insisted so vehemently in their constitutional arguments.[48] Governor Joseph W. Mathews of Mississippi summed up just about everything of importance which seemed to be at stake on the constitutional question when he said in his inaugural speech of January 10, 1848: "We must know whether the compromises of the constitution are to be respected; whether citizens of the slave states are to be considered as equals with their northern brethren, and whether slavery is regarded as such a crime that they who hold this species of property are unworthy of an association with the inhabitants of the free states."[49] The southern rights movement, centering around the question of slavery in the territories, expressed the southern demand for the repudiation of the idea that the development of southern society ran contrary to the mainstream of national development. As the famous "Alabama Platform" put it: "We declare our unalterable determination . . . [not] to hold fellowship or communion with those who attempt to denationalize the South and its institutions by its [their] restrictions upon its citizens."[50]

The galling insult of relegating the South to a position of definite inferiority was all the more difficult to bear because it appeared to project the ultimate triumph of the northern over the southern social system and the ultimate extinction of the slaveholding institution itself. It was this basic fear to which the southern people as a whole responded in their fight against the Wilmot Proviso. It may be true that slavery would not have continued to survive in the ante-bellum South if it had not been economically profitable, but its emotional value for most southerners, and particularly those with no direct economic interest in it, was as a social institution.

The emotional appeal of slavery as an institution of social control has been aptly described by Ulrich Bonnell Phillips as one facet of the "central theme of southern history":

> [The South is,] above all, as to the white folk a people with a common resolve indomitably maintained—that it shall be and remain a white man's country. The consciousness of a function in these premises, whether expressed with the frenzy of a demogogue or maintained with a patrician's quietude, is the cardinal test of a Southerner and the central theme of Southern history. It arose as soon as the negroes became numerous enough to create a problem of race control in the interest of orderly government and the maintenance of Caucasian civilization. Slavery was instituted not merely to provide control of labor but also as a system of racial adjustment and social order. And when in the course of time slavery was attacked, it was defended not only as a vested interest, but with vigor and vehemence as a guarantee of white supremacy and civilization.[51]

The commitment to maintain white supremacy via Negro slavery explains the deep emotional attachment that nonslaveholders had to the institution, an attachment that all southerners recognized and some puzzled over. "It is not perfectly farcical," wrote a Georgian in 1849, "that the people who own slaves should be perfectly quiet, and we who own none should be lashing ourselves into a rage about their wrongs and injuries?"[52] The nature of the nonslaveholder's attachment to slavery is vividly illustrated in the opinion which a poor white in Alabama expressed on the subject of emancipation:

> I'd like it if we could get rid of 'em to yonst. I wouldn't like to have 'em freed, if they was gwine to hang 'round. They ought to get some country, and put 'em war they could be by themselves. . . . Now suppose they was free, you'd see they'd all think themselves as good as we; of course they would, if they was free. Now just suppose you had a family of children, how would you like to hev a niggar feelin' just as good as a white man? how'd you like to hev a niggar steppin' up to your darter? Of course you wouldn't, and that's the reason I wouldn't like to hev 'em free.[53]

Nearly all southerners believed that the presence of large numbers of Negroes in the South made Negro slavery an absolute requirement for the peaceful coexistence of the two races.[54] Just how strong this conviction was that slavery was a social necessity is revealed in a series of articles in the Charleston *Mercury* in the summer of 1847 designed to appeal to southern fears in order to arouse the South to the dangers of free soil. Although one of the articles admitted that the territories were unsuited to slavery,[55] the brunt of the message was the dire consequences which would follow closing off this outlet to the slave population. The Wilmot Proviso was assumed to be the equivalent of abolition because it drew *"a line of political and social demarcation around the Slave States."*[56] This would result in the South being surrounded by a hostile people: "on every side girt round with those who will continually excite our slaves to insubordination and revolt, which it would be folly to suppose would forever be resisted."[57]

The *Mercury's* discussion of the ensuing "servile conflict with all its horrors" suggests the fear and hatred of the Negro which lay behind the belief in the necessity of slavery as an institution of social control: "If the white triumphs, victory itself will be death [for the Negro]. If foreign aid [i.e., aid from the North] make the slave the victor, misery far greater than death will follow him whose unbridled passions will find in the contempt of all restraint, human and divine, a theatre for its display that will make humanity shudder."[58] On the surface, however, the *Mercury* justified the southern position on the ground not of hatred of the Negro but of love for him and a desire to protect him from his real enemies in the North:

Providence, in permitting the removal of a portion of the African race to the shores of America, confided their welfare, temporal and eternal, to *our* keeping; and upon us rests the responsibility of protecting their innocence and helplessness against the rapacious and unscrupulous encroachments of our own race; upon us, in the exercise of that foresight and wisdom with which we are endowed, and not they, devolves the responsibility of securing for them and us, as one family, a just partition of the common territory. They are our family and the world spurns and rejects them. Who feels one throb of love for the negro, but the master who has reared and fostered them?[59]

But this love was evidently absolutely contingent upon the preservation of the institution of Negro slavery which the advocates of the Proviso meant to destroy. "They propose," claimed the *Mercury,* "to circumscribe our territorial limits, and by hemming us in on all sides, and preventing emigration, exhaust our lands while they force upon us a redundant and useless [black] population."[60] This would result in a mass emigration of the non-slaveholding whites and ultimately in the slaves being "left to their own control."[61] The freeing of the slaves would drastically alter the nature of race relations. "They would rapidly return to barbarism," concluded the *Mercury,* "and invite for themselves the fate of the Aborigines of America. That they would soon be exterminated by the white race, under such circumstances, does not admit of reasonable doubt."[62]

As this analysis by the *Mercury* makes clear, the vast majority of southerners considered not the institution of slavery but the large Negro population as the primary problem faced by the South; slavery was rather the solution to this problem.[63] But if the desire for white supremacy was the strongest emotional force behind the southern opposition to the Wilmot Proviso, it seems likewise to have been one of the strongest emotional forces for the movement for the Proviso in the North, particularly among Democrats. Ulrich Bonnell Phillips, the primary advocate of the "white supremacy" interpretation of slavery, uses a quote from a contemporary northern writer to illustrate this striking similarity:

True to his instincts of conquerer, colonizer, founder, the Saxon of the North claims this land [the territories] for himself; he shall occupy it and till it, live on it and by it. Moved by the same inherent spirit, the Saxon of the South makes a similar demand. . . . Why may not he, as well as the northern man, go to the new territories with his property? To this the northern Saxon replies, that these negroes are not property, but men, and bring with them human influences, not of the highest order. But whether property or not, they will occupy the land and consume its produce, both and all of which he wants for his own race.[64]

Closely interwoven with the northern fear of slaveholder dominance was fear of the Negro himself, and the Proviso, commonly called the "White Man's Resolution" by free-soilers,[65] seems to have expressed a northern desire to keep the territories free not only of slaves but of the black race.

The rhetoric of the free-soil movement is replete with expressions of hostility toward the Negro. One of the most notable instances occurs in James Russell Lowell's allegorical treatment of the territorial issue in his enormously popular *Biglow Papers*. In this poem Lowell represents the Negroes as "long-legged swine" who ruin the territories, making them uninhabitable for the northern farmer.[66] Anti-Negro expressions also found their way into free-soil platforms, albeit in muted form. The Barnburners' Utica Convention of June, 1848, called for preserving the western land "for the Caucasian race," or in the more popular parlance of Thomas Hart Benton "keeping the territory clean of negroes."[67] The pronouncements of individual congressmen did not exhibit the same sense of restraint as the platforms. One free-soiler assured the House of Representatives that he had little concern for "the degraded and degenerate blacks."[68]

Northern hostility toward the Negro is likewise revealed in the vehement response to a proposal by Governor William Smith of Virginia to export the state's freedmen to the North. In his speech representing the great dangers involved in rejecting the Wilmot Proviso, George Rathbun referred incidentally to Governor Smith's proposal. "What do we say [to it]?" asked Rathbun. He gave the answer: "That there is no territory in the free States belonging to them [the Negroes]; that there is no place for them. As far as New York is concerned, should the refuse part of the population of Virginia reach our territory, we will carry them back to Virginia."[69] Smith's proposal caused such consternation in Ohio that the Democratic minority in the state legislature was almost able to force through a law prohibiting Negro immigration altogether.[70] One Democratic congressman from Ohio who opposed the Wilmot Proviso, appealing to the fear and hatred of the Negro in the North, used Smith's proposal as a justification for bowing to the will of the South on the Proviso question. Negroes "were as great a curse as would come among any people," declared William Sawyer, and he "would consent to almost anything to keep them out of the bounds of the free states."[71]

Contrary to the peculiar bent of Sawyer's argument, the general effect of the northern fear of the Negro seems to have strengthened sentiment for the Proviso.[72] In the North, where the Negro population was relatively small, the means of assuring white supremacy was to exclude the Negro, and when he could not be physically excluded, he was excluded from civic life.[73] The enforced emigration of southern Negroes did not appear to be as great a threat to white supremacy in the North as the danger of populating the territories with Negroes.[74] In 1848, Lewis Henry Morgan, the anthropologist, wrote to Calhoun from New York in relation to the issue of slavery in the territories:

We are afraid of the indefinite propagation of the colored race, upon which the South seems determined. The feeling towards that race in the North is decidedly that of hostility. There is no respect for them. No wish for their elevation; but on the contrary a strong desire to prevent the multiplication of the race so far as it is possible to do so, by such legislation as shall be constitutional and just. The attachment to the Union is unwavering; and the mass of the people have no disposition to encroach upon the Constitutional rights of the Southern States. But I think it must be regarded as certain, that if a conviction seizes the public mind, that Congress has power to make the territories of the Republic free, without infringing the rights of any portion of the country, this conviction will be persisted in to the last extremity.[75]

These northern fears were fully articulated and integrated into the struggle for the Wilmot Proviso in a speech by John A. Dix on the territorial question, which was reprinted in full in the official summary of the Free-Soil movement. After giving a historical justification of the power of Congress to legislate for the territories, Dix defined what he considered the central matter at stake on the Proviso issue: "One of the most interesting and important problems, both for the American statesman and philosopher, is to determine of what race or races this vast population shall consist; for on the solution which future generations shall give to it will essentially depend the prosperity of the community or communities they will constitute, and their ability to maintain such a form of government as shall secure to them the blessings of political liberty and an advanced civilization."[76] Dix claimed that where slavery existed the colored population tended to increase, so that its extension into the territories would mean a rise in the number of Negroes in the United States, both absolutely and relative to the number of whites. "An enlargement of the surface over which slavery is spread," concluded Dix, "carries with it, by force of invincible laws, a multiplication of the race held in bondage, in other words a substantial increase in the number of slaves."[77] On the other hand, free society suffered from no such liability, according to Dix. He defined the situation of the "inferior caste" there as follows: "Public opinion at the North—call it prejudice if you will—presents an insuperable barrier against its elevation in the social scale. . . . A class thus degraded [first] will not multiply. . . . [Then] it will not be reproduced; and in a few generations the process of extinction is performed. Nor is it the work of inhumanity or wrong. It is the slow but certain process of nature, working out her ends by laws so steady and so silent, that their operation is only seen in their results."[78] Dix would forbear to interfere with slavery where it existed. The speech represented the Proviso not as an attack upon the institution as a solution to the Negro problem in the South, where the black race was numerous, but as a means of preventing the extension of the southern Negro problem to the rest of the nation. By promising that the Proviso would mean the elimination of the Negro everywhere in the republic except in the South, where it would be localized, Dix was able to appeal directly to the hostility which the white man of the North felt for the colored race.

Antagonistic as most northerners were toward the southern institution of Negro slavery, and fearful as they were of slaveholder domination, neither the movement for the Wilmot Proviso nor later free-soil movements represented a direct attack upon the institution where it existed. The nature of the appeal of the Wilmot Proviso in the North suggests that what the northern people wanted was not to destroy slavery in the South but to localize the alleged bad influences emanating not only from the institution itself but also from the presence of large numbers of Negroes. Jacob Brinkerhoff once remarked in connection with the Proviso that he had "selfishness enough greatly to prefer the welfare of my own race, and vindictiveness enough to wish to leave and keep upon the shoulders of the South the burden of the curse which they themselves created and courted."[79] What he seems to have meant by the "curse" which the South "created and courted" was a large Negro population. If slavery and slaves could be kept out of the territories, this "curse," the southern Negro problem, could be isolated and would not encumber the future development of the republic. The key to the strong emotional commitment in the North to free soil was the overwhelming fear of the extension of an alien race, as well as of an alien institution, to the point where they would directly affect the northern people. The Wilmot Proviso had such a strong appeal precisely because it expressed the northern determination to prevent the spread not only of slavery but of the despised Negro as well.

The southern response to the territorial issue contained the same elements of racial fear and hatred. As much as they resented the insult of the Proviso's denial of their moral equality, the southern people were most afraid that they would be isolated within the union, left alone with their Negro problem and their slaveholding solution; thus isolated the South would become an alien and inferior section, and ultimately its social system would yield to that of the North, precipitating a bitter racial conflict.

The southern decision to secede represented an acceptance of southern isolation after the battle for the territories had been irrevocably lost in the election of 1860. The southern people chose to carry this isolation to the logical conclusion of founding a separate nation in order to safeguard the institution on which they thought southern society—and white supremacy—depended.

CHAPTER V

Escape from the Wilmot Proviso: The Emergence of Popular Sovereignty

IN SPITE OF THE GENERAL APPEAL OF THE WILMOT PROVISO IN the North, the Barnburners were much less successful in keeping the territorial issue before the public than Calhoun and his supporters were in the South. Besides having, in the Proviso question, a very popular issue of which they were the principal advocates, the Barnburners had certain other things in common with Calhoun and his South Carolina followers. The party machinery in their own state was in their hands, and they had many Democratic allies outside their state, although in no instance did these allies have complete control over their state organizations. The differences were much more significant, however. The Barnburners were potentially much stronger than the Calhounites; they aspired to their former dominant position within the national Democratic party which they had occupied when Van Buren was the party leader. And because New York was the most important state in Democratic calculations in future national elections, these aspirations were not altogether unrealistic. On the other hand, they were much more deeply committed to the Democratic party than their South Carolina counterparts, and if they were potentially stronger they had correspondingly less freedom of action.

This problem was complicated by their lack of strong and decisive leadership. Of their two leaders of national prominence, Martin Van Buren and Silas Wright, the first had been retired from active politics for three years and the second was anxious to become so after his recent defeat in the gubernatorial election. Neither had been consulted about raising the territorial issue in the first place, and neither approved of this course of action. Both were highly cautious party politicians, not deeply committed, as Calhoun was, to introducing a new major issue into politics. This left the direction of the free-soil issue in the hands of lesser figures who were unable to co-ordinate the actions of the group as a whole. Finally, the Barnburners' hold on the party machinery in New York was precarious and subject to continual challenge from their rivals, the Hunkers.

The fact that the northern struggle for the Wilmot Proviso was intimately bound up with the Barnburners' struggle for political power meant that it was also closely linked with Wright's presidential candidacy, the second lever by which the Barnburners hoped to regain control of the national party. It was essential for their purpose that Wright be identified with the Wilmot Proviso. When one of the Hunker journals contended that Wright was opposed to the Proviso, the New York *Post* vigorously denied the charge, and one of the Barnburners wrote to Wright asking for a public commitment.[1] Wright was reluctant to be drawn into the political struggle. He authorized the *Post* to state that it knew he favored the Proviso, but requested that the letter in which he expounded his views not be published.[2]

The Barnburners waged a covert campaign to advance Wright to the presidency. Some of them tried to win over Hunker and even Calhounite support for Wright.[3] The most important effort to strengthen public sentiment for Wright's candidacy was made by Senator Thomas Hart Benton of Missouri. Next to Van Buren and Wright, Benton had greater national prestige than any political figure associated with the Barnburners, and some of his Missouri followers, feeling that the time had come to advance his claims to the presidency, proposed his nomination in 1848. In a letter rejecting this nomination, Benton attacked Calhoun's Senate resolutions on the Wilmot Proviso as an attempt to exclude northern Democratic candidates from the presidency by instituting a proslavery test for the nominee. Benton advised the party to ignore this "test" and nominate a candidate from the nonslaveholding states, his intention being to influence the public in favor of Wright.[4] The New York *Post* reprinted Benton's letter and soon afterward began to call attention to the support of Wright's candidacy expressed in other northern Democratic journals, but this was the extent of the Barnburners' public advocacy of Wright's nomination.[5]

If the Barnburners did not publicly advance Wright's claims to the presidency, still less did they agitate the territorial issue, in spite of their threat to do so at the end of the congressional session.[6] While they remained determined to press the Wilmot Proviso, only those—like Preston King—most deeply committed to free soil for its own sake tried to keep the question before the general public.[7] Most of them evidently felt that it was unnecessary and perhaps inexpedient to keep the public aroused over the issue, that it was intrinsically popular enough to be revived whenever it suited their purpose.

In the meantime, however, President Polk was making a subtle effort to dissipate support for the Wilmot Proviso. Early in July, Polk made a good will tour through the northeastern states, the center of Proviso sentiment. Although he never specifically referred to the territorial issue, the President pleaded for harmony and union and deprecated sectional conflict everywhere he went.[8] "I would recommend in all parts of our beloved country," he told the Maine legislature, "cultivation of that feeling of brotherhood and mutual regard, between the North and the South, and the East and the West, without which we may not anticipate the perpetuity of our free institutions."[9]

The President's appeal, plus the strong stand of southern Democrats on the Wilmot Proviso, did have a moderating influence on Democratic sentiment in the North. By September, Secretary of State James Buchanan, anxious to acquire southern support for his presidential candidacy, felt that northern opinion was prepared to accept his public advocacy of the extension of the Missouri Compromise line as the solution for the territorial issue.[10] Buchanan's stand tended to undermine still further public sentiment for the Wilmot Proviso in the North upon which the Barnburners were relying in their drive for political power.[11]

The Barnburners suffered an even more severe reversal when Silas Wright died suddenly in late August. This unexpected event deprived them of a popular and prestigious presidential candidate who was irreplaceable, and compounded their leadership problem.[12] Owing to complacency and indifference, the Barnburners had not prepared very thoroughly for the next round in their organizational struggle with the Hunkers.[13] Instead of rousing them from their lethargy, the shock of Wright's death weakened them still further by rendering many of his supporters temporarily apathetic,[14] and the Hunkers were able to make further gains at their expense in rounding up delegates for the forthcoming state convention in October. In addition, the Hunkers elected rival delegates to challenge Barnburners in certain of the districts, a strategy which ultimately won them control of the convention.[15]

In the meantime, the Barnburners' position on the Wilmot Proviso appeared to be further weakened by a speech commemorating Wright given by Francis P. Blair, the former editor of the old Van Buren organ in Washington. Blair maintained that not only had Wright not been responsible for the introduction of the Wilmot Proviso at the last session of Congress but that his views of the territorial question had been incompatible with the measure. "Wright's doctrine," said Blair, was "non-interference on the part of the government with the domestic institutions existing among the people of States in, or coming into, the Union. If this principle be correct, Congress cannot extirpate slavery where it exists nor create it where it does not exist." This meant, according to Blair, that residents of the incipient states which comprised the territory should be able to retain the existing laws on slavery.[16] Wright's position, as delineated by Blair, did not make clear whether existing laws would prevent the taking of slaves into the territories or whether, if they did, the laws were subject to revision by the residents themselves, but it did seem antithetical to the Wilmot Proviso. To refute this suggestion and to shore up the Barnburners' positive stand on the Proviso, the New York *Evening Post* published an excerpt from Wright's letter of the previous spring. The key passage read: "If the question had been propounded to me at any period of my public life—'Shall the arms of the Union be employed to conquer, or the money of the Union be used to purchase, territory now constitutionally free for the purpose of planting slavery upon it'—I should have answered no! And this answer to this question is the Wilmot Proviso, as I understand it."[17] The Barnburners were thus able to identify Wright with the Proviso posthumously much more completely than they had been able to while he was alive.

Confident that they would control the forthcoming state convention, some Barnburners talked of bypassing the territorial issue entirely in order to retain the support of the Hunkers in the ensuing state campaign.[18] But the factional leaders, as well as the dedicated free-soilers, were looking beyond the state election to 1848 and were determined to rely upon "principles," in the absence of a presidential candidate, to advance their political fortunes.[19] In the interest of harmony, however, the leaders were prepared to accept a simple assertion of the free-soil principle and to forego explicit mention of the Wilmot Proviso, in spite of a strong plea from Preston King against such a concession.[20]

When the convention met on September 29, the Hunkers challenged the credentials of a number of the Barnburner delegates, and were able to neutralize enough votes by this means to give them a clear majority.[21] Much to the chagrin of the Barnburners, they were able to replace the incumbent state officers with nominees of their own choosing and reorganize the state central committee to give themselves control.

The rising tension between the two factions came to a head late at night on the fourth and final day of the convention when the platform committee finally reported.[22] Earlier in the evening one of the more outspoken Barnburners proposed resolutions which concluded by declaring "uncompromising hostility to the extension of slavery to territory now free by the act of the general government." Although the resolutions did not mention the Wilmot Proviso and fell short of demanding the prohibition of slavery in the territories, the Hunkers wanted to avoid a direct vote on them. They recognized that they represented a threat to national party unity and would offend the Polk administration, to which the Hunkers looked for support. Moreover, the territorial issue was a political weapon of the opposing faction. On the other hand, the Hunkers did not wish to openly repudiate free soil for fear of offending public opinion in New York. Recognizing that they had a much better chance of bypassing the territorial issue if they postponed consideration of the question until the last possible moment when many of the delegates would be tired and anxious to adjourn, they had no intention of allowing the proposed resolutions to interfere with their delaying tactics.

Following the suggestion of a Hunker who argued that discussion of platform resolutions await the committee report, the convention tabled the resolutions. When at last the committee reported, the platform was completely silent on the territorial issue. David Dudley Field moved that the resolutions proposed earlier be appended to the committee platform, but the Hunkers defeated the move with technical objections. When Field offered a substitute amendment, one Hunker began to complain: "It is now after 12 o'clock—any gentlemen who honor the Sabbath . . . ," a comment interrupted by a shout of derision from the Barnburner partisans. Field made a speech defending his amendment, but before it could be further discussed, one of the Hunkers moved that the previous question on the platform committee's resolutions and address be acted upon. Amid angry protests from the Barnburners, the chairman ruled that the motion cut off Field's amendment and ordered a vote on the motion. Preston King appealed to the convention itself against the ruling and nearly brought the delegates to blows. As one reporter described it:

Of course Mr. K[ing] was violently excited; his language showed that his agitation was extreme. He was called to order by more than a dozen men who stood upon the rostrum, but he paid no heed to their calls; his friends encircled him and cheered him on. Mr. King became so exasperated at the drowning cries of the opposition that he shook his fist at the conservatives [Hunkers] who were standing in a body upon the left of the speaker's chair; the conservatives in turn shook their fists at the radicals, and both sections prepared for a personal conflict—a general and indiscriminate fight. Nearly every delegate in the room was screaming at the top of his voice. Not a syllable spoken could be distinguished. This shouting continued about a quarter of an hour, and happily each of the sections seemed to be satisfied with pugilistic feints, and pushing and crowding. Some idea of the nature of the proceedings may be formed when it is stated that one of the secretaries fainted in his seat from fright.[23]

Order was finally restored and a vote taken. By this time it was nearly three o'clock in the morning and many of the delegates had apparently gone home. The motion for the previous question was carried by a vote of 49 to 32, only slightly more than half of the delegates voting. The convention then approved the committee platform by a voice vote, ignoring Barnburner objections that a quorum was lacking as well as their demands to record the vote. The adjournment of the convention marked a total victory for the Hunkers. Not only had they managed to acquire control of the state party machinery, they had also succeeded, at least temporarily, in completely suppressing the territorial issue.

Outraged at their defeat and confident of popular support, many of the Barnburner delegates wanted to demonstrate their disapproval of the convention proceedings. Under the leadership of Churchill C. Cambreleng and John Van Buren they held a caucus on Sunday afternoon to decide what to do. Preston King proposed that they call a new convention to nominate a separate slate of candidates, but on Cambreleng's advice it was decided instead to remain passive during the campaign, allowing the Whigs to win the election.[24] After a day's delay the Barnburner organ in Albany, the *Atlas,* placed the Syracuse ticket upon its masthead but refrained from an editorial endorsement.[25]

The two emerging Barnburner leaders made an interesting contrast. Short and inclined to portliness, Cambreleng never allowed his dedication to free soil to overcome his sense of restraint. An old associate of former President Van Buren, he was the elder statesman of the antislavery radicals and a steadying influence on the Barnburners.[26] It was precisely this steadiness, which Cambreleng had in common with the elder Van Buren, that "Prince John" lacked. John Van Buren's tall thin figure was most impressive in addressing an audience, and he had the impetuousness which so often accompanies great oratorical skill.[27] The heart and soul of the Barnburners' antislavery movement, he himself seems to have been moved by all the various motives which influenced the faction to follow that course.[28] He was deeply resentful of his father's rejection at the Democratic convention in 1844 and strongly hostile toward those to whom he attributed it.[29] Although he approved of Preston King's reintroduction of the Wilmot Proviso, he developed a strong interest in the territorial issue only on the eve of the Syracuse Convention when it appeared that it might serve as a useful tool with which to smite his Hunker enemies.[30] His humiliation at the convention when the Hunkers successfully challenged his credentials as a delegate led him to act in close concert with the antislavery radicals although he did not seem to be altogether comfortable with them.[31] His subsequent decision to agitate the territorial issue provided the main impetus for the Barnburners' antislavery movement, a movement which he and his associates were to desert in the 1850's.

John Van Buren triggered the movement shortly after the Syracuse Convention, notwithstanding his apparent acquiescence in the decision to remain passive during the campaign. He had participated in a meeting in Albany of the *Atlas* editors and several Barnburners in the state legislature the night after the Syracuse Convention, in which it was decided that the *Atlas* should give a "full and authentic account" of the meeting, exposing the Hunkers' machinations.[32] In addition the *Atlas* was to reprint in each of its succeeding issues the resolution offered to the convention by Field along with the quotation: "The stone which the builders rejected, the same shall be the head of the corner."[33] The meeting had also evidently agreed to refrain from attacking the Syracuse ticket,[34] a policy which John Van Buren quickly violated. He arranged a meeting in Albany for the night of Friday, October 8, at which he denounced the Syracuse nominees as well as the proceedings at the convention.[35] The following day the *Atlas* endorsed the meeting and welcomed the appeals which it claimed were pouring in from all over the state for a state-wide Democratic convention to protest the actions taken at Syracuse.[36] In order to make the convention appear more official, the *Atlas* proposed that the call be issued by the Democratic delegates from the Syracuse Convention itself.

Recognizing that such evidence of party disloyalty would place the Barnburners at a political disadvantage and concerned lest his own name be linked with the movement, the elder Van Buren tried to prevent the calling of the Herkimer meeting.[37] But the older Barnburner leaders responsive to his wishes were incapable of restraining the younger radicals under his son's impetuous leadership. The younger men were prepared to throw off the restraints of party loyalty in the name of the free-soil principle, and the fact that the Whigs were able to fully exploit their protest gave them no more pause than the warnings of their older leaders.[38] On October 18, after ascertaining that a majority of the Barnburner delegation at Syracuse favored a meeting, the *Atlas* issued the call for a mass convention at Herkimer on the 26th over the names of several of the Barnburner delegates at Syracuse.[39] Former President Van Buren did what he could to disassociate himself from the movement. Rejecting a Barnburner plea that he commit himself publicly in favor of the Wilmot Proviso, he wrote an open letter instead, declining to be a presidential candidate and endorsing the Polk administration's war policy without mentioning the territorial issue.[40]

But the Herkimer rebellion was in full swing without the former President. Condemnation of the movement by the Washington *Union* only strengthened the determination of the radical Barnburners.[41] The so-called Herkimer Convention, held just a week before the state election, was almost entirely given over to an execration of the Hunkers for their alleged betrayal of the free-soil principle.[42] The high point of the meeting was John Van Buren's resounding denunciation of the Syracuse Convention. But the general temper of the convention was even more clearly revealed by the reaction to a plea by David Wilmot to support the Syracuse ticket. One observer reported that "here loud cries were raised in opposition in all parts of the House, and after the passage of questions and explanations on both sides . . . the audience begged Mr. Wilmot to leave that part of the subject."[43] It was only with difficulty that Wilmot and John Van Buren managed to prevent independent nominations. John Van Buren assured the convention that he would not vote for the Syracuse nominees, and the platform which he prepared advised the Democratic electors "to vote as they must do when no regular nominations have been made."[44]

The defection led to an overwhelming defeat for the Syracuse ticket. The Herkimer men were generally well pleased with the results. Strong adherents of free soil like Preston King were quite prepared to sacrifice Democratic success to principle. "Against any compromise of freedom," wrote King soon after the election, "the cry of repeal and of liberty will ring out shrill and terrible, and the goths and the vandals will come if they only can be relied upon for liberty."[45] Regular politicians like John Van Buren were less certain about what they had done, but still felt that the election had strengthened their position by demonstrating their drawing power.[46]

Many of the older Barnburner leaders took a different view

of the election. They were deeply concerned about the taint of irregularity which attached to the Herkimer meeting, and were anxious to commence efforts to recapture the regular party machinery lost to the Hunkers at Syracuse.[47] Even they, however, appear to have underestimated the adverse effect of the Herkimer movement on Democratic opinion outside New York. The Barnburners at Herkimer had committed the cardinal sin of party politics, open disloyalty during an election campaign, and even their closest allies in other state parties took a jaundiced view of such proceedings.[48] The result was to strengthen the Hunkers' claim with party politicians outside New York to be the legitimate representatives of the Democratic voters in the state. The outcome of the election might give pause to these politicians since it had demonstrated that Barnburner support was a necessary condition for victory. But it had not demonstrated that it was a sufficient condition. Since there was no way of judging the real preference of the Democratic voters in New York, the Barnburners appeared to most Democratic politicians outside the state to be no more than a minority faction of questionable party loyalty.[49] The shrewdest appraisal of the situation was made by one of Calhoun's New York correspondents who commented: "Our State election is over and the enemies of what they term the 'Southern influence' have destroyed their own influence and placed the matter of the next president in the hands of the South."[50]

The Barnburners' loss of status as well as their loss of control of the state party machinery deprived them of the ability to shape the territorial issue according to their desires, and gave northern Democratic politicians an opportunity to come to an accommodation with their southern associates on the question.[51] This intraparty issue was complicated by the primary interparty issues, the Mexican War and the annexation of Mexican territory. Holding the Democrats responsible for the war in the first place, most Whig politicians opposed Democratic demands for territorial indemnity. By opposing annexation altogether, the Whigs could dispense with the divisive territorial issue. The titular head of the Whig party, Henry Clay, added his weight to the antiannexationist policy in a speech in Lexington, Kentucky, on November 13, which launched his campaign for the Whig presidential nomination.[52] The resolutions Clay presented at the close of his speech condemned the Polk administration for beginning the Mexican War and summarized Whig objections to its current war policy. In an obvious attempt to appeal to antislavery sentiment in the North, Clay included among them the following: "Resolved That we do positively and emphatically disclaim and disavow any foreign territory whatever for the purpose of propagating slavery, or of introducing slavery into such foreign territory."[53]

Confident that Clay would be the Whig nominee for president,[54] the Democratic politicians were anxious to unite their party on an expansionist platform, hoping thereby to repeat their victory of 1844. There were more immediate reasons than the forthcoming presidential contest, however, for the Democrats to unite on an annexationist policy. Negotiations with Mexico had broken down in the autumn of 1847, and the Polk administration seemed to have no choice but to pursue the war to total victory. The prospect of total victory, coupled with the additional sacrifices necessary to achieve it, whetted the appetites of Democratic politicians both in the administration and in Congress for more extensive territorial acquisitions than they had been demanding previously. In fact, a movement sprang up among them for the annexation of all Mexico, a movement which continued to gain momentum in the winter of 1847-48 until it was suddenly deflated by Nicholas Trist's unexpected and unauthorized negotiation of a peace treaty.[55]

Any annexationist platform comprehending the newly aroused acquisitive desires as well as the needs of the presidential campaign had inevitably to deal with the issue of slavery in the territories which so disturbed the Democratic party. Buchanan had already proposed as a solution to the question the extension of the Missouri Compromise line to any territory acquired, but his proposal was unsatisfactory for a number of reasons. By allowing slaves to be taken into the territory south of the 36° 30' line, it directly violated the free-soil principle to which a large segment of northern opinion had committed itself.[56] The editor of the New York *Sun* frankly confessed to Buchanan that "we have much to do here in New York if the mass is to be instructed in its new catechism."[57] Actually, the task of rapidly remolding public opinion to this extent at a time when one of the party factions was pulling in precisely the opposite direction was well nigh impossible. Significantly enough, the Democratic state convention in Pennsylvania which nominated Buchanan for the presidency rejected the extension of the Missouri Compromise line as a party platform.[58] Moreover, although southern Democratic politicians generally (and presumably the southern public) would have been satisfied with the extension of the 36° 30' line,[59] they had largely committed themselves to Calhoun's constitutional argument against prohibiting slavery anywhere in the territory. This did not preclude the Missouri Compromise line as a final legislative settlement of the territorial issue, but the transparent inconsistency of now adopting such a position as a public platform rendered it highly vulnerable to attacks both from the Whigs and from the Calhoun Democrats.

Three weeks after the publication of Buchanan's letter, Vice-President George M. Dallas, a bitter opponent in Pennsylvania politics and a rival candidate for the presidency, had come up with a more promising idea in a speech at Pittsburgh. Apparently rejecting any and all congressional action on the slavery question, Dallas proposed "leaving to the people of the territory to be acquired the business of settling the matter for themselves. They have the right alone," he continued, "to determine their own institutions."[60]

The usefulness of Dallas' "popular sovereignty" idea depended in large part upon its ambiguity. Virtually every Democratic politician recognized the right of the people of a territory to decide the slavery question when they were admitted as a state into the Union. If the Dallas proposal meant no more than this, it was perfectly commonplace except in being a suggestion compatible with Calhoun's constitutional argument to which southern Democrats were firmly committed.[61] But popular sovereignty carried the suggestion that settlers could decide the slavery question as soon as a territorial government was formed, prior to the territory's admission as a state. Since the Mexicans presently living in the territory as well as a majority of American settlers would undoubtedly disapprove of slavery, this would mean that the institution might well be prohibited before it even had a real opportunity to become established. Northern adherents of popular sovereignty were therefore able to present it in this interpretation as essentially a free-soil doctrine.[62] Even the hostile Barnburners preferred it to Buchanan's Missouri Compromise line solution.[63] The compatibility of the two interpretations of popular sovereignty with the radical positions on each side made it seem particularly well fitted to the needs of the northern Democratic politicians.[64]

By the time Congress met in early December, Democratic sentiment had begun to crystallize. After consulting with various Democratic leaders in Congress, Daniel S. Dickinson, the Hunker senator from New York, introduced resolutions which combined Dallas' popular sovereignty idea with a strong endorsement of annexation.[65] Although he did not specifically mention slavery, as Dallas had done, he seemed to clear up the ambiguity associated with popular sovereignty when he maintained that "the true spirit and meaning of the Constitution [will] be observed and the confederacy strengthened by leaving all questions concerning domestic policies [in the territories] to the legislatures chosen by the people thereof."[66] Presumably the settlers could exclude (or establish) slavery as soon as they had been given territorial government. After a careful examination of the resolutions, Calhoun decided that they were intended to trick the South into accepting territory where slavery was to be effectually prohibited and were therefore more pernicious than the Wilmot Proviso itself.[67] He announced his intention to Henry S. Foote, a southern supporter of the resolutions, "to denounce them in the most emphatic manner whenever Mr. Dickinson should call them from the table."[68]

With the assistance of Senator Cass, another supporter of the resolutions, Foote managed to persuade Dickinson not to press his resolutions to a vote for the sake of party harmony. Calhoun also acquiesced in the move when it was represented to him that a fight over the resolutions would divide the opponents of the Proviso and interfere with chances for a satisfactory compromise.[69] He made a special point, however, of calling the attention of his South Carolina followers to the resolutions and their unsound doctrines, and urging an all-out attack upon them in the state press.[70] By the end of the month, the Charleston *Mercury* had denounced the Dickinson resolutions as incompatible with southern constitutional rights, the same treatment meted out to the resolutions by the Barnburners for precisely the opposite reasons.[71]

One of the reasons Calhoun was so deeply concerned about the resolutions was that he recognized them, as he said to a friend, as a point "around which the whole democratic party may rally."[72] "As dangerous as is the concession they make," he wrote to another correspondent, "I find many southern men disposed to make it."[73] Regular southern politicians outside of Congress also responded favorably to the resolutions.[74] A meeting of prominent Virginia Democrats in Richmond unanimously declared: "Resolved, that we most heartily approve the resolutions offered by Senator Dickinson of New York, in the United States Senate, for the true constitutional spirit they evince; and that we utterly condemn the Wilmot Proviso as a gross outrage upon the rights of the South and as an open violation both of the letter and the spirit of the constitution."[75]

But while the Dickinson resolutions satisfied those southern politicians who were more interested in party unity than the territorial issue, their transparent surrender of the territories to the free-soil proclivities of the settlers rendered them vulnerable to attack in the South as a surrender to the antislavery interests. This explicit territorial sovereignty, together with their vague language on the crucial question of the constitutionality of the Wilmot Proviso, gave them the appearance of being a mere sop to political expediency rather than a genuine concession to southern legal rights. Although they seemed to provide an essential basis for accommodation between northern and southern Democrats, the Dickinson resolutions still left a good deal to be desired as a party platform.

No one recognized this more clearly than Lewis Cass, who was pondering a public statement of his own on the territorial issue.[76] Both his presidential ambitions and his commitment to territorial expansion made him extremely anxious to placate the South,[77] and he began to question whether southern politicians were not right in declaring the Wilmot Proviso unconstitutional. Unwilling to trust his own judgment, he found a satisfactory answer in the opinions of John McLean, an associate justice of the United States Supreme Court, whom he consulted late in December.[78] McLean, an aspirant to the Whig presidential nomination, had presented his views to the public a few days earlier in an anonymous article in the Washington *National Intelligencer*.[79] Cass found that upon reading the article his doubts as to the Proviso's constitutionality "ripened into convictions," and he prepared to issue a statement of his position based on this new belief.[80] After having cautiously cleared his views with his friends in Congress, Cass published them in the Washington *Daily Union* of December 30, in an open letter to A. O. P. Nicholson, his leading political supporter in Tennessee.[81]

The letter was a more fully developed exposition of the popular sovereignty doctrine, but it reintroduced the ambiguity about the territorial legislatures which the Dickinson resolutions had apparently disposed of. Beginning with a denial of the constitutionality of the Wilmot Proviso, Cass worked his way to the following conclusion about federal territorial regulation in general: "It should be limited to the creation of proper governments for new countries acquired or settled, and to the necessary provision for their eventual admission into the union, leaving, in the meantime, to [sic] the people inhabiting them, to regulate them in their own way. They are just as capable of doing so as the people of the states; and they can do so at any rate as soon as their political independence is recognized by their admission into the union."[82] This clearly implied the right of settlers to prohibit slavery before statehood was achieved, although it was not clear how they could exercise that right since territorial legislatures were not mentioned. At the same time, the recognition of the settlers' right to prohibit slavery violated the logic of the constitutional argument, in which Cass confessed that the territories differed from the states in that they did "not possess the peculiar attributes of sovereignty."[83] Cass underlined this equivocation in summarizing his position when he said he favored "leaving to the people of any territory which may hereafter be acquired, the right to regulate it themselves, *under the general principles of the constitution* [italics mine]."[84]

Cass's adoption of the southern constitutional argument to obscure the question of territorial regulation was balanced by an equally subtle concession to free-soil opinion. Those free-soilers who wished to dispense with the Wilmot Proviso were turning more and more to the theory expounded by John Quincy Adams during the original congressional debate on the Proviso to the effect that the Proviso was unnecessary because Mexican law prohibiting slavery would remain in force in territory annexed by the United States.[85] The antislavery Washington *National Era* advanced the same idea in the early fall of 1847, and it was subsequently adopted by a substantial portion of the northern Democratic press.[86] It was this idea, in fact, which lay behind McLean's whole argument that the Wilmot Proviso was unconstitutional;[87] and Cass made use of it for his own purposes in the Nicholson letter. He quoted a statement from Buchanan's letter to the effect that it was "morally impossible" that the settlers in the territory would "ever reestablish slavery within its limits."[88] The phrase "reestablish slavery," which appeared three times in the Nicholson letter, seemed to indicate that, like McLean, Cass agreed with Adams' theory. The northern adherents of the theory could be expected to recognize Cass's use of the phrase as a sign of his real attitude, while southern Democrats would presumably overlook its significance.

The Nicholson letter was so framed as to permit southern Democrats to interpret it as perfectly compatible with the southern constitutional position and northern Democrats to interpret it as essentially a free-soil position.[89] Although, like the Dickinson resolutions, the letter encountered the immediate opposition of both the Barnburners and Calhoun and his friends, it was greeted with enthusiasm by most of the Democratic press in the North and the South.[90] By providing the basis for a developing *rapprochement* between southern and western Democrats, it enhanced Cass's standing with the party regulars and made him the leading candidate for the presidential nomination.[91]

CHAPTER VI

The State Conventions

THE IMMEDIATE TEST OF CASS'S SUBSTITUTE PLATFORM FOR THE Wilmot Proviso came in the Democratic state conventions held to select delegates to the national convention at Baltimore in May. Since the resolution of the factional struggle in New York would strongly influence the course of the Democratic party, the state convention there was of particular importance. Hated as he was by the Barnburners, Cass was the favorite candidate of the Hunkers, and his presidential prospects depended upon their maintaining control of the party organization. On the other hand, the state convention would be the last opportunity the Barnburners would have before the presidential election to prevent the suppression of the territorial issue. The Hunkers had used their victory at Syracuse to reconstitute the state central committee, and, in defiance of party tradition, to give it the authority to call future conventions. They also recommended that the New York delegates to the national convention be elected in the congressional districts rather than by a convention, as had been done in the past.

The Barnburners repudiated these moves at their Herkimer meeting and resolved upon a state convention in the same town on February 22, to choose the national delegates.[1] But the older Barnburner leaders wished to bypass the irregular Herkimer meeting and determined to follow the traditional procedure of having a caucus of Democratic legislators call the state convention.[2] A decided majority of the legislators were Barnburners and even some of the Hunkers might well be depended upon to insist upon their traditional prerogative, but to insure against Hunker interference with or boycott of the caucus, the *Atlas* announcement of it did not specify the purpose for which the meeting was called.[3] At the caucus the Barnburners overrode Hunker objections to a call for a state convention. As a conciliatory gesture, the caucus designated a different date and place, February 16, and Utica, respectively, from those chosen at Herkimer, and left the question of the means of selecting national delegates to be settled at the convention itself.[4]

The Hunkers refused to accept the action of the caucus. At Syracuse they had used their majority to vest the power of calling a state convention with their reorganized state central committee; on December 17, the committee issued a call for a meeting at Albany on January 26.[5] The faction experienced considerable difficulty in organizing the necessary political machinery at the local level, and ultimately only forty-three of the fifty-nine counties were represented at the assemblage.[6]

The Hunkers' weakness did not dispose them to compromise, however. At the convention they adopted the congressional district plan for selecting national delegates recommended by the Syracuse meeting. Although there was no formal commitment to a presidential candidate, the Barnburners' chief enemy, Cass, was the obvious preference, and most of the delegates ultimately elected in the districts favored him.[7] In the address the convention carried its appeal against the Barnburners beyond the New York electors to whom it was presumably directed, to the national party, which would ultimately sit in judgment on the two factions at the national convention. The address defended Hunker regularity on the ground that the Barnburners had seceded from the Democratic organization, a secession that "had its origin in the action of the national democratic party itself."[8]

Presumably this "action" was the rejection of the Wilmot Proviso, and the address went on to argue that the Barnburners' advocacy of the Proviso was merely an attempt to regain their power, since the measure was completely unnecessary.

Shortly before the convention met, the New York *Globe,* a Barnburner journal anxious to reconcile the two factions, had printed a letter designed to provide a platform on which they could unite. Reiterating Adams' theory that the Wilmot Proviso was superfluous, the correspondent urged the party to forego the measure in order to safeguard the foremost Democratic aim, annexation.[9] The Hunkers at Albany appropriated this free-soil argument for their own use. The Barnburners, they claimed in the address, conceded that the Mexican territory was legally free and would remain so unless its laws were changed; in spite of this effective admission that the Proviso was unnecessary, the Barnburners, by continuing to advocate it, would disrupt the national party as well as prevent annexation.[10]

In the meantime, the Barnburners had accepted the decision of the caucus for a convention at Utica and abandoned their plans for another meeting at Herkimer. Their sudden concern for party regularity reflected the influence of the elder Van Buren. Although he carefully avoided committing himself publicly to the Proviso movement, the former President moved into New York City shortly after the first of the year and began helping John and other Barnburner leaders to plan the faction's strategy.[11]

At the Utica Convention which met on February 16, John Van Buren assumed the important task of writing the address, and, with the assistance of his father, he prepared a thorough vindication of the Barnburners' position from the point of view of party regularity.[12] The secessionist Herkimer meeting in October, which received so much attention in the Albany address, was played down. Instead, the traditional usages of the party were reviewed at length in order to demonstrate the legitimacy of the convention and of the means which it used to select its national delegates. The address maintained that the Barnburners were fully committed not only to the administration's war policy but to the annexation of territory as well, though not to the dismemberment of Mexico. According to the address, the Barnburners had no desire to impose their own firm commitment to the Wilmot Proviso upon the party as a whole, but wanted instead to avoid making either support for, or opposition to, the measure an article of party faith, as certain of the state parties in the South had done.[13] The eighth resolution of the convention platform expressed the same idea:

That while the democracy of New York feel called upon by their regard for principle and a conviction of duty, to reiterate this emphatic declaration of their sentiment and wishes [on the Wilmot Proviso], they have not now, nor have they ever had any desire to prescribe a test in the Presidential canvass, which might prevent the union of all who sustain the general principles of the democratic creed, and they deeply regret that any of their southern brethren should have unwisely laid down a platform inconsistent with that union, and inevitably tend to break a national party into sectional division.[14]

In spite of the tone of these resolutions and the address, the Barnburners at Utica betrayed their irregular tendencies by their affinity for the same presidential candidate that so interested Calhoun and his followers, Zachary Taylor.[15] Taylor had the same appeal for both factions. As a military hero who stood outside party organization, he had a perfectly clean, not to say blank, political record. This apolitical position, as well as his great popularity, made him the perfect instrument with which to chastise the Democratic organization, bringing about its reformation in accordance with their principles and under their control, provided they could commit him to their cause.

The possibility of using Taylor's candidacy for their own political purposes had been suggested to the Van Burens by one of their associates in Ohio, James W. Taylor, the editor of the Cincinnati *Signal*. The previous spring the Democratic editor, who was no relation to the general, had sent the latter a *Signal* editorial and requested his comments upon it. The editorial urged the general's election as President as an independent candidate, provided he adhered to certain simple principles, among which was the curtailment of the executive's legislative influence. "The extension over the continent beyond the Rio Grande of the Ordinance of 1787," read one statement in the editorial, "is an object too high to be baffled by presidential vetoes."[16] The general tenor of Taylor's reply was that his opinions "were better withheld until the end of the war," but his closing statement was less noncommittal. "With these remarks, I trust you will pardon me for thus briefly replying to you," wrote Taylor, "which I do with a high opinion and approval of the sentiments and views embraced in your editorial."[17]

Vague as this commitment to the Wilmot Proviso was, the editor of the *Signal* thought it sufficient to warrant support for Taylor's presidential pretensions and he was able to persuade the Van Burens to consider taking him up as a candidate.[18] Shortly before the Utica convention met, John Van Buren had the Cincinnati editor write to Taylor again and promise him Barnburner support if he would reaffirm the commitment made in the *Signal* letter. Taylor replied evasively that his views were already sufficiently well known to the public.[19]

Without a firm commitment, the Van Burens had no intention of allowing Taylor to be nominated at Utica. The strong feeling for him in the convention was externally manifested only in the final resolutions which commended him as well as the Barnburner heroes, Thomas Hart Benton and John A. Dix.[20] Exploration of Taylor's position continued behind the scenes. Martin Van Buren asked Blair in Washington to "sound" Jefferson Davis, Taylor's son-in-law, about a Barnburner candidacy for the general; and the chairman of the committee of resolutions at Utica was directed to write again to Taylor asking for a clarification of the *Signal* letter.[21] But the official Barnburner policy announced at Utica totally ignored the dalliance with Taylor. In perfect accordance with the more conciliatory attitude expressed toward the national party, the platform declared merely that the "New York Democrats" (i.e., the Barnburners) had no presidential candidate to present at Baltimore.[22]

Like the Hunker statement, the Utica address and resolutions were designed in large part to persuade the national party of the regularity of the delegates selected. But while the Hunkers appealed directly to the anti-Proviso bias of the southern and southern-oriented Democratic politicians who would decide between the factions at Baltimore, the Van Burens, recognizing the disfavor into which the Proviso had fallen among these politicians, built their case for regularity on strict state party usage and evidence of popular support. Beyond these two sets of claims, however, loomed the same argument which seemed to be equally valid for both factions, that their co-operation was indispensable for victory in New York in the presidential election. For Democratic politicians outside New York the solution appeared to be for the factions to get together and settle their difficulties. But this both factions adamantly refused to do, and the resolution of the struggle was left in the hands of the national convention.

Since the Democratic party in each of the New England states selected most of the delegates to the national convention by means of election in the congressional districts, the conventions in those states were of minor importance. The most significant development was the successful effort to round up support among these delegates for the candidacy of Levi Woodbury, an associate justice of the United States Supreme Court and the favorite son of the New Hampshire Democracy. During the late summer of 1847, a more or less spontaneous movement had sprung up in the South for Woodbury, as a northern candidate who could satisfy southern requirements for a presidential nominee.[23] This development raised his stock among regular party politicians in New England. In October, Woodbury's son, Luke, informed him that the forthcoming New Hampshire state convention would probably nominate him for the presidency. "A northern man who is popular at the South seems to be the candidate required," wrote Luke, "and in this particular you seem to be peculiarly qualified, judging from the tone of the Southern papers."[24]

Concern for victory in the state election in March, however, induced the convention to commend the Wilmot Proviso, a position which the politicians knew to be incompatible with Woodbury's views. In spite of their commitment to Woodbury's candidacy, therefore, a commitment underlined by the convention's selection of an anti-Proviso Woodbury man as the state delegate at large, the convention leaders decided to postpone the presidential question until after the election, in order to prevent the incompatibility from being publicly revealed.[25]

Only after the election was won did the state Democratic leaders feel free to forget the territorial issue and concentrate their attention upon obtaining support for Woodbury's candidacy.[26] They were encouraged by the fact that they had been able to play down their antislavery commitment somewhat during the campaign without disastrous consequences.[27] One New Hampshire Democrat wrote a letter to the Washington *Union* denying the Barnburner claim that the election was a triumph for free soil and warning the Barnburners that they "need expect no support from the delegates from New Hampshire if they come [to the national convention] with their disorganizing schemes which have distracted New York."[28]

Despite their covert disapproval of the Wilmot Proviso, however, Woodbury's New Hampshire managers were hopeful of obtaining Barnburner support for his candidacy.[29] Since he already possessed the confidence of southern politicians, including Calhoun, Woodbury could avoid making the kind of bid for their support on the territorial issue which Buchanan, Dallas, and Cass had made, a bid which had alienated the Barnburners.[30] His managers were able to represent him as a "harmony" candidate around whom all elements in the party, including the extremists on both sides, might coalesce.[31] His candidacy rapidly gathered strength in New England in the spring of 1848 until he became Cass's chief rival for the presidential nomination.[32]

Woodbury's managers scored a particularly successful coup

on March 7, when they got the Democratic members of the Massachusetts legislature to nominate him for the presidency.[33] By the time the national convention met, they had persuaded nearly all the New England delegates to vote for him, in spite of the fact that Cass had many powerful supporters and a certain popularity in the area.[34] Nevertheless, these delegates were not formally committed, and Cass represented an acceptable second choice if the Woodbury candidacy faltered.

Cass's other principal rival for the nomination, Buchanan, drew his strength from his control of the Democratic machinery in Pennsylvania. The adherents of Vice-President Dallas, who held a commanding influence in the Philadelphia area, contested that control in a campaign for delegates to a state convention in the winter of 1847-48. But Buchanan had carefully laid the groundwork for his presidential drive in the state by remaining aloof from the factional struggle between the Democratic politicians closely associated with the gubernatorial administration of Francis Shunk and a group led by Simon Cameron, who were strong proponents of an internal improvements program. It had required all the tact and skill which Buchanan possessed to maintain his neutralist position when the improvements men boycotted the Democratic caucus in the spring of 1845 and combined with the Whigs and Native Americans in the state legislature to elect Cameron himself to the Senate over the caucus candidate. Enraged officials in the Shunk administration demanded that both Buchanan and Dallas condemn the breach of party regularity, but unlike Dallas, Buchanan refused, in order to avoid alienating Cameron. Although the officials set to work to undermine Buchanan's position in the state, the Secretary of State did manage to remain on good terms with both Cameron and Shunk, neither of whom opposed his presidential candidacy.[35] Since Buchanan possessed a strong personal organization throughout the state, the official neutrality of the two leading factions gave him a tremendous advantage in the contest with Dallas.

The campaign in Pennsylvania was complicated by the fact

that Cass also had a political following in the state. Recognizing that they had no chance of achieving victory alone, his supporters and those of Dallas combined their efforts in a movement to stop Buchanan, a movement which received the covert encouragement of the hostile officials in the Shunk administration.[36] These efforts bore fruit in the state convention which met in Harrisburg on March 6, 1848, despite the fact that a large majority of the delegates supported Buchanan.

The Buchanan managers had no difficulty getting the convention to endorse their candidate, but they were forced by a threat of secession from the Dallas-Cass minority to compromise on the selection of delegates to the national convention.[37] It was finally agreed to allow the convention delegates from the various congressional districts to select national delegates of their own choosing, thereby insuring the minority of representation on the delegation. To offset this concession, the Buchanan managers imposed the unit rule upon the delegation and insisted upon a written pledge from each of the selected delegates that he would continue to vote for Buchanan as long as a majority of them so determined.[38] The state central committee was given the authority to replace delegates who refused to take the pledge, but some of Buchanan's supporters distrusted the committee and feared that unreliable delegates whom the committee failed to challenge might lose them control of the delegation.[39]

These fears were intensified in the second day of the convention when a resolution was accepted which gave each national delegate the right to designate a substitute should he be unable to attend the national convention.[40] Nor was the delegation chosen that day wholly acceptable to the Buchanan leaders. There was a strong antagonism between Buchanan and Wilmot, which had induced the latter to declare that he preferred any other candidate.[41] The Buchanan managers tried to have the convention challenge a supporter of Wilmot's who had been selected as delegate from his congressional district, but Wilmot himself successfully defended the selection in a speech in which he also defended his famous Proviso.[42] While the convention was validating all the delegates selected, including Wilmot's friend, the specter of the Proviso induced the platform committee to reject by a vote of twenty-two to two the resolution framed by Buchanan's managers which endorsed Buchanan's Missouri Compromise solution of the territorial issue.[43] But the gravest setback of all was the platform committee's acceptance and the convention's ratification of a resolution commending Cass, which seemed to say that Pennsylvania would acquiesce with pleasure in his nomination.[44] The resolution gravely weakened Buchanan's position outside Pennsylvania, where it was inferred that the state's votes would ultimately go to Cass.[45]

After the convention, Buchanan's managers labored strenuously to regain the lost ground. In accordance with the convention decision, the state central committee submitted written pledges to all of the national delegates, requiring them to continue supporting Buchanan until a majority decided otherwise. The pledge sent to the strong Buchanan supporters on the delegation was accompanied by private letters encouraging them to give "warm answers" to the official notifications, which would then be published in the Pennsylvania newspapers.[46] The committee decided against requiring the delegates to pledge not to send substitutes, preferring to run the risk of substitution rather than that of stirring up new dissension.[47] On the eve of the national convention, Buchanan's friends were able to assure him that they had a safe majority on the delegation, but the mere presence of delegates opposed to Buchanan could not help but undermine his position at Baltimore.

Buchanan also won a very precarious victory in the neighboring state of New Jersey. Immediately after the Harrisburg convention, the Trenton *Daily News,* the principal Democratic journal in the state, came out for Cass and it appeared that he would capture the delegates.[48] The proximity of the state, plus the similarity of Buchanan's tariff views with those of Democrats in New Jersey, gave his managers an opportunity to redeem the situation, however.[49] The state convention in May made no formal commitment as to a candidate but the unit rule was adopted and four of the seven unpledged delegates favored Buchanan.[50] The unpledged delegates from Pennsylvania's other neighboring states, Maryland and Delaware, on the other hand, were divided between Cass and Woodbury.[51]

The first and most significant real test of Cass and his popular sovereignty doctrine came in the Democratic convention in Ohio, which met the second week in January. Of all the state parties, the organization in Ohio had been most closely identified with Martin Van Buren and his followers in New York. The state delegation had stood firm for Van Buren at the national convention in 1844 until the New Yorkers themselves gave way.[52] Since then, however, the followers of Cass had been gaining political strength at the expense of the Van Burenites. Cass's insistence upon the United States claim for the whole of the Oregon territory was one of the most important reasons for these impressive gains. The defeat and death of Silas Wright further strengthened the shift in sentiment to Cass, and the Barnburner secession gave the *coup de grâce* to the Van Burenite fortunes in Ohio.[53]

Without a Van Burenite candidate to oppose him, Cass swept the local Democratic conventions in the late fall of 1847 by default.[54] Many of the conventions deprecated agitation of the slavery question and endorsed popular sovereignty,[55] another indication of the weakness of the Van Burenites. This apparently irresistible trend evidently convinced Samuel Medary, editor of the official state Democratic organ and formerly one of Van Buren's closest allies in Ohio, that he must support Cass and popular sovereignty.[56] He was helped to this decision by his bitter feud with former Senator Benjamin Tappan, editor of the rival *Ohio Press*. Tappan, who had tried to wrest control of the *Ohio Statesman* from Medary early in 1847, was an ardent free-soiler.[57] On the eve of the state convention Medary was hard at work among free-soil delegates, persuading them to forego the Wilmot Proviso.[58]

At the same time, a group of Liberty party politicians, under the leadership of Salmon P. Chase, had been urging free-soil

Democrats to make a stiff fight for the Wilmot Proviso principle at the convention, as they had promised to do.[59] The question arose shortly after the convention opened when one of the delegates suddenly introduced a motion endorsing Cass for the presidency. Jacob Brinkerhoff immediately voiced his opposition to the motion, saying that although he had not yet seen the Nicholson letter, he understood that in it Cass had denied the power of Congress to legislate for the territories on the subject of slavery and that if this were so, he was opposed to Cass. Brinkerhoff's statement created a tremendous uproar, but he accomplished his purpose of having the resolution tabled.[60]

In the meantime, the platform committee was trying to agree on a statement on the territorial issue. This proved so difficult that it was decided to make no recommendation to the convention.[61] The determination of the free-soil delegates to raise the issue evidently caused the committee to reverse this decision, however, and a clever evasion of the question was worked out. The resolutions condemned slavery as an evil and committed the state party "to use all power, clearly given by the terms of the National compact, to prevent its increase, and finally to eradicate the evil." After this expression of antislavery sentiment, the statement went on in the next resolution to recognize "that to each State belongs the right to adopt and modify its own municipal laws; to regulate its own internal affairs, to hold and maintain an equal and independent sovereignty with each and every State; and that upon these rights, the National Legislature can neither legislate nor encroach."[62] Since these rights of the existing states were not at issue in the Proviso question, the second resolution technically did not apply to it, but it could be interpreted to mean that these rights also belonged to the territories as embryo states. In other words, the national legislature was not to interfere with the territories' potential sovereignty by passing the Wilmot Proviso.

This statement, more vague and ambiguous even than the Nicholson letter, the free-soilers in the convention were willing to accept.[63] But the nomination of Cass, also recommended to the convention by the platform committee, was another matter. Tappan, Brinkerhoff, and other free-soilers objected to the nomination on the ground that Cass was opposed to the Wilmot Proviso and claimed that the nomination was a betrayal of their Van Burenite allies in New York.[64] Finally, Brinkerhoff demanded an opportunity for the opposition to record its votes. Notwithstanding the free-soilers' arguments, the convention sustained the nomination by a vote of 237 to 22.[65]

This overwhelming endorsement of Cass gave his candidacy a tremendous impetus throughout the country.[66] News of dissension at the convention reduced the impact somewhat, particularly after it became known that the delegations of two counties had refused to vote for his nomination, one of them having already deserted the convention.[67] Rumors circulated that it had required some kind of bargain to put Cass over, and it was even claimed that the national delegation was unfriendly to him, despite the nomination.[68] While these stories helped to blunt the force of Cass's victory outside Ohio, his supporters were actually in firm control of the state organization. Salmon P. Chase, who had been an independent observer at the convention, hoped that his Democratic friends might organize "another Herkimer," but since the convention's clever straddle prevented a clear issue being made on the question of slavery in the territories, there was neither a candidate nor an issue around which the opposition could crystallize.[69] The defeat of the free-soilers in Ohio was a decisive one. It not only deprived the Barnburners of their most formidable allies in the national convention, it also provided Cass, their leading enemy, with a solid political base for his drive to the presidential nomination.

There was less dissension in Michigan, Cass's own state, than in Ohio. The radical faction of the state party, which comprised the more ardent supporters of the Wilmot Proviso, rallied to the Cass candidacy.[70] On January 28, the same day the lower house of the state legislature passed a free-soil resolution fifty-two to three, sixty-six of the seventy-one Democratic legislators signed a statement endorsing Cass.[71] Many of the signers remained fully committed to the Wilmot Proviso and were ready to oppose any attempt to impose popular sovereignty as a party creed.[72] In this situation the Democratic state convention confined itself to nominating Cass and urging a vigorous prosecution of the war; the divisive question of slavery in the territories was totally ignored.[73] The state convention in Wisconsin likewise avoided the territorial issue and elected unpledged delegates who were, however, reported to favor Cass.[74]

Democratic sentiment for the Wilmot Proviso was weaker in Indiana than elsewhere in the Northwest. The Democratic state convention there dealt with the territorial issue boldly and squarely, resolving that "We regard every and any effort on the part of the National Legislature (under present circumstances) to bind the future inhabitants of any portion of our territory as to their local institutions or internal affairs which are to exist in states hereafter to be formed, as improper and calculated to create local and sectional divisions and weaken the bonds and ties of this great confederacy."[75] Although the resolution did not go as far as the Nicholson letter and declare the Wilmot Proviso unconstitutional, it was perfectly compatible with Cass's popular sovereignty doctrine. The temper of the convention was very favorable to Cass's candidacy, so much so that a premature report was issued that he had been nominated.[76] The nomination was arrested at the last minute, however, by an order from the national administration. Following instructions, the convention instead selected unpledged delegates favorable to Cass's candidacy. Presumably the purpose in keeping the delegates uncommitted was to keep them available for the candidacy of the President or some other member of his administration.[77]

The last Democratic state convention in the Northwest was held in Illinois on April 25. Free-soil sentiment in that state was centered around Chicago, a district represented in Congress by a close associate of the Barnburners, John Wentworth. All spring Wentworth's newspaper, the Chicago *Journal,* had engaged the official party organ, the *Illinois State Register,* in a running battle over the Wilmot Proviso.[78] At the state convention, the anti-Proviso forces, which inclined toward Cass as a candidate, were in the ascendancy. A resolution was passed on the territorial issue which was a milder version of the evasive stand taken by the Ohio convention: "Resolved, That while we sincerely regret the existence of the institution of slavery, we are constrained to believe that by the compromises of the constitution the subject is wholly given over to the jurisdiction of those states which have the misfortune to be burdened with the system; we therefore deprecate and condemn all intemperate and unnecessary agitation of the subject as calculated to endanger the permanence of the Union without effecting any corresponding good."[79]

Cass was the overwhelming favorite of the convention, but the Wentworth forces helped a skillful Woodbury manipulator to dilute the commitment to him.[80] Although the convention expressed its preference for Cass by a vote of sixty to fifty-one for the combined opposition, it did not bind the delegates to the national convention to vote for him, and it commended Woodbury as being also worthy of the nomination.[81] The delegation was committed to voting as a unit, but the inclusion of delegates opposed to Cass rendered his majority uncertain and gave Woodbury's managers hopes of obtaining the state's vote.[82] Nevertheless, the delegates still had a moral commitment to try to secure Cass's nomination. Moreover, despite the dissatisfaction of Wentworth and his followers with the state convention's presidential preference and its stand on the territorial issue, the Chicago congressman had already made it clear that he did not intend to participate in an independent movement.[83] Neither in Illinois nor in any other state in the Northwest was there any sign of a major party defection on the slavery question.

In the southwestern states the progression of events was equally favorable to Cass and his popular sovereignty doctrine. Although party members in these states as elsewhere in the South were virtually unanimous in their opposition to the Wilmot Proviso, the question, compared with the issue of territorial extension, was of less importance there than in the Southeast.

The general pattern of action of the Democratic conventions in the southwestern states was to make a territorial pronouncement condemning the Proviso but leaving the way open for an accommodation on the popular sovereignty policy. Thus the Mississippi convention, meeting on January 8, declared that "Congress does not possess the power to prohibit slavery [in the territories] . . . and that such question belongs exclusively to the citizens of such territory."[84] An effort to make Dallas the official nominee of the convention was unsuccessful, and the timely arrival of news of the Nicholson letter enabled Cass to displace Dallas as the favorite of the unpledged delegates.[85]

The same week, the Arkansas convention announced that it was prepared to support Cass, Woodbury, Buchanan, or Dallas, and resolved that: "As to any territory acquired by us it is the right of the people inhabiting such territory to decide at the proper time whether the institution of slavery shall exist there or not; and any attempt by Congress to control that matter would be a violation of the compromises of the Constitution and an insult to the sovereignty of the States."[86] The convention refrained from specifying "the proper time," leaving, like Cass, the popular sovereignty doctrine ambiguously open to either of its two interpretations. The Texas convention, which met in February, was even less clear on the question, declaring its willingness to support any candidate "as will maintain the federal compromises on slavery."[87] In Louisiana the state convention limited itself to repudiating the Wilmot Proviso and to expressing its "heart-felt gratitude" to those Democrats of the North whose votes had helped to defeat the measure in Congress.[88] All of these states sent unpledged delegations to the national convention, but Cass's position as the frontrunning candidate who met the southern demands on the Proviso, as well as his expansionist views, so popular in the Southwest, made him the natural candidate for them. On the first ballot of the convention he eventually was to receive the votes of every one of these four states.

Elsewhere in the Southwest the results were mixed. In Tennessee, where Cass was extremely popular with the party, he had reason to be disappointed with the outcome. Meeting on January 8, the state convention disavowed "all wish or desire to acquire any territory from Mexico *for the purpose of propagating slavery,*" but denounced the prohibition of slavery there as unjust. "We believe that the people who may hereafter inhabit such territory as may be ceded," declared the convention, "will have the sole and exclusive right under the Constitution, to determine whether they will or will not have the institution of slavery."[89] As this endorsement of popular sovereignty suggests, Cass was the overwhelming favorite of the convention, but despite this the Polk forces were able to prevent his nomination.[90] The delegates were undoubtedly reluctant to repudiate the President even though his renomination was extremely unlikely. A few Polk men managed to get on the delegation notwithstanding the convention's preference, but most of the delegates favored Cass.[91]

The Barnburners had some potential allies in Missouri in the St. Louis area from which Senator Benton drew his main support. Living in a slaveholding state where public sentiment was strongly opposed to obstacles to annexation, however, Benton's followers were severely embarrassed by the territorial issue. The best they could do, even in their own local convention, was to deprecate "disputes in Congress over such abstractions as the Wilmot Proviso."[92] The Cass forces were dominant throughout the rest of the state,[93] but the St. Louis delegates managed to keep the state formally uncommitted at the Democratic convention which met on April 10. The convention address, written by Blair's son Frank, totally ignored the territorial issue, and several Woodbury men were placed on the unpledged delegation, including Blair's other son, Montgomery, who had married Woodbury's daughter.[94] Most of the delegates, however, were inclined toward Cass and could bind the others with the unit rule.[95] The unpledged delegates from neighboring Kentucky also leaned toward Cass, although there was some sentiment for a favorite-son candidate, William O. Butler.[96]

In the southeastern states the question of slavery in the territories could not be so easily evaded. The Georgia Democrats had held their convention prior to the issuance of the Nicholson letter and were able to avoid facing directly the question of popular sovereignty as expounded by Cass. The convention merely reiterated the strong party stand against the Proviso of the previous July and repeated its determination to disavow any candidate who would not repudiate the measure.[97] Congressman Howell Cobb evidently tried, from Washington, to arrange for the selection of Cass delegates, but his request did not arrive until after the convention had already chosen an unpledged slate.[98] The Cass forces could gather some consolation from the opportunity which Cobb would have to influence the delegates directly when they arrived in Baltimore.

The state party in Alabama was the first to take a clear and unequivocal stand against Cass's popular sovereignty doctrine. The state convention was the culmination of a long struggle between the party regulars and the Chivalry, of which the most recent phase had been the contest to elect a United States Senator. The Chivalry were anxious to re-elect Dixon H. Lewis, Yancey's political mentor, who had the same commitment to strong proslavery principles. Lewis had been one of Calhoun's strongest supporters outside South Carolina before a disagreement over the Mexican War separated them, and like other Calhounites he had toyed with the idea of supporting Taylor for the presidency on a no-party platform in the summer of 1847.[99] When news of his correspondence inquiring into the general's political beliefs leaked out, however, Lewis issued an open letter denying that he had pledged his support to Taylor. For the benefit of critical party regulars, he also assured the public that he was fully committed to the policies of the Polk administration.[100] His followers were able to use these assurances to gain support among party regulars for his candidacy.[101]

Many of the party regulars were strongly opposed to Lewis, however, and turned to their foremost leader, William R. King, to try to defeat him.[102] The contest for the Senate seat, fought out in the Alabama press in the fall of 1847, had become a very bitter one by the time the state legislature assembled in early December. After the first day's balloting, in which Lewis led both King and the Whig candidate, the party regulars tried to embarrass him by submitting to both Democratic candidates a questionnaire asking whether they supported the administration's war program, whether they approved of Ritchie's expulsion from the Senate, whether they favored Calhoun for the presidency, and whether they would pledge support in advance for the nominees of the Democratic national convention.[103]

The questionnaire was designed to give Lewis a Hobson's choice between Calhoun on the one hand and complete party regularity on the other. Lewis was prepared at this point, however, to opt for the latter. Disenchanted with Taylor and the no-party movement, Lewis and his followers in north Alabama thought that the Barnburners' revolt in New York provided them an opportunity to make Woodbury the Democratic nominee, and it was necessary for them to work within the regular party organization to seize the opportunity.[104] Lewis therefore openly repudiated Calhoun and his antiadministration policies and pledged himself to support the Democratic nominees "if they were sound on the subject of the Wilmot Proviso." He went on to give Woodbury's presidential candidacy a subtle boost by expressing his preference for "the soundest democrat from the free states—taking the highest, boldest, and most decided grounds against the Wilmot Proviso."[105] Lewis won the senatorial contest with ease, but his commitment sullied the victory for some of the more extreme proslavery men from southern Alabama.[106] Calhoun was bitterly disappointed with what he called "the defection of the state-rights party in and around Montgomery with Lewis at their head," and thought it precluded the triumph of correct principles in Alabama.[107]

When Lewis went to Washington to take his seat in the Senate, he left the Chivalry's co-operationist movement in the hands of Yancey, whom he had recently converted to it. As late as November 16, Yancey had attended a bipartisan Taylor rally, although he refused to make a speech.[108] But Yancey was disillusioned by the Whigs' transparent intention to appropriate Taylor as a partisan while using the Democrats to help secure his election. Moreover, he thought that the Whigs elected to Congress in the no-party movement the previous summer had violated their proslavery commitments by helping to elect Robert C. Winthrop, a Massachusetts Whig, Speaker of the House of Representatives.[109] This evidence of bad faith on the part of the Whigs drove Yancey back into the Democratic party, where he embraced Lewis' co-operationist scheme.

At Yancey's instance, the Democrats at Montgomery held a harmony meeting on January 3, to bind up the wounds caused by the recent party strife. The principal speech was Yancey's glowing eulogy of the national administration and of the northern Democratic friends of the South on the slavery question.[110] Yancey's resolutions, unanimously adopted by the meeting, reiterated the commitment of the Alabama Democracy not to support a Wilmot Proviso man for President or Vice-President, and went on to commend the northern Democrats who had stood up for the rights of the South by opposing the Proviso. Over the objections of Percy Walker, one of Calhoun's supporters from southern Alabama, Buchanan and Dickinson were included among those to be commended.[111] (Since news of the Nicholson letter had not reached Montgomery, Cass was not mentioned.) Even more significant was the veiled reference to the Hunkers in New York: "Resolved, That we hail with unalloyed delight the evidences which recent events have developed, of a disposition in a large and respectable portion of our fellow citizens of the northern section of the Union, to stand firmly by the constitution in this matter [of the Wilmot Proviso] no matter what may be the effect upon their old party organizations."[112] The address of the meeting concluded that Alabama should be represented at the Democratic national convention in order to insure that these "friends at the North" would be seated.[113]

Yancey's resolutions had called for a state convention on

February 14, and he threw himself into the campaign to prepare for it. At the local convention which selected him as a delegate to the state meeting, he undertook to answer the charges of Whig adherents of Taylor that he was prepared to consort with enemies of the South.[114] According to Yancey, there had been a great reaction among northern Democrats against the "Winthrop Proviso," as he called it, and the Whigs were distorting the position of such friends of the South as Dallas and Buchanan for purely partisan reasons. He concluded that, under the circumstances, "there was no reason why democrats should abandon their party organization, but on the contrary as strong a reason as ever why they should abide by the time-honored usages of party."[115]

By the time the state convention met, however, the dissatisfied Chivalry from southern Alabama had exposed the free-soil interpretations of the stands of northern Democrats against the Wilmot Proviso, placing Yancey in an embarrassing position. Early in February, John A. Campbell wrote an article for the Mobile *Herald* designed to show that Buchanan and Cass had surrendered southern rights in the territories in their statements on the question.[116] On the eve of the state convention, the Montgomery *Flag and Advertiser,* the leading Democratic journal in Alabama, ran an even more explosive article by Percy Walker which called attention to the address of the recent convention of the Hunkers at Albany. Walker protested that the convention's declaration that slavery would be prevented from going into the territories by local law as well as by geography was the same "moral impossibility" idea so devastating to southern rights that had been propounded by Buchanan and Cass.[117]

Walker repeated his attack on the anti-Proviso Democrats in the North in the next issue of the *Flag and Advertiser* after the convention had begun. Now including Dallas among the enemies of southern rights along with Cass, Buchanan, and the Hunkers, he asked rhetorically: "Are these the men to whom Mr. Yancey in his speech at the late democratic meeting at the capital referred, as being with the South on the slavery question?"[118] By now it was clear to Yancey that the northern Democrats he had looked to for help were completely unreliable. The Hunkers had not only pronounced for free soil, they were also supporting Cass and could not be used to secure Woodbury's nomination.[119]

Yancey was also concerned about the strength of the opposition to Woodbury in the Alabama convention. The loyalties of the party regulars were divided among Buchanan, Cass, and Dallas. Of the three, Buchanan was the favorite, partly because of his early pronouncement against the Wilmot Proviso and partly because of his close friendship with King, whom the regulars wanted to make Vice-President, although any of the three was acceptable to them.[120] The regulars planned to pass anti-Proviso resolutions and select unpledged delegates instructed merely to oppose any candidate who had not repudiated the measure.[121]

The greatest danger to their plans was that the Chivalry might control the convention and force the selection of a solid slate of Woodbury delegates. The Chivalry did, in fact, win the first round in the struggle for control, securing the election of one of their faction as president of the convention. This loss of organizational control was partly redressed by the regulars' successful move to have most of the delegates selected by the congressional districts rather than by the convention itself.[122]

With the selection of delegates removed from the convention's control, the factional conflict devolved upon the platform. The progress of the popular sovereignty doctrine in the North had given the Chivalry a new issue by which to test the regulars' proslavery principles. In Congress Alabama's senior Senator, Arthur P. Bagby, had answered Dickinson's resolutions with some of his own, denying that either Congress *or* a territorial legislature had the power to prohibit slavery in the territories.[123] On the eve of the convention, the *Flag and Advertiser* had commended Bagby's resolutions to the delegates.[124] Unable to ignore this issue, the party regulars in committee were forced to allow the incorporation of Bagby's idea into the resolutions recommended to the convention. This new statement of principle was rather vaguely worded, however, and was not incorporated into the instructions to the national delegates. Instead they were merely precluded from voting for men who had not disavowed the Wilmot Proviso.[125]

In the meantime, Yancey, after consulting with John A. Campbell and other members of the Chivalry, had prepared a comprehensive set of six resolutions which explicitly repudiated the new northern "free-soil" doctrines and their authors. The first two resolutions, written by Campbell, dealt with the subtle threat of the Hunker claim that the local law of the Mexican territories would continue in force after annexation. Campbell thought that the existence of slavery in the territories required positive legal guarantees, and he demanded in the resolutions that such guarantees be either incorporated into the treaty annexing the territories or provided through congressional action.[126] Yancey's third resolution restated Bagby's denial of the authority of a territorial legislature to prohibit slavery, and the fourth declared the state party's determination "neither to recognize as Democrats or to hold fellowship or communion with those who attempt to denationalize the South and its institutions."[127]

Yancey intended not only to commit the convention explicitly to a strict proslavery position on the territorial issue but to impose this commitment upon the party in its selection of candidates as well, thus eliminating Woodbury's Democratic rivals for the nomination.[128] His two final resolutions read:

Resolved, That this Convention pledges itself to the country, and its members pledge themselves to each other, *under no political necessity whatever,* to support for the offices of President and Vice President of the United States any persons who shall not openly and avowedly be opposed to either of the forms of excluding slavery from the territories of the United States mentioned in the resolutions [i.e., either the Wilmot Proviso or territorial prohibition], as being alike treason to party faith and to the perpetuity of the Union of these States.

Resolved, That these resolutions be considered as instructions to our delegates to the Baltimore Convention, to guide them in their votes in that body; and that they vote for no men for President or Vice President, who will not unequivocally avow themselves to be opposed to either of the forms of restricting slavery, which are described in these resolutions.[129]

Lewis had sent Yancey a private statement by Woodbury to his supporters in the Alabama congressional delegation which fit these specifications, and, armed with this, Yancey made a motion, when the platform committee finally brought in its report, that his resolutions be added as an amendment. After a spirited debate on the motion, Yancey himself was given an opportunity to display his oratorical talents before the convention. In a long and fiery speech, he called attention to the threat from the new northern "free-soil" doctrines and demanded that the Alabama Democracy give an appropriate reply. In the course of his speech Yancey also quoted excerpts from Woodbury's statement and contrasted them with the public statements of Buchanan, Cass, and Dallas, in order to show that only Woodbury could satisfy the requirements of the proper southern position laid down in his resolutions.[130]

Yancey's speech swept away all opposition to his resolutions. Convinced by Yancey's co-operationist activities that they had nothing to fear from him, the party regulars were caught completely off guard by his motion, and none of them was prepared to challenge his inspired defense of proslavery principles.[131] Most of them, like most of the other delegates, were blinded to the complexities of the argument by Yancey's fiery rhetoric and did not grasp the implications of the resolutions, even after they had been explained.[132] Those party regulars who did understand the import of the resolutions had another reason for acquiescing in Yancey's demands. Their desire for Chivalry support for King's vice-presidential candidacy discouraged them from making a fight over the platform, which would inevitably prevent a unanimous nomination.[133] They therefore tried to slur over the differences between the resolutions and the platform committee's report. One regular who was a member of the committee announced to the convention after Yancey had finished speaking that the report and the resolutions covered essentially the same ground. The confused and weary delegates welcomed the statement as a resolution of a perplexing question and enthusiastically gave their unanimous approval to the resolutions.[134] The convention then completed its business, including a unanimous nomination of King for Vice-President, and adjourned. The bitter dissensions in the convention had been successfully concealed in an outward show of harmony.

The resolutions which the convention had adopted were greeted with great enthusiasm in the southern press and quickly came to be known as the Alabama Platform.[135] The lack of opposition to it was owing to the failure of most of the regular party press to perceive that it was intended to prevent southern Democrats from supporting any of the leading party candidates except Woodbury for the presidency.[136] Recognizing the confusion which befogged the issue, the regular party men in the Alabama delegation made it clear that they would not allow the instructions to prevent them from supporting the candidate of their choice.[137] Yancey wrote to Woodbury urging him to make his views public immediately in order to bring the Alabama delegates back into line, and to obtain the support of other southeastern states.[138] Woodbury had no intention, however, of alienating his northern supporters as well as the Barnburners by making an open commitment on the territorial issue, and Lewis was able to persuade Yancey it would be unfair to require Woodbury to clearly define his position on the question in public before the other candidates had done so.[139] Yancey decided to wait until the eve of the convention and submit all four candidates simultaneously to the same test.

In the meantime the widespread popularity of the Alabama Platform in the Southeast gave strong proslavery Democrats an effective tool with which to commit their party to a radical stand on the presidential question. Fortunately for the party regulars the state convention in Georgia had already met. But the Florida convention, responding to the Alabama stimulus, instructed its delegates to withhold support from any candidates who would sanction interference with the right to take slaves into the territories, "whether such interference or restrictions are imposed by Congress directly through its own acts or *mediately* through powers conferred on or conceded to, the inhabitants of such territory."[140]

The Alabama Platform also played a significant role in the state convention in Virginia, which met on the last day of February. The proslavery minority was able to force the party regulars to accept a platform resolution declaring:

That this convention heartily responds to the noble resolutions of the Alabama State Democratic Convention and will "under no necessity whatever," support either for the Presidency or the Vice Presidency, any person who shall not be the firm and avowed opponent of any plan or doctrine which in any way interferes with the right of citizens of any one state to possess and enjoy all their property in any territory which may be acquired by the Union as fully, completely, and securely as citizens of any other state shall enjoy theirs, —except so far as that being unwilling to disturb the Missouri Compromise we are content with adherence to its principles.[141]

The resolution was a source of embarrassment for the party regulars, but the last phrase gave the national delegation an excuse for supporting Buchanan, who was the favorite of a majority of the party regulars at the convention.[142] The convention failed to nominate Buchanan when the friends of John Y. Mason, Polk's Secretary of the Navy, combined with the Chivalry to prevent it.[143] Mason was hoping to be nominated as Cass's running mate and the Chivalry were Woodbury supporters.[144] The unpledged delegation to the national convention was inclined toward but by no means firmly committed to Buchanan.[145] The official party organ, the Richmond *Enquirer,* whose editor was one of the national delegates, made a point of insisting that the party platform did not preclude the support of Cass or Dallas, as well as Buchanan.[146]

In neighboring North Carolina, where the Chivalry was much weaker and where the Buchanan forces had very carefully prepared the way for their candidate,[147] they were much more firmly in control of things. The state convention in April simply repudiated the Wilmot Proviso, and its further declaration that Congress had "no control directly or indirectly, mediately or immediately, over the institution of slavery" contained only the vaguest hint of the Alabama Platform.[148] Although the convention made no official nomination, the delegates selected to go to Baltimore favored Buchanan.[149]

The attempt to use the Alabama Platform to dictate a Democratic presidential candidate received its greatest setback by the refusal of Calhoun to allow the South Carolina party to participate in the national convention. This deprived the southern state rights factions of any leadership of recognized importance in the South, leaving the task of representing the extreme pro-southern position to Yancey, who was at this time a local rather than a national figure. Calhoun's decision was unpopular among South Carolina Democrats.[150] One district revolted and sent a delegate to the convention notwithstanding his wishes.[151] But with this exception, the state party abided by his will and remained outside the national convention. Calhoun disapproved of national party conventions on principle and felt that merely by participating South Carolina would be yielding part of her freedom of action on the presidential question.[152] He did not exclude the possibility of supporting the Democratic nominee, if it should be someone satisfactory like Woodbury.[153] But his expectation that the Virginia delegation would not adhere strictly to its instructions convinced him that such a nomination was extremely unlikely, and he refused to be drawn into the convention to fight for a remote possibility.[154] Calhoun and his southern followers still had a strong affinity for Taylor in spite of the general's recent commitment to the Whig party. They were hoping that the Whig national convention would reject Taylor, allowing them to support him as a man above party.[155] When the Democratic national convention met on May 22, Calhoun and his friends assumed the role of mere observers.

In his Nicholson letter, Cass had made a bid for the presidency by trying to reunite the party on a popular sovereignty platform, thereby restoring the alliance between northern and

southern Democrats which had been disrupted by the Barnburners' advocacy of the Wilmot Proviso. By the eve of the national
convention he had taken a long, though not a commanding, lead
over his rivals for the Democratic nomination. Most of the
delegates from the West were favorably disposed toward his
candidacy where they were not formally committed to him. He
had, in addition, secondary sources of strength in the citadels of
his opponents. He was the first choice of a few and the second
choice of many delegates from New England and Pennsylvania.
And he was the candidate of the Hunkers, who had the good will
of most of the southern delegates as well as of his own friends
from the North.

There remained only three barriers in Cass's path to the
nomination. The first was the two-thirds rule which had been
used to defeat Van Buren four years before. If the rule were
again adopted, it would be much more difficult to nominate him.
The second was the Barnburner delegation which was totally
opposed to his nomination. And the third was the Alabama
Platform, which seemed to preclude the delegates from the
Southeast from voting for him. The most significant political
maneuvers both before and during the convention centered
around the efforts of Cass's opponents to strengthen these barriers.

CHAPTER VII

The Baltimore Convention

THE DEMOCRATIC NATIONAL CONVENTION WAS DUE TO MEET on May 22. In the weeks preceding this date, the New York situation provided the most fertile ground for preconvention intrigue. The Barnburners' inveterate hostility toward Cass, which encouraged other candidates, had been forcibly expressed at the Utica Convention by George Rathbun. Amid the cheers of the delegates, Rathbun had recounted the story of Cass's recreancy on the Wilmot Proviso.[1] In order to offset this accusation of betrayal and to demonstrate the inconsistency of the Barnburners, Cass published excerpts of a friendly letter from Rathbun, which had intimated that the Barnburners might support him for the presidency.[2] In reply, Rathbun pointed out that he had written the letter while Cass was still an advocate of the Wilmot Proviso and went on to compare Cass unfavorably to Benedict Arnold. "So far as I know," said Rathbun, "[Arnold] never published parts of letters written to him before his desertion while he [still] appeared an honest man, to prove the inconsistency of his friends because they had condemned him when he had demonstrated that he was no longer honest or worthy of confidence."[3]

Buchanan and Woodbury were both hoping to benefit by

[121]

the Barnburners' strong antagonism toward Cass.[4] Buchanan's efforts to obtain their direct assistance for his candidacy were rather limited, however. Early in April his campaign manager surveyed the conditions in New York but the report was far from encouraging, since the Barnburners' hostility seemed to extend to Buchanan as well.[5] Notwithstanding this, Buchanan had one of his lieutenants, who had remained faithful to Van Buren in 1844, request Barnburner support from John Van Buren, with whom Buchanan himself was on fairly good terms.[6] John Van Buren's reply was noncommittal, but Buchanan's friends were hopeful that the Barnburners would acquiesce in his nomination.[7] With their help, the Buchanan forces could kill off Cass and inherit his delegates.

Woodbury's managers were much more active in trying to exploit the situation in New York. Shortly after their election victory in New Hampshire, they approached the Barnburners about an "arrangement" for their support.[8] The Barnburners were of a divided mind about Woodbury, however, and even in the doubtful event that an accommodation could be reached, it was evident that the price would be high.[9] Moreover, the threat of the more radical Barnburners like Preston King and John Van Buren to bolt the party tended to discredit the faction with the national organization, making a direct alliance with them of dubious value.[10] Woodbury's bid had also disturbed the Hunkers, who threatened to denounce him if he became the Barnburners' candidate.[11]

These developments persuaded Woodbury and his followers to try instead to bring about an agreement between the two factions to share seats in the national convention and to unite on a single candidate.[12] In the event of such an agreement, the Hunkers would presumably have to recognize the futility of supporting Cass and would fall back upon another candidate, and there was evidence that Woodbury was, in fact, the Hunkers' second choice.[13] Combined with the support which the Barnburners would presumably give him, this would make Woodbury the natural choice of the combined delegations.[14] The Barnburners' threat to bolt the party and the Hunkers' penchant for Cass would thus be neatly neutralized. The bitter antagonism between the two factions made it impossible to carry out the scheme immediately, but Woodbury's managers were hopeful that the pressure of the national convention would enable them to effect it at Baltimore.[15] They determined to have Woodbury's delegates at the convention vote for the admission of both factions, which they tried in the meantime to cultivate.[16]

Their simultaneous bid for support from southern Democrats rendered the task extremely difficult so far as the Barnburners were concerned. The news of Yancey's performance in the Alabama Convention had already disturbed those Barnburners who were inclined toward Woodbury, since they could never support him if he committed himself to the principles of the Alabama Platform.[17] John Van Buren, who disliked Woodbury almost as much as he did Cass, was hopeful that the situation would present him with an opportunity to ruin the judge's chances for the nomination. He asked the Buchanan lieutenant who had written him to give him concrete evidence of Woodbury's alleged proslavery views.[18] Buchanan and his henchmen were not immediately able to provide any such information,[19] but they eventually discovered in the Alabama newspapers an open letter from Yancey which referred explicitly to Woodbury's private commitment. A few days before the Barnburners' caucus met in New York, Buchanan had the Washington *Union* reprint excerpts from Yancey's letter.[20] The *Evening Post,* the Barnburners' leading organ, responded to the *Union*'s story by announcing: "If the statements of Mr. Yancey and the author of the letter on whose authority he relies be not grossly mistaken, Mr. Woodbury has given himself his political death wound."[21]

Woodbury's managers moved quickly to try to heal the wound. They disavowed Yancey's statement in Woodbury's name and had Woodbury send them private disclaimers which they could show to interested delegates.[22] In the meantime, pressure had been building up among Woodbury's southern supporters for an open expression of his proslavery sentiments on the territorial issue.[23] Early in May, Yancey had written to him, as well as to Cass, Buchanan, and Dallas, asking them to state publicly their views on the Alabama Platform.[24] At the urging of his managers, Woodbury returned the same noncommittal answer as the others.[25] Woodbury's friends in Washington were able to persuade Dixon H. Lewis that this course was absolutely necessary to avoid the destruction of his chances for the nomination, and Lewis in turn convinced Yancey.[26] The Alabama congressman to whom Woodbury had originally confided his views was even persuaded to disclaim his commitment in order to reassure northern delegates.[27] The Woodbury forces managed in this way to blunt the force of Buchanan's disclosure of Yancey's letter, but they were unable to offset its effect completely. The incident disconcerted Woodbury's northern supporters and made the Barnburners more wary of him than ever.

The plans of Woodbury's managers were frustrated even more, however, by the Barnburners' determination not to participate in a convention which accepted the Hunkers as delegates.[28] This demand for exclusive recognition not only pleased the more radical Barnburners like Preston King, who refused to countenance any hint of compromise, it also suited the purposes of the more conservative politicians like Martin Van Buren, whose primary concern was control of the state party as a base of political operations.[29] The Barnburners had an opportunity to demonstrate their hold on the Democratic electorate in New York when one of them was nominated for mayor of New York City over the protest of the Hunkers. Despite the continued opposition of the Hunkers in the election campaign, the Democratic nominee was victorious.[30] Pleased with this show of popular support the Van Burens took the occasion to issue a new Barnburner manifesto. The statement was largely the work of the elder Van Buren, with emendations by his son John and Samuel J. Tilden. Van Buren still wanted to avoid committing himself publicly on the territorial issue, and it was decided that the best way to present it to the public was to have it adopted by the

Democratic legislative caucus as its official address to the voters.[31]

The purpose of the statement was to puncture, once and for all, the pretensions of the Hunkers to speak for the Democratic party in New York. The issue of slavery in the territories was the only one dealt with at length; for the validation of the Barnburners' claims to regularity, readers were referred to the Utica Address, which the legislative address was designed to supplement. Van Buren began by pointing out that the recent treaty with Mexico, by which the United States had finally acquired California and New Mexico, disposed of the objections previously urged against the Wilmot Proviso—that it was premature and would prevent annexation.[32] He then undertook an elaborate defense of the constitutionality and expediency of the Proviso which brought him to the crux of his argument.[33] Referring specifically to the actions of the Alabama, Florida, and Virginia conventions, he pointed out that the southern wing of the party was demanding that northern Democrats adopt the view that the right to hold slaves in the territories was guaranteed. "We are called upon to do so," read the address, "under the menace of political disenfranchisement and degradation if we refuse to believe, or profess to believe, this new and startling doctrine."[34] Van Buren went on to argue that this southern demand was an impossible one: "We ask them to believe that the principle of extending slavery to territories now free from it can never be made acceptable to the freemen of the North, and assure them, in the most absolute confidence, that the few persons at the North who for sinister objects strive to make it so, will soon, very soon, be buried under a load of public obloquy in a grave from which there will be no resurrection."[35] This confident declaration of the weakness of the Hunkers and other alleged northern friends of the South prepared the way for an inflexible assertion of the Barnburner demand for exclusive recognition at Baltimore:

We are conscientiously satisfied that there is no room for an honest difference of opinion in regard to the right of the Delegates selected by the Utica Convention to sit in the National Convention which is to assemble at Baltimore for the nomination of Democratic candidates for President and Vice President. If a question is made to their right it must be decided, not compromised. Those delegates should not be insulted by the request that they should yield one particle of the weight to which, as sole representatives of the Democracy of this state, they are justly entitled.[36]

"The simple question," concluded Van Buren, "which the Baltimore convention will be called upon to decide, will be the exclusion or admission of those delegates."[37] The address, in short, was designed to give the national party a straightforward choice, a choice in which its failure to give exclusive recognition to the Barnburners would inevitably lose it the state of New York.

Most of the Barnburner delegates were anxious to be admitted to the national convention on the terms laid down in the legislative address and were prepared to play down, as the address suggested, the conflict over the Wilmot Proviso.[38] They were coming to recognize that their position was more precarious than they had supposed and that despite their threats many of the delegates to the national convention would welcome a pretext either to reject them altogether or to admit them along with the Hunkers. As the time of the convention approached they set to work to prepare an airtight legal case for their admission, including a comparison of the elections of delegates to the Utica and Albany Conventions.[39] At the same time radicals like Preston King, who still had no doubts about their being admitted, were calling the delegation's attention to a problem which they considered even more serious: how to avoid being compromised in the convention on either the territorial issue or the presidential candidate. To resolve this problem John Van Buren proposed to his father that the delegation nominate him after it had been admitted. He maintained that this would give the convention the same kind of clear choice as the legislative address presented on the seating question. If the former President was rejected by the convention, the Barnburners could assume it was because of his suspected views on the territorial issue. The Barnburners could then test the convention with a free-soil resolution and, if that failed, withdraw and nominate Taylor or some other independent candidate. John Van Buren was especially insistent upon the need to make an independent nomination in the event of a secession from the convention. "We can sweep the state with Taylor," he wrote his father in reference to New York, "and we must have a candidate, or you, Wadsworth, Flagg, and other such irregular regulars will vote [for] the Baltimore nominee."[40]

The elder Van Buren vetoed his son's suggestion and explained to him why he considered it precisely the wrong move in the faction's struggle for supremacy in the state and nation. "A single rash and unadvised step," he commented, "which would give the Democracy of the other free states reason to assume that you are indifferent to the general success of the party, that you used this subject for private ends to revenge past injuries or indulge personal piques, might be fatal to your usefulness and success."[41] In place of his son's plan, he offered detailed advice on what the delegation should do at Baltimore, advice which he later incorporated into a memorandum which the delegates used as a guide at Baltimore.[42] Unlike his son, Van Buren was interested above all in the recognition by the national party of the Barnburner faction. Only on one condition should the delegation be prepared to repudiate the convention in its entirety: "The delegation will not submit to the slightest diminution of their power [i.e., by admitting Hunker delegates along with them], but will if that is attempted withdraw their claim for admission and appeal to the people. The nature and character of that appeal must be governed by the circumstances as they shall be found to exist."[43] Van Buren had suggested to his son that in this event the Barnburners might disavow the Baltimore nominations and "take Gen. Taylor if he is in a state to be taken up by you, or some other person."[44] The memorandum did insist too that "every attempt to extract a pledge to support the nomination as a condition or inducement to admission should be repelled as insulting."[45] On the other hand,

Van Buren advised the delegates, once they were admitted, to acquiesce in the nomination of Cass, Buchanan, Dallas, or Woodbury—even though each of them had submitted to a southern test on the territorial issue—should one of the four be selected over the protest of New York.[46]

Van Buren's memorandum provided the Barnburners with answers to every question but one, whom to support in the convention. In spite of Van Buren's obvious reluctance to be a candidate, the delegation made a direct request to use his name, but his emphatic refusal required them to look elsewhere.[47] They expressed interest in Governor Francis Shunk of Pennsylvania, who had remained uncommitted on the territorial issue, but in spite of some encouragement from members of his administration, his deteriorating health appeared to rule him out as a possibility.[48] Their best chance of success seemed to be with General William O. Butler, a Mexican War hero from Kentucky. Butler was a slaveholder, like Zachary Taylor, but he was also, like Taylor, totally uncommitted on the territorial issue, and a good Democrat in the bargain. Some members of the Utica delegation, however, had strong objections to supporting Butler.[49] The Barnburners' confusion over a candidate proved a severe handicap, since it prevented them from designating to the convention a positive alternative to the men they opposed.[50]

The inability of the Barnburners to unite on a candidate rendered the situation in New York even more chaotic than it was already and worked directly to the advantage of Cass, since he was not absolutely dependent upon the votes of the state for his nomination. Cass's managers sought to pursue this advantage by disarming the ultimate weapon of the Barnburners, their ability to deny Cass their state's electoral votes. Shortly before the convention met, Cass's supporters began to argue that he could win the election without New York.[51] "The divisions in New York have now reached a point," said the Detroit *Free Press,* the principal Cass organ, "that it would seem to show that no man likely to be nominated by the Democratic National Convention can hope to get the electoral vote of that state." "Be it so," the *Free Press* concluded, "we do not stand in need of her vote. We can and shall elect the nominee of the Baltimore convention without that vote."[52]

In the meantime, Cass's friends in Congress had been trying to advance his candidacy by reconstructing the alliance between southern and western Democrats which had been so successful four years before. They were seeking an accommodation between the two groups on the popular sovereignty doctrine, and in order to do this they had to circumvent the barrier which Yancey had erected to such an accommodation, the Alabama Platform. On the very eve of the convention, Thomas Bayly, an influential congressman from Virginia, came up with a satisfactory solution to the problem. In a long speech in the House of Representatives condemning the Wilmot Proviso as unconstitutional, Bayly concluded with these remarks:

I have confined myself, as the committee will perceive, to the discussion of the question as to the power of Congress, under the Constitution, to prohibit slavery in the territories. There are other interesting questions which have been mooted of late, which I have purposely avoided debating. They are first, whether if we acquire territory where slavery does not exist, it will be legalized there by the very act of acquisition? and second, whether the people of the territories, through their Territorial Legislatures, can prohibit slavery in the event of the first question being decided one way, or legalize it in the event it is decided the other. These questions, however interesting, are not for us to decide. They are strictly judicial questions, and to the courts I am willing, as I shall be bound, to leave them. They are questions which Congress has no authority to settle, and they are questions which I do not wish to see introduced here or in the politics of the country. Neither the Congress nor the President can have anything to do in their solution.[53]

The point of Bayly's speech, which was printed as a pamphlet and widely distributed in the South,[54] was to remove the differences in interpretation of the popular sovereignty doctrine from the sphere of politics, thus enabling southern as well as western Democrats to support the doctrine in spite of the Alabama Platform. "In truth," wrote one of the delegates from

Tennessee to the national convention, "Judge B. has taken a load from the mind of our friends from all sections of the country sincerely anxious to remain united for the sake of principles so long holding them together as a party."[55] It remained for the Cass forces to persuade the southern delegations to ratify this accommodation in the convention. As the delegate from Tennessee pointed out, however, this would most likely be done implicitly rather than explicitly. "It is evidently the present determination of the delegates here," he said, "not to permit the question to be discussed if it can possibly be avoided."[56] When the convention opened, the strong position of the Cass forces with respect to their platform seemed to augur well for the success of their candidate.

The Baltimore Convention was called to order at five minutes before noon on May 22. The New York question arose immediately in the first order of business, the establishment of the identity of the delegates. One of the Georgia delegates proposed that a committee be set up whose duties would include passing judgment upon the contesting delegations from New York. The first of his resolutions read: "Resolved, That a committee be appointed to examine the credentials of delegates and to report to this body the number of votes to which each state is entitled, and the number and names of the delegates present from each state who are entitled to seats in this convention."[57] During the debate on these resolutions, Senator Hannegan of Indiana moved to postpone them until after everyone claiming to be a delegate "pledged himself to support the nominees" of the convention.[58] Preston King objected for the Barnburners, at whom the move was aimed, that the convention must first be constituted, and, despite widespread approval of Hannegan's motion, the convention as a whole agreed. At the instance of Yancey, to whom such a pledge was anathema, the motion was laid upon the table and consideration of the original resolutions resumed.[59]

New York was excluded from representation on the committee to the mutual satisfaction of both the contesting delegations, but the Barnburners had a more serious complaint. They wanted their case decided, not by the committee, but by an open vote in the convention in which the delegates would be presented with a clear choice between accepting and rejecting them. They expected that the northern delegations, which would weigh more heavily in convention than in a committee where each state had one vote, would hesitate to reject them and run the risk of offending public opinion at home on the slavery question. On the other hand, if they should be rejected under such circumstances, it would strengthen their prestige and prepare the way for their independent movement. They therefore tried to get the convention to accept an amendment which would have limited the committee to ascertaining the "facts" of the dispute and reporting them to the convention. The temper of the convention was against them, however, and their amendment was rejected.[60] The convention revealed its bias again in constituting the committee when it refused to allow one of the members to withdraw in spite of his open avowal of opposition to the Barnburners.[61]

At the evening session the credentials committee made a partial report. It designated the number of votes to which each state was entitled and the names of the legitimate delegates from all the states but New York. Since the New York case would require a special hearing, that part of the report was postponed until the next day. In the discussion of the report, an Ohio delegate challenged the right, affirmed by the committee, of the delegate from South Carolina to cast the state's entire nine votes. Because of the difficulties in New York, most of the delegates were inclined to cultivate South Carolina, and the committee report was eventually approved intact.[62]

The committee took up the New York case at a meeting at eight o'clock that night. It was proposed that the two delegations be given an hour and a half apiece to present their arguments for admission, but only after each had pledged to support the nominees of the convention. The committee's debate over the proposed pledge consumed the entire three hours allotted for the presentation of the arguments, before the motion was finally approved by a vote of fifteen to fourteen. The Hunkers professed their readiness to support the nominees, but the Barnburners, acting in accordance with Van Buren's instructions, protested against the pledge and insisted that their admission must be unconditional.[63] When the committee reassembled at eight o'clock the next morning, the question of the propriety of exacting a pledge was again debated at length, but the committee ultimately sustained the decision and voted to admit the Hunkers on the ground that they were willing to take the pledge while the Barnburners were not.[64]

In the meantime, the convention had met and begun to discuss the adoption of rules. The decision on the two-thirds rule was of special significance, since its adoption would make it more difficult for Cass to obtain the nomination. Unfortunately for him, many of his supporters, as well as most of the southern delegates, were committed to the rule, having advocated it four years before in order to stop Van Buren, and would feel compelled to vote for it on a direct test.[65] Notwithstanding this, the Cass managers thought they saw an opportunity to defeat the measure when the credentials committee asked to interrupt the proceedings to report on the New York case.[66] If the convention adopted the committee's recommendation and seated Cass's Hunker supporters, it might be possible to defeat the two-thirds rule. Virtually every Cass delegate in the convention voted for a motion to postpone consideration of the two-thirds rule until after the disposition of the New York case, but it failed for lack of support from the Pennsylvania delegation, in spite of the fact that they were formally committed to defeat the rule.[67] Buchanan's managers persuaded the delegation that the commitment did not apply to collateral questions.[68] When the vote occurred on the two-thirds rule itself, the Pennsylvanians voted against it, but it was adopted by an overwhelming majority, most of Cass's supporters reverting to their original commitment.[69]

The credentials committee's report on New York was taken up at the afternoon session. The recommendation of the committee to admit the Hunkers was opposed by a friend of the

Barnburners from New England, who objected to the exaction of a pledge. Congressman Bayly of Virginia defended the committee's action, but his argument was answered with telling effect by Yancey, who was not only opposed in principle to a pledge, but apparently hopeful of using the Barnburners to help Woodbury.[70] Maintaining that the exaction of a pledge exceeded the authority of both the committee and the convention itself, Yancey concluded by offering a resolution which defined his conception of how far the power of the convention extended: "Resolved, That as a voluntary association of the Democracy we have no right to sit upon the conflicting claims of the Democracy of any State, and that therefore the Democracy of New York must determine for themselves which delegation from that State is their representative."[71] Presumably, this would require the two delegations to get together, giving Woodbury an opportunity to secure their combined vote. Yancey's resolution was put aside for the moment, but his speech helped persuade the convention to table the committee report and agree instead to hear the two delegations present their respective arguments the following day.[72]

The Barnburners' victory, together with the adoption of the two-thirds rule, weakened Cass's position, and apparently strengthened their influence on the selection of the nominee.[73] They were still having difficulty, however, settling on a candidate. Blair, who had been elected as a delegate from Maryland, suggested William Allen of Ohio. A Barnburner delegation visited Allen in Baltimore late that night to offer him their support, but the Ohio senator was committed to Cass and refused to accept the offer.[74] Having failed with Allen, Blair turned back to his original favorite, General Butler. Although some of the Utica delegates were dubious about Butler, it was agreed that if they were admitted Blair would initiate a movement for Butler among the Kentucky and Maryland delegates to which they would eventually rally.[75]

The Barnburners suffered a severe reverse, however, during the arguments before the convention the next day. The two

Hunker speakers tried to throw the onus of disorganization upon the Barnburners for their refusal to abide by the decisions of the Syracuse Convention and their subsequent meeting at Herkimer. They emphasized that this was a result of the Barnburners' commitment to the Wilmot Proviso, which they stigmatized as anti-Democratic.[76] Most of the Barnburners were anxious to avoid making their commitment to the Wilmot Proviso the primary issue in the dispute.[77] Their first speaker denied that the party split originated in the actions taken at Syracuse on the territorial issue, claiming that it long antedated that convention. He disassociated his delegation from the "irregular" Herkimer meeting and emphasized the regularity of their Utica Convention, in contrast with the Hunkers' Albany Convention. He further insisted that the Barnburners were firmly committed to the Democratic principle of state rights and should not be excluded from the convention merely because of their commitment to the Wilmot Proviso.[78]

This moderate line of argument did not appeal to Preston King, who was the Barnburners' second speaker. Unlike most of his colleagues, he wanted to throw down the gauntlet to the South and, although he was obviously operating under restrictions imposed by the delegation, he managed to communicate his opinions very clearly to the convention.[79] He was determined above all to expose the difference in principle, according to which he expected the convention to decide the case. He therefore concentrated his attention on the injustice, and the inexpediency, of excluding his delegation because of their views on the Wilmot Proviso. Such a move, according to King, would not only logically require the expulsion of many Democrats outside New York, it would also call down the wrath of northern public opinion upon the party. The Barnburners, he continued, would never submit to a test on the territorial issue such as the southern delegates had imposed upon the presidential candidates. He maintained that "If all the other States were prepared to make the democratic party the carrier of slavery over this continent, the democracy of New York would take no part in such an alliance for such an object."[80] He concluded by saying that "alone or in company they [the Barnburners] would fight this battle of freedom from beginning to end."[81]

King's overt introduction of the slavery question, which the convention was trying to suppress, infuriated most of the delegates, and destroyed whatever chance the Barnburners might have had of securing exclusive admission, incidentally removing the danger that the delegation would be compromised.[82] The patient Cambreleng, who spoke after King, tried to recover the lost ground by reminding the delegates of his own and his associates' past services to the party and appealing for conciliation between the sections. While rejecting a formal pledge, he intimated that the delegation if admitted would acquiesce in the nomination regardless of the candidate. "By our past acts," he argued, "we stand pledged to support the nominees of this convention."[83] He concluded by proclaiming the Barnburner dedication to the constitutional rights of the South and deploring a sectional split in the party.[84]

But it was King's speech, rather than Cambreleng's, that struck home to the southern delegates; they were determined now to exclude the Barnburners at all costs. When the arguments were finished, Yancey obtained the floor and substituted for the motion he had proposed the day before a resolution admitting the Hunkers as the regularly constituted delegates from New York. Yancey justified his change in position by claiming that King had made the delegations' dispute the "test of a great principle" (i.e., the Wilmot Proviso). "No men," said Yancey, "proclaiming such a principle can be democrats; they must be factious conspirators or whigs in disguise."[85] He demanded that an immediate vote be taken on his resolution. Yancey's speech, agitating as it did the explosive territorial issue, brought the convention to the brink of chaos. Delegates were milling around, shouting at each other in an unsuccessful effort to make themselves heard over the uproar. It was only with great difficulty that the president was able to restore order sufficiently to allow a motion for adjournment to pass.[86]

When the convention reconvened at five o'clock, tempers had had time to cool. Most of the southern delegates still demanded that the Barnburners be excluded, but they recognized the inexpediency of placing exclusion upon the grounds that Yancey had laid down.[87] Most of the northern delegates, on the other hand, in spite of their sympathy with the southern point of view, recognized the inexpediency of excluding the Barnburners upon any grounds whatsoever. Senator Hopkins Turney from Tennessee, who was hoping to use the Utica delegation to obtain Polk's renomination,[88] made a particularly effective plea against exclusion, arguing that it would not only insure a defection, but would strengthen the defectors' ability to hurt the party.[89]

The crucial vote came on a compromise amendment to admit both delegations. The orientation of the vote was primarily sectional, although candidate preference was also a factor. Nearly all the southern delegations gave unanimous votes against the compromise, while the Woodbury delegates from the Northeast, whose sectional bias was identical with the interest of their candidate, were equally unanimous in favor of it. Cass's northwestern supporters split rather evenly on the issue. For a majority of them the inexpediency of rejecting the Barnburners outweighed their desire to obtain votes for Cass in New York. The three slaveholding states, Kentucky, Tennessee, and Texas, gave most of their votes for the compromise in the hope of eventually obtaining Barnburner support for their favorite son candidates, should Cass fail to win the nomination. The Pennsylvania delegation, having waited until all of the other states had cast their ballots, gave just enough votes for the compromise to pass. Buchanan's managers thought that they could earn some good will toward their candidate among the southern delegates by casting some of their votes against the compromise.[90] With the compromise tentatively approved, the convention adjourned for the day.

Both New York delegations objected very strongly to the convention's action as an effort to cancel out the state's influence altogether.[91] The Hunkers prepared a strong protest to be read to the convention the next day. The Barnburners intended to refuse the proffered seats and leave the convention, but, believing the Hunker protest to be a mere ruse, they wanted to remain long enough to make certain that Hunker votes would not be used to give Cass the nomination.[92] They were still hoping, moreover, to influence the convention's choice of a candidate. If Cass could be stopped and General Butler nominated, they were prepared to support the ticket.[93]

Although the adoption of the compromise appeared to be a setback for Cass, it actually left him in a stronger position than the alternative would have, as many of his western followers perceived.[94] To them rejection of the compromise to gain Hunker votes was a self-defeating strategy. It would injure him as a candidate, not just in New York, but in the Northwest as well. Since southern delegates must be convinced that he could win the election if they were to be induced to support him, the result of his being undermined in the area of his greatest strength, the area on which he depended for victory, would be to encourage delegates to abandon him and his strategy of a southern-western alliance for a combination with brighter prospects. From this point of view, the acceptance of the compromise was essential to Cass's success.[95]

But the adoption of the compromise was also a positive gain for Cass in that it was a sign that the convention had decided to disregard New York in making the nomination. The delegates had had to face up to the fact that the Barnburners and Hunkers were so badly divided that victory in New York was unlikely regardless of what they did. Acceptance of the compromise was essentially a decision to give up the effort to resolve the dispute and proceed to the nominations irrespective of New York, as well as an attempt to minimize the Barnburners' capacity for mischief.[96] The elimination of New York as a factor in political calculations undermined Cass's rivals, whose main strength derived from their claims to be able to carry the state while Cass could not. With his capability of reviving the southern-western alliance, Cass was unquestionably the strongest candidate outside New York.[97] Once the compromise had been approved, the Ohio delegation was able to guarantee a victory in their state, which was absolutely essential to Democratic success without New York, but only if Cass were the nominee.[98]

When the convention proceeded to the nominations the next morning, after having first ratified the New York compromise, the Cass men were in a very strong position. They had already obtained the votes of virtually all the delegates from the Southwest and had persuaded the Mississippi delegation to place Cass in nomination. They still had no sure adherents from the Southeast, however, and it remained to be seen whether delegates from that section would support Cass. Their chief hope was the key Virginia delegation, which retired for consultation when the balloting began.

The sixty-nine Virginia delegates comprised the largest delegation in the convention, but they had agreed to cast their seventeen votes for whichever candidate the majority approved.[99] The delegation was fairly evenly divided among the three leading candidates, Cass, Buchanan, and Woodbury. Woodbury's prospects of getting the state's votes appeared so dim that his Chivalry supporters had resorted to the desperate expedient of circulating a handbill designed to show that, with New York lost, the Democratic party could not succeed without South Carolina, and only Woodbury could carry the state.[100] In the meantime, Buchanan's supporters, who had come to the convention confident that they could convert their plurality in the delegation to a majority by the time the voting began, were dismayed to find that their position was being undermined by members of the state administration in Pennsylvania, who were telling southern delegates that Buchanan would be a weak candidate.[101] This was all the more dismaying, since one of their principal arguments was that Buchanan was the only candidate who could be depended upon to carry his home state.[102]

But it was the leadership of the Virginia delegation which played the most crucial role in determining their ultimate decision. The delegation was headed by Thomas Bayly, the congressman who had laid down the essential conditions of the southern-western alliance in his speech a few days before. Together with John Y. Mason and Andrew Stevenson, an old friend of Cass's who had been elected president of the convention, Bayly managed to win over many delegates to his point of view. The evening before, one of the delegates had telegraphed Buchanan that the younger Ritchie, editor of the *Enquirer,* had gone over to Cass and that the entire delegation seemed to be giving way.[103]

Nevertheless, the final vote was extremely close. On the first poll of the delegation Cass had twenty-six votes to twenty-two for Buchanan and twenty for Woodbury. Recognizing that they could not win, the Chivalry divided their votes between Cass and Buchanan, outraging the latter's followers, who expected their support. The second vote was a tie, broken by Stevenson's timely arrival and his vote in favor of Cass.[104]

The delegation re-entered the convention just as the states had finished casting their ballots. Its vote for Cass was greeted with loud applause and gave him almost one-half of the delegates voting.[105] On the second ballot Cass gained eight votes, as four of his New England supporters emerged and four of the Georgia delegates followed Virginia's example. The breakthrough came on the third ballot when Cass increased his strength by twenty-three votes. The southern-western alliance, with its promise of Ohio, won over North Carolina's eleven votes[106] as well as four more from Georgia. Cass also picked up six more delegates from New England and three from Iowa, who had previously voted for Buchanan. It seemed evident now that the strategy of the Cass men was a success and that their candidate could not be stopped. On the fourth and final ballot, Buchanan's precarious majority on the New Jersey delegation gave way, and the state's seven votes went to Cass, along with South Carolina's nine votes cast by her single delegate, the two remaining votes from Georgia, and a half dozen more from New England.

Since neither delegation from New York had answered the

roll call, the two-thirds rule by common agreement was interpreted to mean two-thirds of the participating delegates, and Cass's one hundred and seventy-nine votes were adjudged to give him the nomination.[107] When the delegations were called upon to ratify the choice of the convention, only Yancey and one other Alabama delegate refused to pledge their support.[108] The joy and relief at having made a successful nomination—there had been a great deal of concern lest the convention break up[109]— was scarcely affected by the Barnburners' statement rejecting their seats in the convention.

In the afternoon General Butler was easily nominated for the office of Vice-President. The convention had determined upon the selection of a southern slaveholder to balance the ticket, and, aside from his being a war hero with no political enemies, Butler had the additional advantage that his nomination might serve as a sop to the Barnburners.[110] While the nomination for Vice-President was being made, the committee on resolutions, which had been established earlier, met to frame a platform for the convention. The most important article in the platform was obviously to be the one dealing with slavery.

It was proposed in the committee to implement a suggestion of Thomas Ritchie's[111] and merely reiterate the platform resolution of 1840 and 1844 on slavery:

That Congress has no power under the constitution to interfere with or control the domestic institutions of the several States, and that such States are the sole and proper judges of everything appertaining to their own affairs, not prohibited by the constitution; that all efforts of the abolitionists or others made to induce Congress to interfere with slavery, or to take incipient steps in relation thereto, are calculated to lead to the most alarming and dangerous consequences, and that all such efforts have an inevitable tendency to diminish the happiness of the people, and endanger the stability and permanency of the Union, and ought not to be countenanced by any friend of our political institutions.[112]

The great appeal of the resolution was its extreme vagueness with reference to the question of slavery in the territories, a

quality which would enable the northern and southern wings of
the party to construe it as best suited their local needs. It failed
to make any direct statement on the Wilmot Proviso, let alone
take up the constitutionality of the question. The resolution had
been originally intended to deal with the question of slavery in
the states, and, like the similar statement of the Ohio convention,
it was only by inference that it could be interpreted as disavow-
ing the Proviso.[113]

Yancey, who was representing Alabama on the committee, was extremely dissatisfied with the resolution, and
proposed to add the following amendment: *"Resolved further,*
That the doctrine of non-interference with the rights of
property of any portion of the people of this confederacy, be it
in the States or Territories, by any other than the parties interested in them, is the true republican doctrine recognized by this
body."[114] In the light of his Alabama Platform, this was a very
mild resolution. It appears perfectly compatible with Cass's
popular sovereignty doctrine and could have been interpreted in
the North as allowing the settlers to prohibit slavery during the
territorial stage of government.[115] Yancey evidently explained
that such was not his interpretation, however, because one of
the committee members, John Slidell of Louisiana, objected that
Cass "entertained opinions directly the reverse of the resolution
[amendment]; and therefore if the Convention should adopt the
resolution, it would rebuke the opinions of Gen. Cass and be
inconsistent with itself."[116] The committee rejected Yancey's
amendment by a vote of twenty to nine, only two northern states,
Pennsylvania and Wisconsin, supporting it. A second effort to
amend the resolution to declare the Wilmot Proviso unconstitutional by adding the words "or territories" after the words, "the
several states," was likewise voted down.[117]

Having failed to carry his point in committee, Yancey raised
the question in the convention after the committee had made its
report. Along with the delegates of Florida and South Carolina,
he submitted a minority report which pointed out that the resolutions of the majority waived the question of slavery in the

territories. Yancey further contended in his report that since, in the absence of a direct statement by the convention on the question, the party would be judged by the opinion of the presidential nominee, the majority platform pronounced, "in substance, against the political equality of the people," i.e., against the right to take slaves into the territories.[118] The minority report concluded with the amendment which Yancey had offered in committee and which he now proceeded to defend in a speech to the convention. In the speech Yancey clarified his objections to Cass's opinions. They were plainly intended, he claimed, to permit settlers to prohibit slavery before the territory became a state, a position which was unsatisfactory to the South.[119] Before the vote was taken, one of the delegates asked whether the amendment was "intended to deny the right of the territorial legislatures to regulate slavery within their limits," to which Yancey replied that it certainly was.[120] With the issue explicitly stated, the convention began balloting on the amendment.

The amendment had no chance of success. It was intended rather to force the southern delegates to decide between their professed slavery principles and political expediency. If, as Yancey expected, they waived a clear statement of their principles in order to aid the election chances of the Democratic nominee, they would render themselves vulnerable to attack from the state rights forces in the forthcoming campaign. In spite of the clear statement of his intention in his speech, however, Yancey's amendment was still open to more than one interpretation, and the southern delegates were able to use this ambiguity to obscure the distinction Yancey was trying to make. Yancey was able to secure all nine of the votes of his own state for his amendment although one Alabama delegate maintained that the opinions of Cass were "approved by the people of Alabama" and that the majority report was "sufficient for the south."[121] But the only other important delegation to vote for the amendment, that of Georgia, explained that, in supporting the measure, "the majority of the delegation did not concur in the construction placed upon the resolution [Yancey's amendment] by the mover of it."[122] Presumably this meant that they did not consider the amendment incompatible with Cass's popular sovereignty doctrine. In a similar interpretation, the North Carolina delegates justified their opposition to the amendment on the ground that, notwithstanding Yancey's intention, it did *not* preclude territorial prohibition as the Alabama Platform demanded, and the "more comprehensive" committee resolution did.[123] Altogether, the amendment received only thirty-six votes, most of the southerners recognizing the inexpediency of demanding from the North the more explicit statement.[124] After Yancey's amendment was rejected, the convention adopted the committee platform, with only Yancey, one other Alabama delegate, and the Florida delegation withholding approval. The convention then created a national committee to co-ordinate the election campaign and, its business completed, adjourned.

Threatened with disruption on the explosive territorial issue, the party had succeeded in the convention in rehabilitating the old alliance between the South and the West on an ambiguous popular sovereignty platform. This doctrine, as expounded by Cass, satisfied the southerners' demand that the northern wing of the party surrender the Wilmot Proviso principle as the price of their continued participation in the party organization and seemed to offer a formula for victory in the forthcoming election. The platform was likewise understood to repudiate the Proviso, although for reasons of expediency it did not openly do so and was far from satisfying the more extreme demands of the Alabama Platform which embodied the views of a great many southerners. The expectation was that the repudiation of the Wilmot Proviso principle would enable Cass to carry most of the southern states. At the same time it was calculated that his popularity in the Northwest was sufficient, if accompanied by a free-soil interpretation of popular sovereignty, to win this region for him, particularly in view of the fact that the Whigs seemed about to nominate a southern slaveholder. With enough southern and northwestern states, along with the traditional Democratic strongholds, Pennsylvania, New Hampshire, and

Maine, the party could win the election and thus triumph over the threat posed to it by the Wilmot Proviso. The controversy over the "abstract" right to take slaves into the territories had evidently lost the Democrats the state of New York, but, despite this loss, the Cass forces thought that they had succeeded in limiting the damage to that state alone with their popular sovereignty solution. The election was to prove that they were mistaken.

CHAPTER VIII

The Election Campaign

ALTHOUGH THE PRESIDENTIAL NOMINATION HAD BEEN MADE
without reference to New York, the Cass leaders had not given
up hope of obtaining the co-operation of both New York factions in an effort to carry the state for the party.[1] But while the
Hunkers announced their willingness to support the ticket, notwithstanding their pique at the convention's failure to recognize
them as the legitimate representatives of New York,[2] the Barnburners initiated their independent movement. They held a caucus on May 25, the very night of the nominations, and decided
to hold a convention to select candidates of their own. There
was talk of their accepting Butler as the vice-presidential candidate and running him with John A. Dix.[3]

On his way home, Preston King stopped off in Baltimore to
talk with Dix about a possible nomination, but found him wary
of an independent movement.[4] The delegation was determined
to act, however, and issued a call from Philadelphia on the 26th
for another convention at Utica on June 22, to nominate candidates for President and Vice-President.[5] A committee was appointed to prepare an address to the Democratic electors which
was published a few days later in the Barnburner journals.[6]

The Barnburners were hoping to strengthen the impetus for

an independent movement by having the general committee of the party in New York City call a mass meeting to protest the actions of the Baltimore Convention. In spite of the committee's disapproval of the convention's handling of the New York dispute, however, it accepted the nominations and called a ratification meeting instead. The Barnburners called their own meeting on June 7, to hear the report of the Utica delegates from the New York City district.[7]

The protest meeting was also an effort to prevent the Whigs from nominating Zachary Taylor, as it seemed likely they would do. In a recent letter to his brother-in-law, Captain John S. Allison, Taylor had identified himself as "a Whig but not an ultra Whig," and this letter, together with another written at almost the same time in which he said that he would be a candidate for the presidency even if rejected by the Whigs, left him in a very strong position on the eve of the Whig convention.[8] Notwithstanding the Allison letter, John Van Buren and other Barnburners were still extremely eager to make Taylor their candidate.[9] By running Taylor for the presidency, they expected not only to beat Cass but to elect their state ticket as well, leaving them in a position to regain control of the national party, which would be purged by its defeat of its proslavery bias.[10]

Since this plan involved supporting Taylor as an independent candidate rather than as the Whig nominee, they had to find some way to bring about his defeat in the Whig convention. With the help of Thurlow Weed, the Whig political boss in New York, who was subtly plotting against Taylor, they arranged to have northern Whig delegates on their way to Philadelphia stop off in New York and attend their protest meeting. The idea was to convince the delegates that the Democratic divisions in New York would enable Henry Clay or some northern candidate to carry the state, encouraging them to hold out against Taylor's nomination.[11]

In his speech to the meeting, John Van Buren made it clear that he would resolutely oppose Taylor if the Whigs nominated him. And he went on to pour scorn on the Whigs for their apparent readiness to abandon their principles and reject Clay for the general.[12] However impressed they were with John Van Buren's reasoning, the Whig delegates were unwilling or unable to prevent Taylor's nomination at Philadelphia, and the Taylor supporters among the Barnburners had to abandon their plans.[13]

In the meantime, the Cass men at Washington were doing everything in their power to discourage the independent movement. Following a ratification meeting in Washington on May 29, Thomas Ritchie led a crowd of Cass well-wishers to call upon the two most influential associates of the Barnburners in Congress, Dix and Benton. Benton responded by pledging his support to Cass and promising success in Missouri in November. Dix was more noncommittal, but intimated that he wished to support Cass and would try to persuade his Barnburner friends to do so.[14] The same night Benton wrote to Van Buren on behalf of Dix, Blair, and himself, advising against an independent movement.[15] Dix himself wired similar advice to William Cullen Bryant, the editor of the *Evening Post*.[16]

In order to bring further pressure to bear on the Barnburners, the party leaders persuaded Benton and Allen, as well as other senators, to accompany Cass on a visit to New York. Benton's attendance was particularly important. It would not only give him an opportunity to consult privately with Barnburner leaders, including his old friend Van Buren, and show them the advantages of coming to terms with the national party, it would also hold out to the faction the promise that through Benton they could exercise considerable influence over Cass.[17]

The trip appeared to be a great success. Cass departed for Detroit after a short visit, leaving Benton and his associates to win over the Barnburners. Well satisfied with his talks with Barnburner leaders in New York City, Benton decided against pressing matters too far and returned to Washington rather than proceed with the rest of the party to Albany, which was only a few miles from Van Buren's home. He had not received an invitation to visit the former President, and although he told Cass he had bypassed Albany in order to avoid being identified too closely with the Barnburners, he evidently feared a direct rebuff. His tactics seemed vindicated, nonetheless, when he received a letter from Van Buren in which the former President concurred in his opinion regarding the inexpediency of a separate nomination.[18]

The Barnburners were determined to have their own presidential candidate, however, and Van Buren ultimately acquiesced in this determination,[19] although he continued to insist that the Utica Convention should limit itself to New York as far as possible. While he did not rule out eventual participation in a national movement, he thought that for the Barnburners themselves to initiate the movement would be self-defeating.[20]

The immediate problem for the Barnburners was whom to nominate. Van Buren himself seemed the most natural choice, but he was strongly opposed to this. He tried to persuade Dix to make himself available and suggested the names of four other men as possible nominees.[21]

By the time the convention met on June 22, three of Van Buren's five suggestions had already been ruled out; another, Addison Gardiner, a former lieutenant-governor, considered himself merely a stand-in candidate in case Dix should refuse the nomination.[22] The delegates rebelled against the selection of Dix, however, because of his coolness toward the independent movement.[23] Notwithstanding his refusal to be a candidate, Van Buren's nomination was virtually assured when one of the delegates read to the convention a letter which he had written for the occasion, ably defending the course of the Barnburners and their adherence to the Wilmot Proviso principle.[24] Sentiment for Van Buren became overwhelming as more and more delegates became convinced that he would not refuse the nomination, in spite of his reluctance to be run.[25] An informal ballot taken on the evening of the 22nd gave Van Buren sixty-nine votes to fourteen for Gardiner and two for Dix.[26] John Van Buren and his immediate associates voted for Gardiner as a preventive against the charge that he was trying to engineer his father's nomination.[27] By the next day the delegates had agreed among themselves to nominate Van Buren by acclamation, and the "thunderous applause" which accompanied the nomination made it clear that they were highly pleased with their selection. The convention then nominated Henry Dodge, a senator from Wisconsin, for Vice-President and adopted a platform devoted largely to the affirmation of the Wilmot Proviso principle.[28]

In spite of their shock at Van Buren's "treason," the national party leaders still anticipated a Democratic victory in November; they had not included New York in their electoral calculations, and they expected the free-soil movement to cut more heavily into Whig than Democratic strength outside the state.[29] These expectations were strengthened by the strong protest of many northern Whigs against Taylor's nomination at Philadelphia, an event which caused one delegate from Massachusetts to declare to the convention that the Whig party was dissolved.[30] Immediately after the nomination, a dozen Whigs who had walked out of the convention held a meeting to plan the establishment of an independent antislavery movement. They decided to work for a national convention of all the opponents of the extension of slavery, regardless of previous party affiliation, and they delegated one of their number to attend a mass meeting of free-soilers being held in Columbus, Ohio, on June 22, and have the meeting issue the call.[31]

The leading spirit behind the Columbus meeting was Salmon P. Chase, a Liberty party man who had long been working to bring about a concert of free-soil forces.[32] Much to Chase's dismay, the Liberty party had nominated its own candidates, John P. Hale and Horatio King, the previous December, making it more difficult to merge the organization into a unified movement with disaffected Whigs and Democrats; but Chase was hard at work trying to overcome this obstacle.[33] He had arranged the free-soil meeting in Columbus to coincide with a meeting of the Liberty party in order to allow the delegates to fraternize with each other.[34] He also wrote to Hale, suggesting that he withdraw as a candidate and endorse a national free-soil movement.[35]

On the evening before the two conventions were formally assembled, the delegates held a common meeting under the leadership of Chase to co-ordinate their actions.[36] The next day the free-soil convention adopted resolutions drawn up by the representative of the Whig dissidents at Philadelphia protesting against the nominations of both major parties and calling for a national convention of free-soil forces in Buffalo, on August 9, to nominate satisfactory candidates for the offices of President and Vice-President.[37] The Liberty party convention approved the Buffalo meeting but, in order to make it more palatable to the party, recommended Hale as a candidate and reserved the right to withhold support from the nominees if they failed to measure up to Liberty principles.[38] Some of the more radical Liberty leaders refused to sanction participation in the Buffalo Convention, but they were a small minority.[39] Both Hale and the Liberty organ at Washington endorsed the call, and the party rank and file signified their approval in local conventions.[40]

In the meantime, the Whig delegates from Massachusetts who had rebelled against Taylor's nomination had returned home to rouse their constituents against the ticket. The "conscience Whigs" of Massachusetts, the faction to which these delegates belonged, had already agreed to hold a protest meeting if Taylor were nominated, and, as soon as the delegates arrived, a call went out for a free-soil convention at Worcester, on June 28, a date purposely selected to allow the convention to respond to the initiative of the Columbus meeting.[41] The Worcester Convention, attended by Liberty men and Democratic free-soilers, as well as by conscience Whigs, selected delegates to go to Buffalo and made overtures to the Barnburners to participate in the movement.[42]

Chase had already approached the Barnburners about participating in a national convention, and he wrote them again after the Utica Convention asking whether they would be represented at Buffalo.[43] Despite the fact that they had obtained from the Utica Convention permission for the Baltimore delegates to attend a national convention "for the purpose of collecting and concentrating the popular will in respect to the question of the Presidency,"[44] the Barnburner leaders were having a difficult time agreeing on whether they should go to Buffalo. Radical free-soilers like Preston King were extremely anxious to unite with Whig and Liberty men in a national antislavery movement, but some Barnburners had strong doubts about the expediency of such a move.[45]

Shortly after the Worcester Convention, John Van Buren and several other Barnburner leaders held a meeting in Albany to decide the matter. Unable to reach an agreement among themselves, they consulted the elder Van Buren, who convinced them of the wisdom of going to Buffalo by pointing out the political advantage to be gained in the accession of Whig and Liberty votes.[46]

In order to fully exploit this advantage, the Barnburners would have to impose their presidential candidate upon the Buffalo Convention, and they had every intention of doing so. Chase was told that they would attend the Buffalo meeting but would not surrender their commitment to Van Buren.[47] The *Evening Post* publicly reiterated the commitment on the eve of the convention. After expressing confidence that Van Buren would be the Buffalo nominee, the *Post* went on to say: "If the convention nominates someone else it will be for the democratic delegates from this state to consider how they might give it to understand they do not concur in the proceeding."[48] Chase was prepared to acquiesce in the Barnburners' demand in order to achieve his desired union of free-soil forces, and so too was Charles Sumner, one of the leaders of the conscience Whigs in Massachusetts.[49] Many of the Massachusetts men had strong objections to the Barnburners' nominee, however. "It is asking too much," wrote one of them, "to require Whigs to vote for Van Buren."[50]

The main objection of the conscience Whigs to Van Buren, aside from his past politics, was his commitment, made originally in 1837 and reiterated in his recent letter to the Barnburners at Utica, to veto a congressional act abolishing slavery in the District of Columbia.[51] After hearing from Preston King that Van Buren would probably not insist upon this commitment, Charles Francis Adams, the most influential of the conscience Whig leaders, wrote the former President intimating that he and his followers would support him at Buffalo if he would abandon it.[52] The Barnburner leaders had already become aware of the importance of the issue to Van Buren's prospects, owing to the objections raised by the Liberty organ in Washington, and were considering how best to deal with it.[53] Van Buren decided he should return a noncommittal reply to Adams, and the conscience Whigs determined to support Judge McLean in the convention.[54]

Chase, who was handling McLean's candidacy, had almost despaired of his accepting the nomination.[55] Convinced as he was of the likelihood of Van Buren's triumph at Buffalo, he had been trying to persuade McLean to take the vice-presidential nomination.[56] The Barnburners were also pressing McLean to accept second place on the ticket, suggesting that he would lead it to victory in 1852.[57] McLean not only declined the vice-presidential nomination, he also told Chase not to let his name go before the convention as a presidential candidate unless Van Buren withdrew.[58] When Chase learned of the decision of the conscience Whigs from Massachusetts and that Van Buren himself was willing to acquiesce in another nomination, he tried to get McLean to change his mind about being a candidate, but the judge refused.[59] By the time the Buffalo Convention met, the field of presidential candidates had been narrowed to Van Buren and Hale, whose nomination was being urged by most of the Liberty men.

The night before the convention, a committee met to try to hammer out some kind of preliminary agreement on the platform. When a platform modeled on that of the recent free-soil convention in Columbus was proposed, some of the Barnburners objected to it as too radical, including as it did a direct commitment to abolish slavery in the District of Columbia. At this delicate moment Chase shrewdly called upon Preston King, whom the committee had selected as its chairman, for a speech. King made an eloquent plea in favor of a declaration that the federal government "should rid itself of all responsibility for [slavery's] existence."[60] King's address struck a responsive chord in the committee; a motion to adopt it as the basis of the platform on slavery was unanimously approved, the Barnburners acquiescing in his implied commitment on the subject of slavery in the District.[61] Chase had undoubtedly informed them that they could expect his help in nominating Van Buren if they would accept a strong platform.

The results of the committee meeting were reported to the convention the following day immediately after it had been called to order. King had reduced the ideas of his speech to three resolutions, which were offered for the consideration of the convention:

Resolved, That it is the duty of the Federal Government to relieve itself of all responsibility for the extension or continuance of slavery, whenever that Government possesses Constitutional authority, and is responsible for its existence.

Resolved, That the States within which slavery exists, are alone responsible for the continuance or existence of slavery within such States, and the Federal Government has neither responsibility nor Constitutional authority to establish or regulate slavery within the States.

Resolved, That the true, and in the judgment of this Convention, the only safe means of preventing the extension of slavery into territory now free, is to prohibit its existence in all such territory by an act of Congress.[62]

King's resolutions, adding the commitment of abolishing slavery in the District of Columbia to the central article of common faith, the prohibition of slavery in the territories, were directly incorporated into the statement of principles which the convention unanimously adopted as its platform. The Barnburners' acceptance of the platform, whose adoption preceded the nominations, stirred up rumors of a deal among insiders to nominate

Van Buren on a platform which would satisfy Whigs and Liberty men. Joshua R. Giddings, the Whig abolitionist, lent credence to the rumors when he announced his willingness to accept Van Buren as a candidate in a plea to the convention for harmony.[63]

Since the convention was actually a conglomeration of antislavery well-wishers from all parts of the North, a more formal and more representative body called the Committee of Conference was established to handle the significant business. The committee ratified the report of the platform committee and submitted it to the convention at large for final approval on the morning of the second day, and then turned to the question of nominations in the afternoon.[64]

Even after they learned of McLean's extreme reluctance to be a candidate, the conscience Whigs of Massachusetts were still inclined to support him, and the judge might have won the nomination had he changed his mind and allowed Chase to submit his name to the convention with those of the other candidates.[65] He refused, however, and Chase withdrew him as a candidate before the balloting began.[66] A Liberty party delegate submitted Hale's name to the committee with the promise that he and his party would abide by the nomination. Chase then called upon Benjamin F. Butler, who was handling Van Buren's candidacy, to define the position of the Barnburners' nominee.

In a long speech to the committee, Butler attempted to overcome Whig and Liberty prejudice against Van Buren by emphasizing the disinterested nature of the former President's views on current politics and the prestige which his nomination would give the movement.[67] One of the delegates later described the climax of Butler's remarks:

In his speech Butler was getting around thorny points in Van Buren's career very skillfully. While graphically describing a recent visit to the ex-President's Kinderhook farm and telling how he was now pursuing bucolic pursuits like Cincinnatus, the model yeoman of his epoch, Butler spoke of the agility with which Van Buren leaped a fence to show his visitor a field of sprouting turnips. A Whig who remembered the veto pledge and was totally opposed to nominating its author broke in upon Butler with the startling exclamation: "Damn his turnips! What are his opinions about the abolition of slavery in the District of Columbia?"[68]

Butler was equal to the occasion and was able to turn it to his advantage. Although he did not make an explicit commitment on the issue, he suggested that Van Buren would accept the convention platform. And to demonstrate the former President's good faith, he read a letter from him endorsing the convention and offering to withdraw as a candidate if it would help achieve unity.[69]

Butler's speech and his reading of the Van Buren letter was, as one delegate remarked, "the turning point of the convention."[70] It won over the conscience Whigs who had decided to refuse to participate in the voting unless the Barnburners committed themselves to support the nominee. Most of them now voted for Van Buren, along with the Barnburners and a few Liberty men like Chase, giving him a clear majority on the first ballot.[71] After the vote had been announced, one of the Liberty party leaders moved that the nomination be made unanimous. His speech to the committee, telling of the sacrifices by which the Liberty organization had been created, now to be surrendered in the interests of harmony, was so moving that it brought tears to the eyes of many of the delegates.[72] "The Liberty Party is not dead," he concluded, "but *translated*."[73]

After a short adjournment the committee reassembled and nominated Charles Francis Adams for the vice-presidency. It then reported its selections to the full convention where they were ratified by acclamation.[74] Ecstatic over the unity achieved, the convention unanimously approved a resolution commending Hale and one inviting John Van Buren "to stump the United States generally" in favor of the free-soil ticket.[75] After several more speeches and a final reading of Van Buren's letter, the convention was permanently adjourned. A new political organization, known as the Free-Soil party, had been born.

The successful union of antislavery forces at Buffalo thwarted the efforts of leaders of both the major parties to suppress the

Wilmot Proviso question, making it instead the major issue in the presidential campaign. Northern Democratic and Whig politicians tried to minimize the Free-Soilers' inroads on their party strength by themselves espousing free soil and representing their respective organizations as the most effective instrument for achieving it.[76] The principal argument of northern Whigs was that Taylor would not veto the Wilmot Proviso.[77] Some northern Democrats made the same claim for Cass, his evident commitment to the contrary notwithstanding.[78] Most of them, however, tried to demonstrate that Cass, unlike Taylor, was a friend of free soil in spite of his commitment against the Proviso. "We know from the frequent declarations made in private conversation," said the Cleveland *Plain Dealer,* "that [Cass] is as strongly opposed to the further extension of slavery as we are."[79] Cass's popular sovereignty doctrine was represented as securing free soil without congressional action.[80] "We think General Cass' construction of the Constitution," the *Plain Dealer* continued, is an ample proviso against the further extension of slavery."[81] A vote for Cass would therefore be the most effective means of achieving freedom in the territories, while a vote for Van Buren would help to defeat that object by making the election of Taylor more likely. "Shall we have a slavemonger for President?" asked the Augusta *Age* rhetorically in reference to Taylor.[82]

In spite of their concern about the territorial issue, however, the Democratic leaders remained hopeful of winning the election. They felt that the union of antislavery forces at Buffalo would make the free-soil movement more attractive than ever to northern Whig voters, who generally felt more strongly about the slavery question than Democrats did. This strengthened their conviction that the movement would injure the Whigs more than it would their own party.[83] They were particularly sanguine about Whig defections in the Northwest which promised to help them in the entire area and deliver to them the traditional Whig stronghold, Ohio.[84] By early September, Senator Allen was writing Cass that Ohio was as certain for him as any state in the Union.[85]

With Ohio apparently assured, the key to northern Democratic hopes was Pennsylvania. There the free-soil issue was much less important than elsewhere in the North,[86] but the Democrats labored under the handicap of having passed the "free trade" Walker Tariff of 1846. In the immediate reaction against the tariff in Pennsylvania, every incumbent Democratic congressman except Wilmot had been defeated for re-election. In 1847, the Democrats had won the gubernatorial campaign, however, and the party leaders were hoping that the Pennsylvanians had forgotten the tariff, which had not produced the ill effects in the state that the Whigs had predicted.[87] Buchanan and other state leaders expressed their confidence that the powerful Democratic political machine could deliver the state again in November.[88] According to Buchanan's election calculations, which of course included Pennsylvania, the Democrats were certain of carrying enough states to give them 144 electoral votes, only two short of a majority. The additional votes, he concluded, must come from one of the doubtful southern states, South Carolina, Florida, Georgia, Louisiana, or Tennessee.[89] The greatest threat to accomplishing this was Yancey's effort to bring about an independent state rights nomination in the South.

Yancey left the Baltimore Convention determined that the Democratic ticket should not succeed. On his way home he stopped off in Charleston to address a meeting held to protest the actions of the convention. So strong was the local feeling against the proceedings at Baltimore that Calhoun himself was unable to have the meeting postponed until after the Whigs held their convention.[90] Calhoun wanted to see if the Whig convention would reject Taylor, in which case he was hoping that the southern Whigs would "break off from the party on extreme southern grounds."[91] He felt that otherwise Taylor would not be an acceptable nominee, and he warned the leaders of the South Carolina meeting to refrain from nominating the general.

At the meeting on June 6, the Charlestonians listened indignantly to Yancey's account of the betrayal of principles by the southern delegates at Baltimore. Yancey went on to call upon the meeting to thwart the efforts of the southern traitors by launching an independent movement built around the Alabama Platform: "With this great southern principle as a nucleus, let us call upon the South to rally as one man—to meet in their primary assemblies—to meet in Southern Convention—to consult and agree upon a ticket for President and Vice President which should be acceptable to all by reason of its talent, its purity, its devotion to the Constitution."[92] Yancey agreed, however, that no immediate move should be made with respect to the presidency. Following this line of action, the meeting tabled a resolution nominating Taylor and limited itself to denouncing the Baltimore proceedings as "unsatisfactory and objectionable."[93]

After the meeting Yancey went on to Alabama to try to persuade the electors to follow the Charlestonians' lead. He was disappointed to find Democratic sentiment overwhelmingly opposed to "any action against the nomination," and more than nine-tenths of the voters "determined to vote the regular ticket."[94] "I find nearly all ready to award praise to me for my course," he wrote to Calhoun, "but not bold enough to face the storm."[95] He himself was determined to persist in his efforts to launch an independent movement nonetheless, in order to try to prevent the South from acquiescing in Cass's dangerous opinions on the territorial issue.

On June 19, Yancey addressed a Democratic meeting in Montgomery assembled to hear the report of the local delegates to the national convention. Although he roundly denounced the entire Baltimore proceedings, Yancey reserved his strongest criticisms for his fellow delegates from Alabama and the convention's presidential nominee. He insisted that the delegates had violated their commitment to the Alabama Platform and betrayed the interests of the South in pledging their support to Cass. According to Yancey, Cass was still committed to the nonextension of slavery notwithstanding his attempt to buy southern votes for the presidency by abandoning the Wilmot Proviso; his popular sovereignty platform, in fact, represented a more objectionable form of the free-soil doctrine than the Proviso itself, since it gave the "Mexican negroes" presently living in the territories the right to decide the slavery question, with the result that southern emigrants would be required "to take passes, instead of to give them, from these degraded beings."[96]

His own course Yancey described as the only one consistent with the commitment to southern rights laid down in the Alabama Platform:

I was instructed by the organized Democracy of Alabama to proceed to Baltimore and be guided by the specific injunction, unanimously imposed, to vote for no men for President and Vice-President who would not unequivocally avow themselves to be opposed to either of the forms of restricting slavery described in the instructions. I rendered faithful obedience to these instructions, and the Democratic Party of Alabama pledged itself to the country and the members of the Convention pledged themselves to each other under no circumstance whatever to support for the offices of President and Vice-President of the United States any person who shall not be opposed openly and avowedly to either of these forms of restricting slavery. I shall stand immovably by the Alabama Platform. I cannot support General Cass for the Presidency.[97]

Yancey ended by calling upon the meeting to repudiate the Baltimore Convention and recommended a state convention to nominate a separate ticket.[98]

As Yancey had predicted, the meeting was ready and anxious to praise his actions. A resolution was passed thanking him and the Montgomery delegate who had acted with him "for their bold manly course in the late Baltimore Convention."[99] But the meeting had no intention of endorsing an independent movement. It had, in fact, already ratified the nominations and pledged support for the nominees in the coming election.[100] The following evening the meeting reassembled and clarified its motion praising the actions of Yancey and his cohort, in order to remove any trace of ambiguity from its position. The resolution, it stated, "applied only to services in the Convention and not to any other act done or position taken by them after their legitimate duties ceased as such delegates."[101] The meeting went on to depreciate efforts "being made to disorganize and dissolve the Democratic party of Alabama and to misrepresent Cass's opinions"; the members pledged themselves to oppose such efforts and to work for the election of the Democratic ticket.[102]

Yancey had suffered a similar rebuff at the hands of his fellow townsmen in Wetumpka. The meeting there, after hearing him speak, had expressed confidence in his integrity but challenged his judgment; Cass was not only approved as a candidate but his Nicholson letter singled out for special approbation.[103] Undaunted, Yancey continued to work for an independent nomination. He began to collect funds to establish a newspaper, since none of the state journals was willing to break with the party, and made plans to issue a call for a mass convention at Montgomery to nominate an independent southern candidate.[104]

Only in South Carolina, however, did the Democratic organization repudiate the Baltimore Convention. Elsewhere in the South, Democrats turned their backs on an independent movement and rallied instead to the regular party nominees. Democrats in the southwestern states had been friendly to Cass even before his nomination, and they welcomed him as a candidate.[105] The organizations in the southeastern states also remained completely loyal, in spite of the approval of the Alabama Platform in the area. The Chivalry in Virginia joined party regulars in pledging support for the nominees and began actively canvassing the state on their behalf.[106] This union was facilitated by the official party line that neither the Baltimore Platform nor Cass's Nicholson letter gave the territorial legislatures the right to prohibit slavery.[107] The Democratic politicians in neighboring North Carolina, less infected by the spirit of the Alabama Platform, simply rejected Yancey's objections to the Baltimore Convention as "hairsplitting," and the party had no difficulty uniting behind the ticket.[108]

In Georgia, the party was divided by the territorial question posed by the Alabama Platform. Two Democratic journals, the Macon *Telegraph* and the Augusta *Constitutionalist,* were firmly committed to the Platform, and as it was commonly recognized in Georgia that Cass's popular sovereignty doctrine was actually designed to permit territorial prohibition, this seemed to preclude their supporting him for the presidency.[109] But the two editors were ultimately persuaded to acquiesce in Bayly's solution, leaving the entire question to the judiciary.[110] As a result, harmony was achieved at the state convention held on June 21. A unanimous platform commended Cass and the Nicholson letter to the Georgia voters. One resolution directly repudiated an independent movement in either section of the country: "Resolved That the advocacy of the claims of any candidate for the Presidency upon grounds other than broad and national—grounds based solely on sectional and local considerations is, in its very nature, fraught with evil and with danger, undemocratic, and contrary to the design and spirit of our institutions."[111]

Notwithstanding a stronger Calhoun influence in the party in Florida and Alabama, there the nominations were also ratified. On June 16, the Florida state central committee unanimously endorsed Cass and the Baltimore Platform.[112] The state press fell into line, contending that Cass's popular sovereignty doctrine was perfectly compatible with the earlier commitment to the Alabama Platform.[113] The Democratic journals in Alabama took a similar position.[114] When it became clear that the state party would unite behind the nominees, Dixon H. Lewis, who was being pressed by the party regulars for a public statement,[115] wrote to Yancey advising him to discard his plans for an independent nomination. Arguing that lack of support outside of South Carolina rendered the effort hopeless, Lewis suggested that Yancey simply remain neutral during the campaign and await the reformation of the state party. For his own part, said Lewis, he felt that his obligation to the party required him to support its nominees.[116] He announced his support a few days later in a letter printed in the Alabama newspapers.[117] Yancey, bowing to the inevitable, gave up his efforts to launch an independent movement.

He was still determined to vindicate his own position and bring about the defeat of Cass, however. After his assaults on the actions of the Alabama delegates at Charleston and Montgomery, several of them had published letters defending their position and attacking Yancey for his inconsistency in supporting Woodbury in violation of his own Alabama Platform; they also undertook to defend Cass's position on the question of slavery in the territories and to justify their support of him in the election campaign.[118] The Democratic newspapers in Alabama, most of which were inimical to Yancey and all of which ultimately supported Cass, used these arguments against Yancey and in favor of the Democratic ticket.[119] Early in August, Yancey answered his critics in a seventy-nine page pamphlet giving the history of the inception of the Alabama Platform and his unsuccessful attempt to implement it in the national convention.[120] The pamphlet indicated all Cass's weaknesses as a candidate from the southern point of view and concluded by urging southern Democratic voters not to cast their ballots for the party nominee.[121] The election of Taylor would be a lesser evil by far for the South, according to Yancey.[122] To the delight of the southern Whigs who had heartily applauded all his actions, Yancey distributed his pamphlet throughout the South.[123]

Although Yancey's attack on the Democratic nominee gave aid and comfort to the Whigs, the Democratic organization had at least neutralized his effort for an independent nomination. But the failure of Yancey's project did not completely kill the idea for a southern convention. When it appeared infeasible to run a separate southern candidate, Calhoun turned his attention to diverting the southern people from the election campaign which was tending to divide them. In order to unify the South irrespective of party, Calhoun wanted a southern convention to demand from the North a recognition of southern rights.[124] He offered to co-operate with the southern Whigs in Congress against an administration measure for settling the territorial question if they would join him in issuing an address to the people of the South calling for such a convention.[125] But the southern

Whig congressmen were themselves too deeply engrossed in the campaign to bring about the election of their favorite, Taylor, to co-operate with Calhoun. Congress adjourned without any action being taken, and Calhoun was forced to postpone his plans until after the election. In South Carolina, where his supporters were dividing over the candidacies of Cass and Taylor, Calhoun urged them "to conduct the canvass with moderation" in order that they might be "reconciled immediately after its termination" for a united nonpartisan effort on behalf of southern rights.[126] With his eye on his ultimate goal of southern unity, Calhoun refused to take any part whatever in the election campaign.[127] For the Democrats the specter of a southern convention was removed and the party organization seemed unimpaired.[128]

In the meantime, Congress had been wrestling with the problem of a territorial government for Oregon, an issue which could not fail to have an impact on the election campaign. The House had passed a territorial bill for Oregon as early as August of 1846, a few days before the Wilmot Proviso was first introduced. This measure, which included a clause prohibiting slavery, had been allowed to die in the Senate for that session, and the subsequent agitation over the Wilmot Proviso had prevented congressional action thereafter. The northern advocates of free soil in Oregon had retained a clear majority in the House of Representatives, and the agitation over the Proviso made them more determined than ever to prohibit slavery there. On the other hand, the southerners' commitment against congressional prohibition anywhere in the territories, as a result of the Proviso agitation, made them equally determined to prevent prohibition in Oregon, unless they could wring some concession from the North regarding the territories in the Southwest. The southerners and northern friends of the South who controlled the Senate refused to accept a measure incorporating naked prohibition but were unable to induce the House to recede from its demand. The result was an impasse between the two houses which prevented the passage of a territorial bill for Oregon.

The independent free-soil movement during the election campaign gave the Polk administration a strong incentive to try to break the impasse and give Oregon its long overdue territorial government. Administration leaders thought that if they could settle the Oregon question they could allay much of the excitement which was dividing the party in New York and elsewhere.[129] Polk finally decided to try to get Congress to extend the Missouri Compromise line to the new territories. Late in June, he had Senator Bright of Indiana propose an amendment to the Oregon bill prohibiting slavery in all territories north of the 36° 30' line; the amendment implied, just as the original Missouri Compromise had, that slavery would be permitted south of the line where it was not prohibited.[130] The amended bill was opposed by many southerners, however, who were committed to the position that congressional prohibition anywhere in the territories was unconstitutional. This, combined with the opposition of the free-soilers, prevented the bill from making any progress.[131]

On July 12, as a result of an agreement among southern senators of both parties, John M. Clayton of Delaware proposed that the territorial issue be referred to a special committee consisting of eight senators, two northern Democrats, two southern Democrats, two northern Whigs, and two southern Whigs.[132] The committee was established and finally agreed to a complicated scheme proposed by Senator Dickinson which ultimately came to be known as the Clayton Compromise. The measure provided a territorial government for Oregon and validated the existing laws in the territory, including one prohibiting slavery, unless the territorial legislature chose to alter them. In California and New Mexico, the legislative power was to reside with a governor, secretary, and three judges, all of whom were to be appointed by the President. They were expressly forbidden, however, to pass a law respecting slavery, which was to be treated, as Bayly had suggested in May, as a judicial question. Finally, provision was made for appeal of the slavery question from the territorial courts to the Supreme Court.[133]

Calhoun, who was serving on the committee, tried to elicit a pledge from Polk that he would appoint southern men as officials in California and New Mexico "who would maintain the southern views on the subject of slavery," but the President was noncommittal.[134] Calhoun decided to support the measure nonetheless when he failed to get southern Whig support for calling a convention.[135] His influence proved decisive in the Senate. In spite of strong opposition from free-soilers, the compromise was passed by a combination of northern Democratic and southern votes.[136]

The Whigs had already prepared the way for the defeat of the compromise settlement in the House, however. At a conference on July 22, the northern Whig congressmen, who feared passage of the compromise would enable Van Buren to sweep most of the northern states, persuaded a handful of their southern colleagues, under the leadership of Alexander Stephens of Georgia, to join them in opposing the measure. These southern Whigs were convinced that the defeat of the measure would strengthen Taylor's prospects in their own section, as well as in the North.[137] When the Senate bill came up in the House on the 27th, Stephens immediately moved to table the motion on the grounds that it merely postponed, rather than settled, the territorial issue; he added that "he had no belief that the question could be settled during the present session."[138] Stephens and seven other southern Whigs combined with the northern Whigs and Democratic free-soilers to carry the motion by a vote of 112 to 97.[139]

Having rejected the Clayton Compromise, the House finally passed its own measure extending the provisions of the Northwest Ordinance and recognizing the existing Oregon law prohibiting slavery.[140] The Senate now amended the House bill to extend the Missouri Compromise line to the Pacific Ocean, Calhoun voting for the amendment though not the final bill.[141] The House refused to accept the amendment, however, and the Senate finally yielded when two Democratic Senators from slaveholding states, Benton and Sam Houston of Texas, voted with the free-soil men to accept the House bill.[142] With the unanimous approval of his cabinet, Polk decided that since the Oregon territory was situated north of the Missouri Compromise line, he ought to sign the bill.[143] He and his advisors recognized that a veto would strengthen the hands of the free-soilers in the North.[144] But the President insisted, over Buchanan's strong protest, upon accompanying his signature with a message explaining his reasons for signing, so that he would not be misunderstood to approve a bill prohibiting slavery in the territories south of the 36° 30' line.[145] With the Oregon question settled, Congress at last adjourned.

One result of the defeat of the Clayton Compromise was to convince the South Carolina delegation in the House of Representatives of the perfidy of the southern Whigs and the impossibility of co-operating with them politically.[146] The most important member of the delegation was Robert Barnwell Rhett, erstwhile editor of the Charleston *Mercury*. Both Rhett and the *Mercury* had been hostile to Cass and neutral in the presidential campaign until the defeat of the compromise, but then the journal, under the influence of Rhett, began denouncing the southern Whigs and drifting toward the Democratic nominee.[147]

By the time Rhett arrived in Charleston after the adjournment of Congress, he had decided that he must prevent the Whigs from electing Taylor, the worse of two evils. On August 20, Rhett managed to get the Democratic executive committee to propose resolutions endorsing Cass and Butler to the district meeting in Charleston to be held the following day.[148] The meeting, under Rhett's control, rejected a motion to support a mixed ticket of Taylor and Butler, and endorsed the committee resolutions.[149] The same day the *Mercury* pronounced for Cass.[150] The impact of these developments was such that the *Mercury* could announce that South Carolina's vote was "morally certain for Cass," and Taylor's supporters gave up all hope of carrying the state.[151]

The commitment of the South Carolina Democrats brought the last of the state party organizations in the South into line.

Since the Democratic party was the majority party in most of the southern states, the effect of the support for Cass in South Carolina, combined with the collapse of the movement for a southern convention, was to send Democratic hopes soaring. Late in August, Polk wrote to Cass congratulating him upon almost certain victory. "The present prospect is," said the President, "that you may receive the support of every southern state except Kentucky."[152] Even Calhoun reluctantly admitted that the election indications favored Cass.[153]

But the Democratic leaders had failed to reckon with Taylor's popularity in areas in the North like Pennsylvania, where the slavery question was of secondary importance.[154] As the Whig leaders came to recognize that they could not save Ohio, they began to concentrate their efforts on taking Pennsylvania away from the Democrats.[155] The tariff issue was effectively revived and local Democrats realized that they were in for a real contest.[156] In spite of the need for a maximum effort, however, difficulties developed in the party organization. These were underlined when Governor Shunk resigned because of ill health, requiring a gubernatorial election in October. The Democrats were divided on a candidate to succeed Shunk and many of the party leaders in the state called upon Buchanan to run. "I have come to the conclusion after much reflection," wrote Senator Simon Cameron, "that you should be the candidate. It can be presented in such a shape as to make your acceptance the result of a wish to save the party—as Wright did in 1844."[157] Buchanan, perhaps remembering Wright's fate, chose to remain Secretary of State.[158] The nominee chosen did not succeed either in unifying the disparate party elements or in revitalizing the party organization. The result was a narrow victory for the united Whigs in the October election.[159]

The setback in Pennsylvania struck consternation in the hearts of the Democratic leaders. "Last night I gave up Pennsylvania," wrote Secretary of War Marcy, "and with it many of my high hopes for Cass's election."[160] President Polk made a desperate effort to get Wilmot to transfer his support from Van

Buren to Cass, but it proved a failure.[161] The continued profes-
sions of the Democratic leaders of their belief that the state
would be redeemed in November did not belie the fact that their
confidence had been visibly shaken.[162]

With Pennsylvania in doubt, southern Democratic politicians
who had been claiming that Cass would receive a strong vote in
their section began to calculate precisely how many electoral
votes in the South would be required to make up the deficit from
the loss of Pennsylvania.[163] The doubtful slaveholding states, on
which the Democratic leaders had not depended but for which
they had high hopes, were Georgia, Florida, Louisiana, Tennessee, and Maryland.[164] These states had a total of forty electors,
of which Cass would have to win nineteen along with his other
expected votes in order to win without Pennsylvania. The Wilmot Proviso question was the major issue in these states, and
Democrats were relying upon Cass's explicit commitment to veto
the Proviso as well as the fidelity of the party organization to
produce the necessary votes.[165] The southern Democratic journals contrasted the position of acquiescence in the Wilmot Proviso, which they claimed Taylor had taken in the Signal letter,
unfavorably with that of Cass in his Nicholson letter.[166] In the
Southeast, where the Alabama Platform's denial of the power
of a territorial legislature to prohibit slavery was a vital issue,
Democrats either argued that the Nicholson letter was compatible with the Alabama Platform or else took the position of Congressman Bayly that this, unlike the Proviso question, was a
matter for the judiciary to decide.[167] Southern Democrats also
launched strong attacks on the Whig vice-presidential nominee,
Millard Fillmore, as an antislavery man, particularly after the
publication in the Washington *Union* of a letter written by Fillmore in 1838, expressing his approval of the aims of an abolition society in Buffalo.[168]

As the campaign went on, however, it gradually became evident that the Whigs were having the better of the slavery argument. One of the turning points of the campaign in the South
seems to have been Polk's decision not to veto the bill providing

a territorial government for Oregon. This created a deep resentment among many southerners who felt that the President had
signed the bill to propitiate northern opinion.[169] The southern
Whigs had been attacking the Democratic party as untrustworthy
on the slavery question, and Polk's action was grist for their
mill.[170] Sergeant S. Prentiss, the leading Whig campaigner in
the doubtful state of Louisiana, wrote that while he was not now
"over-sanguine as to the general result" of the election, Polk's
signing the Oregon Bill would undoubtedly prove a real boon.
"This is a heavy blow to the Southern Democracy who have
made this their leading question," said Prentiss, "and I am of
the opinion that it will result in the decided advantage to the
Whigs."[171] The Whigs pressed their advantage, claiming that
Polk had "yielded up the rights of the South."[172] Drawing the
moral of the story for southern voters, one Whig journal asked:
"If Mr. Polk has deserted the South in its utmost need, what can
we expect from Mr. Cass?"[173]

Whig efforts to undermine southern confidence in northern
Democrats were also strengthened by Van Buren's Free-Soil
candidacy. Many southern Democratic leaders expected the
Barnburners' defection to aid the party in the South, and it does
seem to have helped solidify the party organization.[174] But the
Democratic rank and file were apparently more impressed with
the fact that a man whom the organization had once recommended to them as a northern man with southern principles
was now leading a movement which seemed directed against the
South.[175] Hard as the Democratic politicians labored to prove
that Cass was completely committed to the South on the Proviso
question, the logic of their argument was no match for the emotional appeal of a southern over a northern candidate, all the
more so in the face of Van Buren's example.[176]

Moreover, the attack upon Cass's views on the question of
slavery in the territories by Whigs and Democratic mavericks
like Yancey helped to raise additional doubts about the Democratic nominee's friendliness to the South. These attacks emphasized the free-soil implications of popular sovereignty, but even

more important they revealed to southern voters Cass's initial enthusiasm for the Wilmot Proviso and the political reasons for his ultimate opposition to it.[177] Given Cass's evident propensity to yield to public opinion, could he be trusted to remain faithful to the South on the Proviso question? A state rights Democrat from Alabama articulated the feelings of many southern voters when he said of Cass: "What confidence can we have in him that even under the most positive pledges he may not change his position on the Wilmot Proviso within the next year and go back to his old original position?"[178] This danger seemed all the greater to the many southerners who believed that Cass's real views on the slavery question were represented by a quotation from his protest against the Quintuple Treaty in 1842, widely circulated in the southern Whig press during the campaign: "We are not slaveholders. We never have been. We never shall be. We deprecate its existence and pray for its obliteration everywhere."[179] Under the circumstances, the effectiveness of the Whig argument that since General Taylor was a southern slaveholder the South did not require pledges on the slavery question to vote for him is not surprising.[180] Cass's opposition to the Wilmot Proviso and his popular sovereignty doctrine were logically satisfactory to most southern Democratic politicians,[181] but for the southern voters it lacked the emotional appeal of the simple, indisputable fact that Zachary Taylor lived in the South and owned slaves.

This became clear on election day when the southern Democratic voters deserted the party en masse to vote for Taylor. One Democratic leader in Georgia commented on the election in his state: "As to the turnout our expectations were realized, but hundreds of democrats have come to the polls only to vote against us. . . . Is it not extraordinary that so large a wing of the democratic party has deserted without a solitary leader at their head? The rank and file have rebelled by regiments, and yet we do not know and never shall know the individual traitors. . . . This wholesale defection is entirely unexplained and unexplainable."[182]

Considering the strength of the Democratic organizations in the South, Taylor polled a tremendous southern vote.[183] He won eight of the fifteen slaveholding states, including all those considered doubtful, and came very close to carrying the traditional southern Democratic strongholds, Virginia, Alabama, and Mississippi.[184] The failure to make up in the South the loss of Pennsylvania, which Taylor swept by a large majority, cost the Democrats the election. They did manage to win two New England states as well as the entire Northwest, but without Pennsylvania or the doubtful southern states, it was not enough. The articulated ambiguities of the Democrats were no match for Taylor's eloquent silence on the territorial issue.

The Democratic defeat in the election of 1848 shattered the tenuous bonds which had been forged at the Baltimore Convention, releasing a new impulse toward sectional antagonism in both branches of the party. Freed by the party failure from the restraints imposed by their candidate's Nicholson letter, Democrats in both sections began to gravitate to more extreme positions on the question of slavery in the territories.[185] Northern Democratic politicians, who during the campaign had been forced by the independent movement to advocate free soil at the same time that they preached popular sovereignty, were now able to opt directly for the Wilmot Proviso. Even such state organizations as the Indiana Democracy, which had previously taken a strong pro-southern position on the territorial issue, now declared for congressional prohibition of slavery in the territories.[186]

This development was nourished by the resentment of Cass's northern supporters, particularly those in the Northwest, against southern Democratic defections to Taylor on election day, to which they attributed the defeat of the party. They felt that they had been betrayed by the southern rejection of the author of the Nicholson letter for an unpledged southern slaveholder, and they were no longer willing to make concessions to their southern colleagues for the sake of party harmony. On December 15, the correspondent of the Charleston *Mercury* com-

mented sadly on the Indiana legislature's replacement of Senator
Hannegan with a free-soil Democrat: "Thus one by one the
supporters of the South and the Constitution fall before the antislavery spirit of the North. To stand by us is now political death
to any statesman at the North. By our imbecility we have earned
a most glorious isolation and united the whole North and Northwest against us on the slavery question."[187]

The new impulse of antislavery feeling in the North, accompanied as it was by an equal and opposite reaction in the
South,[188] shook the foundations of the Union before it finally
subsided. It required the immediate threat of disunion, in the
crisis of 1849-50, to force the Democratic politicians to fall back
once again on the popular sovereignty solution to the territorial
issue. Democrats in the first session of the Thirty-first Congress
embodied the doctrine as well as other mutual concessions in
the Compromise of 1850.[189] But while the compromise temporarily preserved the Union, it failed to resolve the sectional conflict over the territorial issue. It represented rather an evasion
of that issue, an impossible promise to both sections that the
attitude of each toward slavery in the territories would be upheld. This became clear when the Kansas-Nebraska Act applied
the principle to an area which would soon enter the Union and
therefore directly affected the sectional balance of power. The
struggle for control of the territories was renewed and was characterized by a new intensity as the entire society became caught
up in it. This time the culmination of the struggle was not an
evasive compromise but a confrontation of the issue which led
to disunion and civil war.

The election of 1848 presaged the ultimate failure of the
Democratic popular sovereignty solution of the territorial dispute. It was clear in 1848 that what the southern voters demanded was a repudiation not of the letter but of the spirit of
the Wilmot Proviso, and this neither Cass nor Douglas nor any
other northern advocate of popular sovereignty could give them.
Within the next twelve years this feeling had so intensified that
the South was prepared to make it not only the paramount con-

sideration in its voting but the requirement for continued union with the North as well. In 1860, the southern Democratic politicians were sufficiently attuned to the temper of their section to recognize the inadequacy of a mere technical concession on the question of slavery in the territories, such as Douglas and his supporters were willing to make, and they themselves took the first step toward disunion by disrupting the Democratic party.[190]

But even southern repudiation of popular sovereignty could not revitalize it as a platform in the North. By 1860, northern voters everywhere were sufficiently aroused to reject even the most palatable popular sovereignty alternative to the Republican commitment to the Wilmot Proviso principle. Lincoln had already demonstrated, in the Illinois senatorial election in 1858, that he could poll more votes than the most prestigious northern champion of popular sovereignty.[191] In spite of the threat of disunion, virtually every northern state made the same choice in 1860. The northern people announced clearly and unmistakably that the northern social system was going to prevail in the territories and in the nation at large. Unwilling to accept this, the South tried to isolate itself from the threat to its own social system by creating a separate nation. The consequence was the tragedy of the Civil War.

Notes

CHAPTER I

1. Eugene Irving McCormac, *James K. Polk, A Political Biography* (Berkeley: University of California Press, 1922), p. 351.

2. Milo Milton Quaife (ed.), *The Diary of James K. Polk, 1845-1849* (4 vols.; Chicago: A. C. McClurg and Company, 1910), I, 303, 305-8; II, 50, 56-57, 59-60.

3. *Ibid.*, II, 70, 72-73.

4. As early as 1842 Van Buren had written: "The truth is, that the Democrats of this State [New York] have suffered so often and so severely in their advocacy of Southern men, and Southern measures, as to make them more sensitive in respect to complaints of their conduct from that quarter than I could wish. They say that . . . their party has suffered in every limb by the abolition question, and all this is undoubtedly true." Quoted in William Ernest Smith, *The Francis Preston Blair Family in Politics* (2 vols.; New York: The Macmillan Company, 1933), I, 157. Cf. Gideon Welles to Martin Van Buren, July 28, 1846, in Martin Van Buren Papers, Library of Congress.

5. See excerpts from various northern Democratic newspapers in 1843 and early 1844 opposing the immediate annexation of Texas reprinted in the *New York Weekly Tribune,* December 14, 1846. See also the confidential letter circulated among important New York Democrats during the election of 1844, and their Joint Letter "to the Democratic-Republican Electors of the State of New York," reprinted with the circumstances of their genesis in Parke Godwin, *A Biography of William Cullen Bryant* (2 vols.; New York: D. Appleton and Company, 1883), I, 411-23. A New York Democratic congressman opposed to the Van Burenites later cited the confidential letter as evidence that the Wilmot Proviso was generated out of their pique over the annexation question. See the *Congressional Globe,* 29 Cong., 2 Sess., Appendix (Washington: Government Printing Office, 1847), pp. 320-21; "Stephen Strong and the Secret Circular," in the *New York Weekly Evening Post,* March 27, 1847.

6. The account of the annexation struggle presented here generally follows that in Justin H. Smith, *The Annexation of Texas* (New York: The Macmillan Company, 1919), pp. 322-55, though Smith does not emphasize the slavery question.

7. Preston King to Azariah C. Flagg, December 21, 1844, and G. Stetson to Azariah C. Flagg, December 31, 1844, in Azariah C. Flagg Papers, New York Public Library; John N. Niles to Gideon Welles, January 24, 1845, in Gideon Welles Papers, Library of Congress.

8. *Congressional Globe,* 28 Cong., 2 Sess., p. 19.

9. John C. Calhoun to R. M. T. Hunter, December 29, 1844, in J. Franklin Jameson (ed.), "Correspondence of John C. Calhoun," Volume II of the *Annual Report of the American Historical Association* (Washington: Government Printing Office, 1900), p. 636; Preston King to Azariah C. Flagg, December 21, 1844, Lemuel G. Stetson to Azariah C. Flagg, December 31, 1844, in Azariah C. Flagg Papers, New York Public Library.

10. Preston King to Azariah C. Flagg, January 11, 1845, in Azariah C. Flagg Papers, New York Public Library. Lemuel Stetson, who spoke for the Van Burenites in opposition to annexation early in January, did not mention the slavery question, concentrating his attention instead upon constitutional objections. See the *Congressional Globe,* 28 Cong., 2 Sess., Appendix, pp. 58-61. For Stetson's real objections, see Lemuel Stetson to Azariah C. Flagg, December 31, 1844, in Azariah C. Flagg Papers, New York Public Library.

11. Preston King to Azariah C. Flagg, January 8, 1845, in Azariah C. Flagg Papers, New York Public Library.

12. *Congressional Globe,* 28 Cong., 2 Sess., p. 121.

13. *Ibid.,* p. 173.

14. Preston King to Azariah C. Flagg, January 11, 1845, in Azariah C. Flagg Papers, New York Public Library.

15. *Congressional Globe,* 28 Cong., 2 Sess., p. 193.

16. *Ibid.,* p. 194; Smith, *Annexation of Texas,* p. 333.

17. Preston King to Martin Van Buren, February 14, 1845, in Martin Van Buren Papers.

18. Silas Wright to John A. Dix, February 17, 1845, in John A. Dix Papers, Columbia University.

19. John A. Dix to Silas Wright, February 27, 1845, in *ibid.*

20. *Congressional Globe,* 28 Cong., 2 Sess., p. 244; Smith, *Annexation of Texas,* pp. 336-37.

21. Preston King to Azariah C. Flagg, February 8, 1845, Lemuel G. Stetson to Azariah C. Flagg, December 31, 1844, in Azariah C. Flagg Papers, New York Public Library; John A. Dix to Silas Wright, February 27, 1845, in John A. Dix Papers.

22. John C. Calhoun to Andrew V. Donelson, May 23, 1845, in Jameson (ed.), "Calhoun Correspondence," pp. 658-59; Smith, *Annexation of Texas,* pp. 337-38.

23. *Congressional Globe,* 28 Cong., 2 Sess., p. 359.

24. The dispute over whether Polk actually gave such assurances, which arose later in the Polk administration and has been continued by historians, appears to be finally settled by the statement by Dix in a letter to Wright the very day the bill combining the House resolution and Benton's proposal was introduced in and passed by the Senate: "I had a conversation with the President-elect whose solicitude on the subject [annexation] is very great, and he assured me if he had any discretion placed in his hands, he would exercise

it in such a manner as to satisfy us." John A. Dix to Silas Wright, February 27, 1845, in John A. Dix Papers. Dix makes clear elsewhere in the letter that he means Polk will implement Benton's proposal. The strongest case against Polk's having given positive assurances, presented in Smith, *Annexation of Texas,* pp. 348-50, n. 34, is based entirely on inference and circumstantial evidence. And even without having seen the Dix letter, Smith concludes from Polk's subsequent course of action that "even if he had not given the pledge . . . he had perhaps used language implying something of the sort." *Ibid.,* p. 354, n. 40.

25. *Congressional Globe,* 28 Cong., 2 Sess., p. 362.

26. *Ibid.,* p. 372.

27. Benjamin Tappan to the New York *Evening Post,* July 21, 1848, in the *New York Weekly Evening Post,* August 11, 1848.

28. John C. Calhoun to Andrew J. Donelson, May 23, 1845, in "Calhoun Correspondence," pp. 658-59.

29. See John Tyler's statement in Lyon G. Tyler, *The Letters and Times of the Tylers* (2 vols.; Richmond: Whittet and Shepperson, 1885), II, 365. Calhoun's version of the events is given in the *Congressional Globe,* 29 Cong., 2 Sess., p. 498.

30. James K. Polk to A. J. Donelson, March 7, 1845, in "Documents: Letters of James K. Polk to Andrew J. Donelson, 1845-1848," *Tennessee Historical Magazine,* III (March, 1917), 62.

31. George Bancroft to James K. Polk, October 13, 1848, in James K. Polk Papers, Library of Congress; James Buchanan to Andrew J. Donelson, March 10, 1845, in John Bassett Moore (ed.), *The Works of James Buchanan* (12 vols.; Philadelphia and London: J. B. Lippincott Company, 1908-11), VI, 120; Smith, *Annexation of Texas,* pp. 353-55.

32. Martin Van Buren to John D. Kellogg, September 2, 1845, in Martin Van Buren Papers. In spite of his objections to the means of accomplishing annexation, Dix commended Van Buren's statement. See John A. Dix to Martin Van Buren, September 13, 1845, in *ibid.*

33. *Congressional Globe,* 29 Cong., 1 Sess., p. 65. Before approving annexation, however, the New York delegation had given almost a unanimous vote for an unsuccessful amendment prohibiting slavery in part of Texas. See *ibid.,* p. 64.

34. Preston King to Azariah C. Flagg, February 8, 1845, in Azariah C. Flagg Papers, New York Public Library; Preston King to Martin Van Buren, February 15, 1845, John A. Dix to Martin Van Buren, September 13, 1845, and March 27, 1846, in Martin Van Buren Papers; Alex Wells to John C. Calhoun, April 7, 1846, in Chauncey S. Boucher and Robert P. Brooks (eds.), "Correspondence Addressed to John C. Calhoun, 1837-1849," *Annual Report of the American Historical Association for the Year 1929* (Washington: Government Printing Office, 1931), p. 341.

35. The account of Polk's cabinet selection, except where noted, is taken from Joseph G. Rayback, "Martin Van Buren's Break with James K. Polk: The Record," *New York History,* XXXVI (January, 1955), 51-62.

36. Van Buren's letter was written February 27, 1845, evidently several days after Van Buren had received Polk's letter of February 22. Moreover, it was not until March 2 that the letter was delivered to Polk by Van Buren's son. See Elizabeth Howard West (ed.), *Calendar of the Papers of Martin Van Buren* (Washington: Government Printing Office, 1910), pp. 550-51.

37. Ivor Debenhorn Spencer, *The Victor and the Spoils, A Life of William*

L. Marcy (Providence, Rhode Island: Brown University Press, 1959), pp. 133-34. Enemies of Van Buren and Wright, both in and out of the state of New York, tried to use the Texas issue to gain political influence with the administration at the expense of the Van Burenites. See John Arthur Garraty, *Silas Wright* (New York: Columbia University Press, 1949), pp. 342-45.

38. Spencer, *Life of Marcy*, p. 134.

39. John A Dix to Azariah C. Flagg, March 3, 1845, in Azariah C. Flagg Papers, New York Public Library; Martin Van Buren to George Bancroft, March 7, 1845, in "Van Buren-Bancroft Correspondence, 1830-1845," *Proceedings of the Massachusetts Historical Society,* XLII (June, 1909), 439-40.

40. Polk had advanced the claim to all Oregon in his inaugural message in March of 1845.

41. Sentiment for 54° 40′ was extremely strong among northwestern Democrats. The state convention in Ohio adopted resolutions that the United States government had no power to modify the claim to the entire Oregon territory. See Elwood Fisher to John C. Calhoun, January 10, 1846, in Boucher and Brooks, "Correspondence Addressed to Calhoun," pp. 316-18.

42. John C. Calhoun to Thomas G. Clemson [Postscript], December 22, 1845, in Jameson, "Calhoun Correspondence," p. 674.

43. *Congressional Globe,* 29 Cong., 1 Sess., p. 109.

44. *Ibid.,* p. 110.

45. *Ibid.,* p. 125.

46. *Ibid.,* p. 131. King clarified his accusation on January 6. See *ibid.,* p. 147. King's move was not an isolated incident. One assemblyman from New York reported to John C. Calhoun that "the Southern Democrats have been repeatedly assaulted during the present sitting of our Legislature, by the Anti-annexationists and the friends of Mr. Van Buren, who have neglected no opportunity to give vent [to] the bitterness of their disappointed hopes"; he went on to ask for a copy of Calhoun's Oregon speech "to reply to the charge that the South, having secured Texas, is now willing to forsake our claim to the Oregon." Alex Wells to John C. Calhoun, April 7, 1846, in Boucher and Brooks, "Correspondence Addressed to Calhoun," p. 341. Cf. "The Administration Reviewed," in the New York *Herald,* September 2, 1846.

47. John C. Calhoun to Henry W. Conner, January 16, 1846, in Henry W. Conner Papers, Manuscript Division, Library of Congress. In his speech on Oregon Giddings predicted that Polk, having extended slavery by acquiring Texas, would compromise on Oregon in order to "save the institutions of the South from the apprehended danger of a war with England." *Congressional Globe,* 29 Cong., 1 Sess., p. 140.

48. *Congressional Globe,* 29 Cong., 1 Sess., Appendix, p. 87. Martin Grover, a Van Buren Democrat from New York, assured the westerners that Yancey's warning was false. See *ibid.,* Appendix, p. 125.

49. One observer in Washington wrote that "there was undoubtedly among the Democratic politicians much disgust over Polk's duplicity on Oregon." Elwood Fisher to John C. Calhoun, October 19, 1846, in John C. Calhoun Papers, South Caroliniana Library. Cf. Gideon Welles to Martin Van Buren, July 28, 1846, Churchill C. Cambreleng to Martin Van Buren, May 16, 1848, in Martin Van Buren Papers.

50. Gideon Welles to Martin Van Buren, July 28, 1846, in Martin Van Buren Papers; "The Mexican Negotiations on Two Millions Bill," in *Niles' Register,* LXX (August 15, 1846), 374; "A Day after the Fair," in the *New*

York Weekly Tribune, July 4, 1846, quoting the Cleveland *Plaindealer;* James Rathbun to Lewis Cass, September 30, 1846, in the Detroit *Daily Free Press,* April 13, 1846.

51. A leading Democratic newspaper in the Northwest, the Chicago *Daily Journal,* responded to Polk's successful veto of the Rivers and Harbors Bill by calling for an alliance between the North and the West against the South. See the editorial quoted in Avery O. Craven, *Edmund Ruffin, Southerner: A Study in Secession* (New York and London: D. Appleton and Company, 1932), pp. 264-65, n. 6.

52. One contemporary Pennsylvania politician thought that this move "did much to inspire David Wilmot to offer the Wilmot Proviso in 1846." Quoted in Richard Stenberg, "The Motivation of the Wilmot Proviso," *The Mississippi Valley Historical Review,* XVIII (March, 1932), 538, n. 11.

53. *New York Weekly Tribune,* June 1, 8, 1846. See also the speech of a New York Whig congressman, attacking the war and taunting the Van Burenites about their loss of influence within the Democratic party, in the *Congressional Globe,* 29 Cong., 1 Sess., p. 979.

54. Martin Van Buren to George Bancroft, February 15, 1845, in "Van Buren-Bancroft Correspondence, 1830-1845," p. 439.

55. Concord *New Hampshire Patriot and State Gazette,* June 11, 1846.

56. *Ibid.,* June 25, 1846.

57. *Ibid.,* July 9, 16, 1846.

58. *Ibid.,* July 9, 1846. The Democratic state convention had deprecated agitation of the slavery question. See *ibid.,* June 18, 1846.

59. John A. Dix to Martin Van Buren, May 16, 1846, Churchill C. Cambreleng to Martin Van Buren, May 16, 1846, in Martin Van Buren Papers; John A. Dix to Azariah C. Flagg, May 15, 1846, Azariah C. Flagg to John A. Dix, July 19, 1846, in Azariah C. Flagg Papers, New York Public Library; "The War With Mexico," "Policy and Right," and "The Prediction—The Result" in the *New York Weekly Tribune,* June 6, 1846. The leading Van Burenite journal expressed doubts about Polk's policy but these were submerged when war came. See "The Threatened War with Mexico," in the New York *Evening Post,* May 8, 1846. The dissatisfaction of northeastern Democrats with the administration was common knowledge among people at Washington. See Andrew Johnson to B. McDaniel, July 22, 1846, in Andrew Johnson Papers, Library of Congress.

60. See Martin Grover's remarks to the House of Representatives in the *Congressional Globe,* 29 Cong., 2 Sess., p. 139. For the Whig charges see *ibid.,* 29 Cong., 1 Sess., pp. 644-45, 827, 916.

61. John A. Dix to Silas Wright, July 10, 1846, in Morgan Dix (ed.), *Memoirs of John Adams Dix* (2 vols.; New York: Harper and Brothers, 1883), I, 202-3. According to Dix, Polk gave the assurances.

62. *Congressional Globe,* 29 Cong., 1 Sess., pp. 1050-51. In his speech on the substitute the introducer reminded the southern congressmen of the northern Democratic sacrifice in giving up their presidential candidate in 1844 and in supporting the annexation of Texas, and pleaded for their support in return. He went on to say that if the southern Democrats should reject his appeal, he might be forced to believe the charge that southerners were "a very selfish people, always asking, but never giving." He concluded by beseeching the southerners "to consider that the North too have rights, and that there is a limit beyond which we cannot go." *Ibid.,* Appendix, p. 1025.

63. *Ibid.,* pp. 1164-65. Most of the Van Buren dissidents can be identified

by the action which they took on the tariff and the $2,000,000 bill. Among the northern Democrats whom he thought were trying to bring about the defeat of the tariff, Polk identified five New Yorkers. See Quaife (ed.), *Polk Diary,* II, 53, 54. Four of the five, Preston King, Bradford R. Wood, George Rathbun, and Martin Grover, voted to table the $2,000,000 bill and became leaders of the Wilmot Proviso movement. The fifth, Charles Goodyear, was evidently absent the day the appropriation was proposed but later supported the Wilmot Proviso. Other northern Democrats who voted with the Whigs on the tariff (though not necessarily against final passage) and to table the appropriation included Jacob Brinkerhoff of Ohio, the self-styled author of the Wilmot Proviso, Timothy Jenkins of New York, Hannibal Hamlin of Maine, Paul Dillingham, Jr., of Vermont, James B. Hunt of Michigan and David Wilmot of Pennsylvania. With the exceptions of Wood, Goodyear, and Hunt, all of these men were mentioned in connection with the origin of the Wilmot Proviso in one or the other or both of the two most complete first-hand accounts of that event, those of David Wilmot and Jacob Brinkerhoff. Moreover, they comprise almost everyone who is mentioned in the accounts. See Charles Buxton Going, *David Wilmot, Free Soiler* (New York: D. Appleton and Company, 1924), pp. 134-35, 138.

64. One Pennsylvania Democrat remarked that he would have "voted for the bill but the South and those who acted with them had the power and they were determined to use it regardless of consequences." Jacob S. Yost to Lewis S. Coryell, November 14, 1846, in Lewis S. Coryell Papers, Historical Society of Pennsylvania. Cf. John M. Niles to Gideon Welles, October 23, 1846, in Gideon Welles Papers; Gideon Welles to Martin Van Buren, July 28, 1846, in Martin Van Buren Papers; "The Administration Reviewed," in the New York *Herald,* October 2, 1846.

65. *Congressional Globe,* 29 Cong., 1 Sess., p. 1211.

66. *Ibid.*; Quaife (ed.), *Polk Diary,* I, 396-99, 495-96, II, 15-16, 56-57, 76-77.

67. Buchanan, who helped prepare the message, was deeply concerned about the political repercussions of acquiring territory in the Southwest. See Quaife (ed.), *Polk Diary,* I, 495-96, II, 15-16, 73.

68. *Congressional Globe,* 29 Cong., 1 Sess., p. 1211; Jacob Brinkerhoff to the Mansfield *Shield and Banner,* September 16, 1846, in the Columbus *Daily Ohio Statesman,* October 2, 1846.

69. *Congressional Globe,* 29 Cong., 1 Sess., pp. 1211-12.

70. In his biography of Wilmot, Charles B. Going presents what appears to be conclusive evidence that the Proviso was Wilmot's own idea and that his account of its origin is essentially correct. This account was given in a speech which Wilmot delivered to his constituents on September 21, 1847, reprinted in the Washington *National Era,* October 21, 1847. The speech, which Wilmot later delivered virtually unchanged to the Herkimer Convention on October 26, 1847, is also reproduced in Oliver Cromwell Gardiner, *The Great Issue: Or the Three Presidential Candidates* (New York: W. C. Bryant and Company, 1848), p. 59. Going has quoted the relevant portion in *David Wilmot,* pp. 134-35. But as Richard Stenberg points out in his article, "The Motivation of the Wilmot Proviso," Going's ascription of the Proviso to Wilmot's moral opposition to slavery is an unsatisfactory explanation of the Pennsylvania congressman's motive. (Stenberg's claim that Wilmot wanted to make political capital at home in order to compensate for his vote in favor of the Walker Tariff, based as it is on weak circumstantial

evidence, is unconvincing, all the more so as it appears the Proviso was not an issue in his campaign for re-election.) Aside from his general association with the Van Buren faction, Wilmot had shown no antislavery tendencies prior to his introduction of the Proviso. On the contrary, the previous December he had voted with the South to annex Texas, and voted against an amendment prohibiting slavery in part of Texas. See the *Congressional Globe,* 29 Cong., 1 Sess., pp. 64-65. The most plausible explanation is that the events of 1846 progressively alienated Wilmot from the Polk administration, with its alleged pro-southern orientation, and that he was now prepared to join other Van Buren Democrats in an antiadministration revolt against its supposedly pro-southern policy of southwestern expansion. (Wilmot, like other Van Burenites, was complaining that the administration was withholding patronage from him and was resolved to do something about it. See David Wilmot to Victor Piollet, July 4, 1846, in Going, *David Wilmot,* pp. 145-46). Testimony that Wilmot was at this time a member of a Van Burenite clique in the House of Representatives, of which Preston King was the leader, was volunteered at the time of King's death by Gideon Welles, a friendly observer of the group. See John T. Morse, Jr. (ed.), *The Diary of Gideon Welles* (3 vols.; New York: Houghton Mifflin Company, 1909), II, 386. It is significant perhaps that Wilmot did not renew the fight for the Proviso in the first session of the thirtieth congress when King and several other of the New York Van Burenites had retired. Cf. the report of the Washington correspondent "Ion," dated January 7, in the Baltimore *Sun,* January 8, 1848.

71. "Slavery Extension Question by Robert Dale Owen, dated September 9," in the Washington *National Era,* October 21, 1847. Significantly enough, Wilmot, in his account, omitted the reasons for Owen's opposition and his statement that he would rather see the appropriation defeated than passed unamended.

72. See Wilmot's speech in the Washington *National Era,* October 21, 1847.

73. *Ibid.* Shortly after the introduction of the Proviso, Jacob Brinkerhoff claimed credit for originating the idea. See Jacob Brinkerhoff to the Mansfield *Shield and Banner,* dated September 16, 1846, in the Columbus *Daily Ohio Statesman,* October 2, 1846. In a more complete account written some two decades later, Brinkerhoff maintained that several persons had simultaneously conceived the idea independently. See Jacob Brinkerhoff to Henry Wilson, April 4, 1868, in the *New York Times,* April 23, 1868.

74. "The Administration Reviewed" in the *New York Herald,* October 2, 1846.

75. See the remarks of Martin Grover to the House of Representatives in the *Congressional Globe,* 29 Cong., 2 Sess., p. 139.

76. See Wilmot's speech in the Washington *National Era,* October 21, 1847.

77. As the leading antislavery Whig newspaper later put it: "The vote of the House has killed the war by destroying the motive for continuing it." "The Position of the North with Regard to the Extension of Slavery," in the *New York Weekly Tribune,* August 19, 1846.

78. *Congressional Globe,* 29 Cong., 1 Sess., p. 1214.

79. *Ibid.,* p. 1217.

80. At the following meeting of Congress, James Dobbin of North Carolina remarked on Wilmot's amendment: "At the last session of Congress, this warlike manifesto made its appearance, an adjournment took place and its achievements were thus far bloodless; we indulged the hope that the war was over; but it seems that this was only the ending of the first campaign."

Congressional Globe, 29 Cong., 2 Sess., p. 383. Only if the amendment was merely a political maneuver which was fraught with danger rather than an expression of a genuine antislavery movement could the South have "indulged the hope that the war was over." This would explain the silence of southern politicians both when the amendment was introduced and afterward, as well as their surprise and dismay when Preston King reintroduced it at the next session of Congress. One northern Democrat later admitted having voted for the amendment "to make the bill odious to our friends in the South and thereby to defeat it if possible." *Congressional Globe,* 29 Cong., 2 Sess., p. 180. On August 10, The Washington correspondent "Civis" of the Van Burenite New York *Evening Post,* who was probably a Democratic congressman, expressed satisfaction at the ultimate failure of the Two Million Bill. See the New York *Evening Post,* August 12, 1846.

81. "Position of the North with Regard to the Extension of Slavery," in the *New York Weekly Tribune,* August 19, 1846; Jacob Brinkerhoff to the Mansfield *Shield and Banner,* September 16, 1846, in the Columbus *Daily Ohio Statesman,* October 2, 1846; "Honorable Moses Norris and Slavery," in the Concord *New Hampshire Patriot and State Gazette,* October 22, 1846.

82. *Congressional Globe,* 29 Cong., 1 Sess., p. 1215.

83. *Ibid.,* p. 1217.

84. *Ibid.,* p. 1214.

85. *Ibid.,* pp. 1215-16.

86. Quaife (ed.), *Polk Diary,* IV, 343; "Position of the North with Regard to the Extension of Slavery," in the *New York Weekly Tribune,* August 19, 1846; Jacob Brinkerhoff to the Mansfield *Shield and Banner,* September 16, 1846, in the Columbus *Daily Ohio Statesman,* October 2, 1846. According to the *Tribune's* account, only six northerners opposed the amendment, according to Brinkerhoff only three. Only the number of votes on each side is recorded in the official records.

87. "Civis," August 9, in the New York *Evening Post,* August 10, 1846.

88. *Congressional Globe,* 29 Cong., 1 Sess., p. 1218.

89. *Niles' Register,* LXX (August 15, 1846), 373-74; *New York Weekly Tribune,* August 19, 1846; New York *Evening Post,* August 15, 1846.

90. *Congressional Globe,* 29 Cong., 1 Sess., pp. 1220-21; New York *Herald,* August 12, 1846; *New York Weekly Tribune,* August 26, 1846. See also Davis' later speech explaining his action in the *Congressional Globe,* 29 Cong., 2 Sess., p. 509.

CHAPTER II

1. "The Two Million Appropriation," in the Washington *Daily Union,* August 12, 1846. Twelve days later the *Union* cited an editorial in the New York *Courier and Journal* deprecating the Proviso as unnecessary and "calculated to increase the fanatical abolition spirit," but the paper still did not oppose it. See *ibid.,* August 24, 1846.

2. Going, *David Wilmot,* pp. 154-55.

3. "Massachusetts," in the *New York Weekly Tribune,* October 3, 1846.

4. "The Democracy in Massachusetts," in the Washington *Daily Union,* September 19, 1846.

5. "The Late Democratic Mass Convention," in the Concord *New Hampshire Patriot and State Gazette,* October 22, 1846.

6. "Democratic Mass State Convention," in *ibid.*

7. "New York Democratic State Convention," in the *Albany Evening Atlas,*

October 6, 1846. There is a set of resolutions dated October 1 in Dix's handwriting, virtually identical with those passed by the convention, in the Azariah C. Flagg Papers at the New York Public Library. Dix apparently forwarded them to Flagg for possible revision. He had earlier told Flagg he was preparing something on national affairs for the convention address which he wished Flagg and Governor Wright to revise. See John A. Dix to Azariah C. Flagg, September 27, 1846, in Azariah C. Flagg Papers, New York Public Library. Whether or not Dix actually did prepare the address as well as the resolutions is less important than the fact that both statements expressed precisely the same cautious sentiment on the Mexican question as his draft resolutions.

8. "Address to the Democratic Electors of the State of New York," in the *Albany Evening Atlas,* October 6, 1846.

9. "Whig State Convention," in the *New York Weekly Tribune,* October 3, 1846. One mass meeting of the Whigs in Buffalo did denounce the administration for waging a war of conquest to strengthen the South, but even this indirect reference to slavery was exceptional. See "Voice of Buffalo for Young," in *ibid.,* October 10, 1846. In its analysis of the Whig victory the leading antislavery Whig journal in New York made no mention of slavery. See "The Meaning of It," in *ibid.,* November 14, 1846. The Brooklyn *Eagle* claimed that its editorial of December 21 was the first mention of Wilmot's amendment by a Democratic journal in New York. See Walt Whitman, *The Gathering of the Forces,* edited by Cleveland Rogers and John Black (2 vols.; New York and London: G. P. Putnam's Sons, 1920), I, 197.

10. Columbus *Tri-Weekly Ohio Statesman,* September 11, 1846; Jacob Brinkerhoff to the Mansfield *Shield and Banner,* September 16, 1846, in *ibid.,* October 2, 1846; New York *Evening Post,* September 28, 1846.

11. Edgar Allan Holt, "Party Politics in Ohio, 1840-1850," *Ohio Archeological and Historical Quarterly,* XXXVIII (January, 1929), pp. 125-37; Edwin M. Stanton to Salmon P. Chase, November 30, 1846, in Salmon P. Chase Papers, Historical Society of Pennsylvania.

12. Phillip May Hamer, *The Secession Movement in South Carolina, 1847-1852* (Allentown, Pennsylvania: H. Ray Haas and Company, 1918), pp. 1-2; Richard Harrison Shryock, *Georgia and the Union in 1850* (Durham: Duke University Press, 1926), pp. 135-36; Joseph Carlyle Sitterson, *The Secession Movement in North Carolina* (Chapel Hill: The University of North Carolina Press, 1939), p. 38; Clarence P. Denman, *The Secession Movement in Alabama* (Montgomery: Alabama State Department of Archives and History, 1933), pp. 3-4. One isolated convention in north Alabama, however, did condemn the Proviso. See *ibid.*

13. See Chapter III, n. 8.

14. The Proviso is not even mentioned in all the surviving Calhoun correspondence, from the time of its introduction until November of 1846, and then only in relation to its possible effects on Democratic unity. See the John C. Calhoun Papers.

15. Hamer, *The Secession Movement in South Carolina,* p. 2.

16. Charleston *Mercury,* December 27, 1846; R. E. Morrill to John C. Calhoun, January 4, 1847, in John C. Calhoun Papers.

17. Garraty, *Silas Wright,* p. 363.

18. Alex. Wells to John C. Calhoun, April 7, 1846, in Boucher and Brooks (eds.), "Correspondence Addressed to Calhoun," p. 341.

19. New York *Evening Post,* September 23, 1846.

20. Silas Wright to James Buchanan, September 10, October 30, 1846, in James Buchanan Papers, Historical Society of Pennsylvania; George Bancroft to James K. Polk, October 4, 1846, in James K. Polk Papers, Library of Congress.

21. Ransom H. Gillet, *The Life and Times of Silas Wright* (2 vols.; Albany: The Argus Company, 1874), 1670-71.

22. Bradford R. Wood to James Buchanan, November 9, 1846, in James Buchanan Papers, Historical Society of Pennsylvania; "Result of the Election —Its Causes and Consequences," in the *Albany Evening Atlas,* December 4-10, 1846. Evidence of Hunker responsibility for the defeat is presented in Garraty, *Silas Wright,* pp. 382-83, and Herbert D. A. Donovan, *The Barnburners* (New York: The New York University Press, 1925), p. 80.

23. Quaife (ed.), *Polk Diary,* II, 218.

24. Bradford R. Wood to James Buchanan, November 9, 1846, in James Buchanan Papers, Historical Society of Pennsylvania; Michael Hoffman to Azariah C. Flagg, November 6, 1846, in Azariah C. Flagg Papers, New York Public Library; Martin Van Buren to Gorham A. Worth, November 6, 1846, Silas Wright to Martin Van Buren, November 10, 1846, Churchill C. Cambreleng to Martin Van Buren, November 30, 1846, in Martin Van Buren Papers. Cf. Gouvener Kemble's "note of a conversation" with Polk, dated January 9, 1847, quoted in Donovan, *Barnburners,* pp. 80-81.

25. William Seward, the most prominent antislavery Whig politician in New York at this time, attributed the Barnburners' fight for the Wilmot Proviso directly to Wright's defeat. See William Seward to Salmon P. Chase, February 2, 1847, in Salmon P. Chase Papers, Library of Congress. Cf. Seward's letter of January 14, 1847, reprinted in Frederick W. Seward (ed.), *Seward at Washington as Senator and Secretary of State* (New York: Derby and Miller, 1891), p. 34. The leading Whig journal in New York took a similar view. See "The Great Issue," in the *New York Weekly Tribune,* January 16, 1847. On the other hand, there is evidence that the radical Barnburners intended all along to make a sectional appeal against the slaveholding interest, in spite of their apparent willingness to forego the slavery question in the state campaign. See George Rathbun to Lewis Cass, September 30, 1846, in the Detroit *Daily Free Press,* April 13, 1848; Eustis Prescott to John C. Calhoun, September 23, 1846, in John C. Calhoun Papers; M. M. Noah to M. C. Mordecai, October 21, 1846, in Franklin H. Elmore Papers, Library of Congress.

26. Morris Longsreth to James Buchanan, February 21, 1847, in James Buchanan Papers, Historical Society of Pennsylvania. Political observers during the elections reported a strong hostility toward the Polk administration in the North which they linked with sectional antislavery feeling. See John Hogan to John C. Calhoun, September 21, 1846, Elwood Fisher to John C. Calhoun, October 19, 1846, in John C. Calhoun Papers.

27. *Ibid.*; Elwood Fisher to John C. Calhoun, December 2, 1846, in Jameson (ed.), "Calhoun Correspondence," pp. 1097-98. Sectional feeling had gone so far in Ohio as to encourage certain politicians to try to make an antislavery appeal which transcended traditional party lines. See Salmon P. Chase to [Adam Jewett], August 15, 1846, Salmon P. Chase to [R. Errett], September 4, 1846, Salmon P. Chase to Joshua R. Giddings, September 23, 1846, in Salmon P. Chase Papers, Library of Congress.

28. John Hogan to John C. Calhoun, December 12, 1846, in John C. Calhoun Papers.

29. More than one political observer perceived the movement in the making even during the election campaign. See M. M. Noah to M. C. Mordecai, October 21, 1846, in Franklin H. Elmore Papers; John Hogan to John C. Calhoun, September 21, 1846, in John C. Calhoun Papers. That the Barnburners did exploit the antislavery appeal of the territorial issue to strengthen Wright as a potential candidate is clear from R. H. Gillet to Azariah C. Flagg, January 15, 1847, in Azariah C. Flagg Papers, New York Public Library.

30. See King's speech in the *Congressional Globe,* 29 Cong., 2 Sess., p. 114.

31. On November 9, John A. Dix wrote to Azariah C. Flagg expressing concern about King's anti-southern feelings and asking Flagg to talk with King when the latter came through Albany on his way to Washington. See Azariah C. Flagg Papers, New York Public Library. Presumably Dix, who thought the Barnburners should remain quiet, wanted Flagg to restrain King as he had once before during the annexation crisis. See Preston King to Azariah C. Flagg, December 21, 1844, February 8, 1845, in *ibid.* Since King assumed the leadership of the movement to prohibit slavery in the territories as soon as he reached Washington, it seems reasonable, although not absolutely necessary, to assume that he was planning some such move beforehand and that the cautious Dix knew about it or at least suspected it. That it was not Wright's intention to raise the slavery question is clear from his letter to Dix of October 12, 1846, in Gillet, *Silas Wright,* II, 1724. Wright was not too happy when he learned what King had done. See *ibid.,* p. 1873. Dix may himself have had a request from Albany to try to restrain King. See John A. Dix to S. J. Tilden, January 2, 1847, in John Bigelow (ed.), *Letters and Literary Memorials of Samuel J. Tilden* (2 vols.; New York and London: Harper and Brothers, 1908), I, 49.

32. Report of the correspondent "Civis," dated December 25, in the New York *Evening Post,* December 26, 1846; report of the correspondent "Civis," January 4, 1847, in the *New York Weekly Evening Post,* January 7, 1847.

33. Preston King to Azariah C. Flagg, January 18, 1847, in the Azariah C. Flagg Papers, New York Public Library.

34. See, for example, Polk's record of his conversation with Senator William S. Archer of Virginia on September 4, in Quaife (ed.), *Polk Diary,* II, 115.

35. James K. Polk to John C. Calhoun, December 19, 1846, in John C. Calhoun Papers.

36. See Elwood Fisher to John C. Calhoun, December 2, 1846, in Jameson (ed.), "Calhoun Correspondence," pp. 1097-98.

37. Quaife (ed.), *Polk Diary,* II, 283-84.

38. *Ibid.* Calhoun was so concerned about the Proviso that he wrote: "If they [southerners] regard their safety, they must defeat it, even should the union be rent asunder." John C. Calhoun to Mrs. Thomas G. Clemson, December 27, 1846, in Jameson (ed.), "Calhoun Correspondence," p. 716.

39. Quaife (ed.), *Polk Diary,* II, 287.

40. *Ibid.,* II, 289-90. Wilmot's version of the interview is given in his speech to Congress on February 17, 1849, in the *Congressional Globe,* 30 Cong., 2 Sess., Appendix, p. 139.

41. "The Right of Search" in *Niles' Register,* LXII (March 26, 1842), 54-60. When the Webster-Ashburton Treaty did not specifically disavow the British right of search, Cass ostentatiously resigned in protest, although he was aware that his earlier request to be relieved of his post had already

been granted. See John Tyler to Robert Tyler, April 14, 1848, in Tyler (ed.), *Tylers Letters,* II, 454-55.

42. See Cass's letter to E. A. Hannegan, May 10, 1844, in *Niles' Register,* LXVI (May 25, 1844), 197; see also J. M. Howard to the editors of the Detroit *Daily Free Press,* September 17, 1844, in *ibid.,* LXVII (October 26, 1844), 122.

43. Samuel Medary to Martin Van Buren, December 27, 1847, in Martin Van Buren Papers.

44. See "Mr. Rathbun's Speech to the Utica Convention," in Gardiner, *The Great Issue,* p. 94. Cf. the exchange between Cass and Jacob W. Miller of New Jersey on the Senate floor, March 1, 1847, as reported in the Washington *Daily Union,* March 2, 1847.

45. Quaife (ed.), *Polk Diary,* II, 291-92.

46. *Congressional Globe,* 29 Cong., 2 Sess., pp. 204, 218; Quaife (ed.), *Polk Diary,* II, 323, 325-27, 331-34, 335-37, 339-40. Polk consulted with the respective chairmen of the two committees shortly before the measure was reported in both houses. See *ibid.,* II, 335.

47. John C. Calhoun to Mrs. T. G. Clemson, December 27, 1846, in Jameson (ed.), "Calhoun Correspondence," pp. 715-16; Cave Johnson to A. O. P. Nicholson, December 25, 1846, in Miscellaneous Papers (Cave Johnson), New York Historical Society.

48. See the report of the Washington correspondent "Civis," dated December 25, in the New York *Evening Post,* December 26, 1846.

49. "Progress of the Plot," in the *New York Weekly Tribune,* November 18, 1846; *Congressional Globe,* 29 Cong., 2 Sess., pp. 51-52, 85-86. For evidence of the sensitiveness of the King clique, see the speeches of David Wilmot and James Rathbun in the *Congressional Globe,* 29 Cong., 2 Sess., Appendix, pp. 178, 316.

50. John C. Calhoun to Wilson Lumpkin, December 13, 1846, in John C. Calhoun Papers.

51. *Congressional Globe,* 29 Cong., 2 Sess., p. 47, Appendix, p. 61. Cf. the remarks of Washington Hunt of New York in *ibid.,* p. 72.

52. Cave Johnson to A. O. P. Nicholson, December 25, 1846, in Miscellaneous Papers (Cave Johnson), New York Historical Society. On January 5, the Washington correspondent "Civis," who was probably a Democratic congressman from New York, wrote that he had been shocked to hear southern congressmen say they would secede if the territory was not annexed with slavery permitted. See the *New York Weekly Evening Post,* January 14, 1847.

53. *Congressional Globe,* 29 Cong., 2 Sess., Appendix, p. 54.

54. *Ibid.,* p. 86, Appendix, p. 225.

55. On December 24, the day Gordon spoke, Joshua R. Giddings, the abolitionist congressman from Ohio, wrote Horace Greely, the antislavery editor of the New York *Tribune,* that the Wilmot Proviso would be presented and probably would be rejected. See the Joshua R. Giddings Papers, Library of Congress. Gordon's apparent unwillingness to help introduce the Proviso had given way by January 4, when he voted to allow King to introduce it. See the *Congressional Globe,* 29 Cong., 2 Sess., p. 105. King thought Gordon's conversion important enough to have attention called to it in the Barnburner press when the Hunkers tried to use his earlier speech to discredit the Proviso. See Preston King to Azariah C. Flagg, February 22, 1847, in the Azariah C. Flagg Papers, New York Public Library.

56. *Congressional Globe,* 29 Cong., 2 Sess., p. 96.

57. *Ibid.,* p. 105. For evidence of an effort by the Barnburners' leaders to stop King, see John A. Dix to S. J. Tilden, January 2, 1847, in Bigelow (ed.), *Tilden Letters,* I, 49. For evidence of the leaders' displeasure with King's move, see Ranson H. Gillet's summary of a letter which he delivered for Silas Wright to King and of King's reception of the letter, in Gillet, *Silas Wright,* II, 1873. However, the effort to stop King evidently did not involve Wright himself, who seems to have been taken completely by surprise by King's move. Once the issue was raised publicly Wright supported King, regretting only that he had not "seen fit to let this move come from someone else." Silas Wright to Martin Van Buren, January 28, 1847, in Martin Van Buren Papers; Silas Wright to John A. Dix, January 19, 1847, in Gillet, *Silas Wright,* II, 1916.

58. *Congressional Globe,* 29 Cong., 2 Sess., p. 114.

59. *Ibid.,* p. 115.

60. See the report of the Washington correspondent "Civis," dated January 5, in the *New York Weekly Evening Post,* January 14, 1847. Cf. "The Great Issue," in the *New York Weekly Tribune,* January 16, 1847; Silas Wright to John A. Dix, January 19, 1847, in Gillet, *Silas Wright,* II, 1916; letter of William Seward [dated January 11, 1847] reprinted in Seward (ed.), *Seward at Washington,* pp. 33-34.

61. Alexander H. Stephens to Linton Stephens, January 5, 1847, quoted in Richard Malcolm Johnston and William Hand Browne, *Life of Alexander H. Stephens* (Philadelphia: J. B. Lippincott and Company, 1878), p. 218; "The Great Issue" in the *New York Weekly Tribune,* January 16, 1847; letters of William Seward on January 11, 1847, and January 14, 1847; reprinted in Seward (ed.), *Seward at Washington,* pp. 33-34.

62. On January 13, Alexander Stephens wrote his brother Linton that Armistead Burt, Calhoun's chief lieutenant in the House, tried to get Robert Toombs to speak on Wilmot's proviso because he was "anxious to get up excitement on the slave question." Quoted in James D. Waddell (ed.), *Biographical Sketch of Linton Stephens* (Atlanta: Dodson and Scott, 1877), p. 93. Calhoun wrote his supporters in Charleston that "as to the slave aspect of the subject" their newspapers "should speak unqualifiedly and wholely." John C. Calhoun to Henry W. Conner, January 17, 1847, in Henry W. Conner Papers.

63. *Congressional Globe,* 29 Cong., 2 Sess., Appendix, p. 76.

64. *Ibid.,* 29 Cong., 1 Sess., p. 1204.

65. *Ibid.,* 29 Cong., 2 Sess., pp. 178, 454.

66. *Ibid.,* pp. 178-80. Even after it had been rejected, Calhoun's followers, like most southerners, were reluctant to give up the extension of the Missouri Compromise line as a solution to the problem, although Calhoun himself wished to require that it be offered to the South by the North. See Henry W. Conner to John C. Calhoun, August 23, 1847, in Jameson (ed.), "Calhoun Correspondence," p. 1129; John C. Calhoun to Benjamin F. Perry, September 20, 1847, in John C. Calhoun Papers. The inconsistency between the southern Democrats' adherence to Calhoun's constitutional argument and their willingness to accept an "unconstitutional" Missouri Compromise solution gave them some difficulties. See Reuben C. Chapman to R. M. T. Hunter, August 12, 1847, in R. M. T. Hunter Papers, University of Virginia.

67. Preston King to Azariah C. Flagg, January 12, 18, 1847, R. H. Gillet to Azariah C. Flagg, January 15, 1847, in Azariah C. Flagg Papers, New York Public Library.

68. On January 15, the correspondent "Civis" hastened to assure his readers of the falsity of the rumor that, as a result of the free-soil movement, Calhoun would oppose a full war effort and thus interfere with the annexation of territories. See the *New York Weekly Evening Post,* January 21, 1847.

69. *Congressional Globe,* 29 Cong., 2 Sess., p. 182. Pettit was merely repeating, in stronger terms, an argument made by the Barnburner, Martin Grover, in answer to Seddon's earlier attack on the free-soil movement. See *ibid.,* p. 137.

70. With reference to the northern resentment one Barnburner wrote: "The southern movement concerning slavery creates great feeling here and is likely to bring a near unanimous vote from the free states against them." R. H. Gillet to Azariah C. Flagg, January 15, 1847, in Azariah C. Flagg Papers, New York Public Library.

71. Armistead Burt to Henry W. Conner, February 1, 1847, in Henry W. Conner Papers, Library of Congress; Wilson Lumpkin to John C. Calhoun, January 6, 1847, Richard K. Crallé to John C. Calhoun, April 18, 1847, in Jameson (ed.), "Calhoun Correspondence," pp. 1102-3, 1112-16; Joseph W. Lesesne to John C. Calhoun, August 21, 1847, Wilson Lumpkin to John C. Calhoun, August 27, 1847, in Boucher and Brooks (eds.), "Correspondence Addressed to Calhoun," pp. 391-93, 395-402.

72. Armistead Burt to Henry W. Conner, February 1, 1847, in Henry W. Conner Papers. Not only did Burt refer specifically to Pettit's remark, so too did Calhoun in his speech in Charleston, March 9, 1847, calling for a unified southern defense of the slaveholding system. See Richard K. Crallé (ed.), *The Works of John C. Calhoun* (6 vols.; New York: D. Appleton and Company, 1854), IV, 390.

73. Preston King to Azariah C. Flagg, January 12, 18, 1847, in Azariah C. Flagg Papers, New York Public Library.

74. *Albany Evening Atlas,* January 16, 1847.

75. *Ibid.,* January 27, 1847.

76. *Ibid.,* February 1, 1847.

77. The resolutions of all the states are reprinted in the *Congressional Globe,* 30 Cong., 1 Sess., Appendix, p. 680.

78. Martin Grover to Azariah C. Flagg, January 15, 1847, Preston King to Azariah C. Flagg, January 18, February 22, 1847, in Azariah C. Flagg Papers, New York Public Library.

79. See Wilmot's speech of February 17, 1849, in the *Congressional Globe,* 30 Cong., 2 Sess., p. 139. The Barnburners considered the idea of a resolution but ultimately rejected it as impractical. See Preston King to Azariah C. Flagg, January 18, 1847, in Azariah C. Flagg Papers, New York Public Library. Wilmot reported that Polk offered him an ambassadorship to abandon his antislavery measure. See James Dunlop to John McLean, March 20, 1847, in John McLean Papers, Library of Congress.

80. *Congressional Globe,* 29 Cong., 2 Sess., pp. 303, 352; Going, *David Wilmot,* pp. 161-63.

81. *Congressional Globe,* 29 Cong., 2 Sess., p. 425. The northern Whigs gave a unanimous vote in favor of the Proviso.

82. *Ibid.,* p. 455.

83. *Ibid.,* 453-55.

84. John C. Calhoun to ―――― [February 19, 1847], in Henry W. Conner Papers. This letter, which was almost certainly written to Conner, begins with Calhoun's statement that he had delivered a speech that day which he

goes on to describe. The only other speech by Calhoun which might equally well be described was his speech in Charleston on March 9, at which Conner was present.

85. Quaife (ed.), *Polk Diary*, II, 304-6, 346-48, 392; "The Wilmot Proviso" in the Washington *Daily Union*, February 19, 1847.

86. Gideon Welles to ———, February 27, 1847, in Gideon Welles Papers.

87. Barnburner hostility to Cass dated back to his attempt to wrest the presidential nomination from Van Buren in 1844.

88. Lewis Cass to R. S. Wilson, February 19, 1847, in the Detroit *Daily Free Press*, August 29, 1848. Cf. Lewis Cass to Alpheus Felch, February 4, 1847, in Alpheus Felch Papers, Detroit Public Library. In an obvious reference to Cass, the Washington correspondent of the Whig *Tribune* reported that Calhoun's speech greatly agitated "one presidential candidate." See the *New York Weekly Tribune*, February 24, 1847. One of the Barnburners later declared that an influential southern political figure had told him that Cass had agreed to oppose the Proviso in return for southern support for his presidential candidacy. See "Mr. Rathbun's Speech to the Utica Convention," in Gardiner, *The Great Issue*, p. 94.

89. "The Wilmot Proviso in the Senate," in the *New York Weekly Evening Post*, February 25, 1847; "Mr. Rathbun's Speech to the Utica Convention," in Gardiner, *The Great Issue*, p. 95; cf. Quaife (ed.), *Polk Diary*, II, 458.

90. *Congressional Globe*, 29 Cong., 2 Sess., pp. 541-43.

91. *Ibid.*, p. 544.

92. *Ibid.*, p. 548.

93. Cass himself had presented the resolutions. See *ibid.*, p. 540. He got around them by assuming that they applied only after the territory had been acquired, when the Congress was establishing a territorial government. See *ibid.*, p. 551.

94. *Ibid.*, p. 550.

95. *Ibid.*

96. See the exchange of remarks on the Senate floor that day between Cass and Jacob W. Miller of New Jersey, as reported in the Washington *Daily Union*, March 2, 1847.

97. The vote was thirty-one to twenty-one. Senator Charles G. Atherton of New Hampshire, who had vacillated, with Cass, when the President approached them on the issue, voted for the Proviso, another indication that the antislavery influence was stronger among Democrats in the Northeast than in the Northwest. See the *Congressional Globe*, 29 Cong., 2 Sess., p. 555.

98. *Ibid.*, p. 573. The influence of Cass appears to have been of much less importance in the House than in the Senate. Of the seven House Democrats who changed their vote, only one was from the Northwest. The Northwest continued to provide a large percentage of northern Democratic votes against the Proviso in the House, however, most of the others coming from Pennsylvania. See the "List of 'Good Samaritans'," in [Augustus Baldwin Longstreet], *A Voice from the South* (Baltimore: Western Continental Press, 1848), p. 56.

CHAPTER III

1. John C. Calhoun to Percy Walker, October 26, 1847, in the *Charleston Mercury*, June 13, 1855. Cf. John C. Calhoun to ——— [February 19, 1847], in Henry W. Conner Papers; John C. Calhoun to Charles James Faulkner,

August 1, 1847, in John C. Calhoun Papers. As early as 1837, Calhoun was saying that "the sooner the [slavery] issue is made the better for us and the country." John C. Calhoun to James Edward Calhoun, December 20, 1837, in Jameson (ed.), "Calhoun Correspondence," p. 386.

2. Crallé (ed.), *Works of Calhoun,* IV, 382-96.

3. *Ibid.,* pp. 394-95.

4. John C. Calhoun to Thomas G. Clemson, April 11, May 6, July 8, 1847, in Jameson (ed.), "Calhoun Correspondence," pp. 726, 728-29, 735.

5. "The Slavery Question," in the Tallahassee *Southern Journal,* March 23, 1847; John Hart to John C. Calhoun, March 10, 1847, William B. Johnson to John C. Calhoun, August 31, 1847, in John C. Calhoun Papers; Washington *National Era,* May 27, 1847.

6. *Charleston Mercury,* March 18, April 13, April 29, 1847; Washington *National Era,* May 27, 1847; Tallahassee *Floridian,* August 7, 1847.

7. "Great Meeting of the People of Lowndes Without Distinction of Party," in the Montgomery *Tri-Weekly Flag and Advertiser,* April 24, 1847; Franklin H. Elmore to John C. Calhoun, April 16, 1847, in John C. Calhoun Papers. Cf. the resolutions of the meeting in Madison County in the Tallahassee *Floridian,* August 7, 1847.

8. H. W. Hilliard to John C. Calhoun, April 16, 1847, in John C. Calhoun Papers.

9. Robert Toombs to John C. Calhoun, April 30, 1847, in Boucher and Brooks (eds.), "Correspondence Addressed to Calhoun," p. 373.

10. Samuel A. Wales to John C. Calhoun, June 17, 1847, in *ibid.,* pp. 382-83.

11. John C. Calhoun to Samuel A. Wales, June 27, 1847, in *Niles' Register,* LXXII (July 24, 1847), 323.

12. The secretary of the convention forwarded the resolutions to Calhoun, evidently in the hope that Calhoun would be pleased by the reference to him. See John H. Y. —— to John C. Calhoun, July 2, 1847, in John C. Calhoun Papers.

13. Calhoun's Charleston clique seriously considered supporting Taylor. See H. W. Conner to John C. Calhoun, May 14, 1847, in John C. Calhoun Papers.

14. One southern Democratic journal, the Athens *Southern Banner,* tried to read Calhoun out of the party. See "Mr. Calhoun's Position," in the *Charleston Mercury,* May 19, 1847.

15. "Mr. Calhoun's Movement against a National Convention," in the Washington *Daily Union,* March 27, 1847. Even some of the strongest pro-slavery advocates accepted the validity of this analysis. See William Gilmore Simms to James H. Hammond, May 1, 1847, in Mary C. Simms, Oliphant Alfred Taylor Odell, and T. C. Duncan Eaves (eds.), *The Letters of William Gilmore Simms* (5 vols.; Columbia: University of South Carolina Press, 1956), II, 312.

16. Washington *Daily Union,* March 15, 27, 29, April 5, August 6, 1847; *Daily Richmond Enquirer,* March 26, 29, August 26, 1847; Milledgeville *Federal Union,* February 23, 1847; Montgomery *Tri-Weekly Flag and Advertiser,* March 23, October 30, 1847; Jackson *Mississippian,* April 16, 1847; Tallahassee *Floridian,* August 7, 1847.

17. Quaife (ed.), *Polk Diary,* II, 458; Washington *Daily Union,* March 16, 1847, and March 29, 1847, quoting the Columbus [Georgia] *Times* and the Warrenton [North Carolina] *Reporter*; Milledgeville *Federal Union,* March

23, 1847; *Charleston Mercury,* April 24, May 13, 1847; H. B. Anthony to Andrew J. Donelson, March 29, 1847, in Andrew J. Donelson Papers, Library of Congress; Beverly Tucker to James H. Hammond, March 13, 1847, James H. Hammond to William Gilmore Simms, April 1, 1847, in James H. Hammond Papers, Library of Congress; J. B. D. DeBow to ———, July 18, 1847, in John C. Calhoun Papers.

18. "The Tactics of Mr. Calhoun," in the Washington *National Era,* February 25, 1847.

19. William Hope Hull to Howell Cobb, May 22, 1846, John B. Lamar to Howell Cobb, June 8, 1846, in Ulrich Bonnell Phillips (ed.), "The Correspondence of Robert Toombs, Alexander H. Stephens, and Howell Cobb," Volume II of the *Annual Report of the American Historical Association for the Year 1911* (Washington: Government Printing Office, 1913), pp. 345-47; James R. Saunders to George S. Houston, February 19, 1847, in George S. Houston Papers, Duke University. Dixon H. Lewis, who had been one of Calhoun's strongest supporters before the war, wrote: "By his self-sacrificing course, particularly on the Mexican War . . . [Calhoun] put himself in a position where not a friend he had outside of South Carolina could sustain him and live." Dixon H. Lewis to Richard K. Crallé, May 11, 1848, in Richard K. Crallé Papers, Library of Congress.

20. Washington *Daily Union,* February 9, 1847.

21. *Congressional Globe,* 29 Cong., 2 Sess., p. 366.

22. David Campbell to William E. Campbell, March 4, 1847, in David Campbell Papers, Duke University; Duff Green to Richard K. Crallé, March 5, 1847, in Richard K. Crallé Papers.

23. See above, n. 19. Cf. Quaife, *Polk Diary,* II, 378-79, 440; John Tyler to Alexander Gardiner, March 2, 1847, in Tyler (ed.), *Tylers Letters,* II, 479; William Gilmore Simms to James Henry Hammond, March 29, [1847], in Oliphant *et al.* (eds.), *Simms Letters,* II, 290; James L. Orr to John C. Calhoun, August 9, 1847, in Boucher and Brooks (eds.), "Correspondence Addressed to Calhoun," pp. 389-90.

24. "Republican State Convention" in the *Daily Richmond Enquirer,* February 26, 1847.

25. "Messrs. Bocock and Leake" in *ibid.,* March 18, 1847; Duff Green to John C. Calhoun, March 6, 1847, in John C. Calhoun Papers; Richard K. Crallé to John C. Calhoun, April 18, 1847, in Jameson (ed.), "Calhoun Correspondence," p. 1112.

26. *Daily Richmond Enquirer,* March 19, 1847.

27. *Ibid.,* January 16, 18, 21, 22; John C. Calhoun to Thomas G. Clemson, January 30, 1847, in Jameson (ed.), "Calhoun Correspondence," p. 1074.

28. Quaife (ed.), *Polk Diary,* II, 457-58; Duff Green to Richard K. Crallé, March 5, 1847, in Richard K. Crallé Papers.

29. Franklin H. Elmore to John C. Calhoun, April 10, 1847, in John C. Calhoun Papers; I. W. Hayne to James H. Hammond, March 31, [1847], in James H. Hammond Papers.

30. "Pennsylvania" in *Niles' Register,* LXXII (March 20, 1847), 35.

31. "Important Legal Opinion" in *ibid.* (May 22, 1847), p. 177.

32. C. J. Faulkner to John C. Calhoun, July 15, 1847, in Boucher and Brooks (eds.), "Correspondence Addressed to Calhoun," pp. 385-87.

33. John C. Calhoun to Charles James Faulkner, August 1, 1847, in John C. Calhoun Papers.

34. Daniel Huger and others to John C. Calhoun, August 2, 1847, in

Boucher and Brooks (eds.), "Correspondence Addressed to Calhoun," pp. 399-402.

35. H. W. Conner to John C. Calhoun, August 23, 1847, in Jameson (ed.), "Calhoun Correspondence," p. 1128.

36. John C. Calhoun to H. Conner, August 25, 1847, in John C. Calhoun Papers.

37. Henry W. Conner to John C. Calhoun, August 8, 1847, in *ibid.*

38. H. W. Conner to John C. Calhoun, August 8, September 7, 1847, in *ibid.*; H. W. Conner to John C. Calhoun, August 23, 1847, in Jameson (ed.), "Calhoun Correspondence," p. 1129.

39. H. W. Peronneau to John C. Calhoun, September 25, 1847, H. W. Conner to John C. Calhoun, October 6, 1847, in Boucher and Brooks (eds.), "Correspondence Addressed to Calhoun," pp. 398-99, 404; H. W. Peronneau to John C. Calhoun, September 29, 1847, in John C. Calhoun Papers.

40. John C. Calhoun to Percy Walker, October 26, 1847, in the *Charleston Mercury,* June 13, 1855. Calhoun had originally planned to have the program of commercial retaliation implemented by the southern association, until that scheme collapsed. See John C. Calhoun to ———, September 28, 1847, in *ibid.,* May 5, 1851.

41. *Charleston Mercury,* September 30, 1847.

42. John C. Calhoun to Charles James Faulkner, August 1, 1847, in John C. Calhoun Papers; Wilson Lumpkin to John C. Calhoun, November 18, 1847, in Jameson (ed.), "Calhoun Correspondence," p. 1137.

43. John C. Calhoun to David Johnson, October 8, November 4, 1847, in John C. Calhoun Papers; "Governor's Message," in the *Charleston Mercury,* November 24, 1847.

44. On November 18, Wilson Lumpkin wrote to Calhoun: "If the Wilmot Proviso (as you anticipate) should receive the sanction of Congress, it will strongly tend to favor the views which we entertain. Indeed the passage of the Wilmot resolutions by Congress, I believe, will be one of those wicked acts which will be overruled for great good. It will enlarge the platform on which we stand." Jameson (ed.), "Calhoun Correspondence," p. 1138. Calhoun himself wrote in December that he expected further developments of the session would bring the South together. See John C. Calhoun to H. W. Conner, December 16, 1847, in Henry W. Conner Papers.

45. "Mr. Calhoun in the South," in the Tallahassee *Southern Journal,* March 23, 1847.

46. "Democratic State Convention," in the *Tri-Weekly Nashville Union,* April 3, 1847. Cf. "Tennessee Democratic Resolutions," in the Jackson *Mississippian,* December 24, 1847.

47. "Democratic State Convention," in the Jackson *Mississippian,* June 11, 1847.

48. John C. Calhoun to Thomas G. Clemson, June 7, 1845, in Jameson (ed.), "Calhoun Correspondence," p. 663; James K. Polk to Cave Johnson, December 21, 1844, in St. George L. Sioussat (ed.), "Letters of James K. Polk to Cave Johnson," *Tennessee Historical Magazine,* I (September, 1915), 254.

49. John C. Calhoun to Thomas G. Clemson, June 7, 1845, in Jameson (ed.), "Calhoun Correspondence," p. 664.

50. "Virginia Legislature," February 17, in the *Daily Richmond Enquirer,* February 18, 1847.

51. *Ibid.* Harvie offered his resolutions before Calhoun offered his in the

Senate, but it seems certain he derived his inspiration from Calhoun nonetheless.

52. *Ibid.,* February 18, March 9, 1847.

53. "Republican State Convention," in *ibid.,* February 26, 1847.

54. "Convention Debates" in *ibid.,* April 7, 1847.

55. "Republican State Convention," in *ibid.,* February 26, 1847.

56. See the speech of Robert Scott in "Convention Debates" in *ibid.,* April 7, 1847.

57. *Ibid.,* March 26, 1847.

58. *Ibid.,* February 24, March 15, April 17, 1847.

59. Edward J. Harden to Howell Cobb, May 3, 1847, in Phillips (ed.), "Toombs, Stephens, Cobb Correspondence," p. 87; Lewis E. Harvie to John C. Calhoun, May 8, 1847, R. K. Crallé to John C. Calhoun, July 20, 1847, in John C. Calhoun Papers.

60. Washington *Daily Union,* August 11, 1846. Part of the address is quoted in John Witherspoon DuBose, *The Life and Times of William Lowndes Yancey* (Birmingham: Roberts and Son, 1892), pp. 153-54.

61. William L. Yancey to William P. Browne, January 31, 1848, in the Montgomery *Tri-Weekly Flag and Advertiser,* February 8, 1848.

62. Albert Burton Moore, *History of Alabama and Her People* (Chicago and New York: The American Historical Society, Inc., 1927), I, 259.

63. Reuben C. Chapman to R. M. T. Hunter, August 12, 1847, in Robert M. T. Hunter Papers; John A. Campbell to John C. Calhoun, November 20, 1847, in Jameson (ed.), "Calhoun Correspondence," p. 1144.

64. "Journal of the Democratic Convention," in the Montgomery *Tri-Weekly Flag and Advertiser,* May 8, 1847; Franklin H. Elmore to John C. Calhoun, April 18, 1847, in John C. Calhoun Papers.

65. Reuben C. Chapman to R. M. T. Hunter, August 12, 1847, in Robert M. T. Hunter Papers.

66. *Ibid.; Huntsville Democrat,* August 25, 1847; Malcolm C. McMillan, "Taylor's Presidential Campaign in Alabama, 1847-1848," *The Alabama Review,* XIII (April, 1960), 86.

67. "Mr. Yancey's Speech," in the Montgomery *Tri-Weekly Flag and Advertiser,* July 22, 1847.

68. "Democratic Convention," in the Milledgeville *Federal Union,* July 6, 1847; "The Old Parties," in the Washington *National Era,* August 5, 1847; "Georgia" in *Niles' Register,* LXXII (July 10, 1847), 293.

69. Edward J. Black to John C. Calhoun [between June and December, 1847], in Boucher and Brooks (eds.), "Correspondence Addressed to Calhoun," pp. 380-81.

70. "Democratic Convention" in the Milledgeville *Federal Union,* July 6, 1847.

71. *Ibid.;* Wilson Lumpkin to John C. Calhoun, August 27, 1847, in Boucher and Brooks (eds.), "Correspondence Addressed to Calhoun," p. 398.

72. "The Wilmot Proviso—A Brighter Prospect," in the Milledgeville *Federal Union,* August 3, 1847.

73. "The True Friends of the South" in *ibid.,* September 28, 1847.

74. "Democratic Convention in Georgia," in the Jackson *Mississippian,* July 9, 1847; "General Taylor's Letter" in the *Daily Richmond Enquirer,* July 7, 1847. Cf. the widely reprinted letter to the people of Mississippi appearing under the title "The Ultimatum," in the *New York Weekly Tribune,* October 30, 1847.

CHAPTER IV

1. See below, n. 3. Even in Kansas, where conditions were most favorable for the successful use of slave labor and where there was strong pressure on the slaveholders to go there to "save" the state for the South, very few emigrated. See William O. Lynch, "Popular Sovereignty and the Colonization of Kansas from 1854 to 1860," *Proceedings of the Mississippi Valley Historical Association,* IX (1917-18), 380-92; Elmer LeRoy Craik, "Southern Interest in Territorial Kansas, 1854-1858," *Collections of the Kansas State Historical Society,* XV (1919-22), 437-48. The well-organized and well-publicized expedition of Major Jefferson Bufford, by far the largest single southern emigration enterprise, could raise only $14,000 in contributions and three hundred prospective settlers, very few of whom were slaveowners. See Walter Lynwood Fleming, "The Bufford Expedition to Kansas," *Publications of the Alabama Historical Society,* IV (1900), 167-92, especially n. 58 and n. 59. The few hundred slaves who were taken to Kansas "were brought very largely, though of course not entirely, as a part of the pro-slavery propaganda—not for profit." Charles Estebrook Cory, "Slavery in Kansas," *Transactions of the Kansas State Historical Society,* VII (1901-2), 242.

2. Tepid opposition to the prohibition of slavery in the territories was usually disastrous in election campaigns in the South. Democrats in Arkansas, for example, won a two to one victory in an election in 1856 when their opponents expressed skepticism about the Kansas-Nebraska Act's repeal of prohibition in the Kansas territory. But successful as they were at the polls, proslavery men found it impossible to persuade Arkansans to go to Kansas in order to protect the institution there. One historian concludes that "the nature of the Arkansas reaction to the parade of tragedies in Kansas demonstrates that Arkansans, as a whole, viewed the turmoil only as it had a bearing upon that abstract principle [of a matter of right]." See Granville R. Davis, "Arkansas and the Blood of Kansas," *The Journal of Southern History,* XVI (November, 1950), 448-49, 455. For evidence of antipathy of southern emigrants to slavery, see Lynch, "Popular Sovereignty in Kansas," pp. 388-90, 391, n. 32; Delilah L. Beesley, "Slavery in California," *The Journal of Negro History,* III (January, 1918), 37; Lloyd Lewis, "Propaganda and the Kansas-Missouri War," *The Missouri Historical Review,* XXXIV (October, 1939), 7.

3. At the height of the excitement over the Wilmot Proviso, the organ of Calhoun's Charleston clique, the *Mercury,* carried an article which admitted that "no slaves can pay in California." The article continued: "As a practical question, the area of slavery will not cover sterile mountains, sandy plains, or mere grain-growing regions. It is the insulting and unprincipled effort that renders it indispensable not to admit a claim, which will be extended to other invasions of the Constitution." "The Wilmot Proviso," in the *Charleston Mercury,* August 13, 1847. Cf. the speeches of Andrew Butler of South Carolina and Reverdy Johnson of Maryland in the *Congressional Globe,* 29 Cong., 2 Sess., pp. 544, 554; Andrew J. Donelson, Francis Wilkinson Pickens, and Thomas B. King to James Buchanan, May 15, June 4, June 11, 1847, in James Buchanan Papers, Historical Society of Pennsylvania; B. Alvord to ——— Marcus, August 21, 1848, in James H. Hammond Papers; "Remarks of Gen. W. Thompson," in the Washington *National Intelligencer,* October 21, 1847.

4. Quoted in Ulrich Bonnell Phillips, *The Course of the South to Secession,*

ed. E. Merton Coulter (New York and London: D. Appleton Century, Inc., 1939), p. 156. Cf. Walter Lippmann, *Public Opinion* (New York: The Macmillan Company, 1947), pp. 220-49.

5. See James G. Randall, "The Civil War Restudied," *The Journal of Southern History,* VI (November, 1940), 447; James G. Randall, "The Blundering Generation," *The Mississippi Valley Historical Review,* XXVII (June, 1940), 13; Avery O. Craven, "Coming of the War between the States: An Interpretation," *The Journal of Southern History,* II (August, 1936), 322; Avery O. Craven, "The 1840's and the Democratic Process," *The Journal of Southern History,* XVI (May, 1950), 162-63, 173-75; Charles W. Ramsdell, "The Natural Limits of Slavery Expansion," *The Mississippi Valley Historical Review,* XVI (September, 1929), 159-63.

6. Avery O. Craven, *The Growth of Southern Nationalism, 1848-1861* (Baton Rouge: Louisiana State University Press, 1953), p. 397.

7. Craven, "Coming of the War Between the States," p. 317.

8. Arthur M. Schlesinger, Jr., "The Inevitability of Violence," in Kenneth M. Stampp (ed.), *The Causes of the Civil War* (Englewood Cliffs, New Jersey: Prentice Hall, Inc., 1959), p. 116.

9. Cf. the contention of another critic of the revisionists: "In the sequence of [historical] cause and effect, of which the human mind will never have complete command, the category of the *imponderabilia,* passion and emotion, conviction, prejudice, misunderstanding, have their organic function. No doubt it is this very fact which makes that command unattainable for us, but we are not therefore entitled to ignore these non-rational factors or to argue them away with the help of wisdom after the event." See Pieter Geyl, "The Problem of Inevitability," in *ibid.,* p. 122.

10. When an amendment was finally moved in the North during the secession crisis, it was to make slavery a permanent part of the Constitution, not subject to future amendment, so that the institution could never be abolished except by individual state action. The fact that the slaveholding states had the power to veto an amendment abolishing slavery scarcely acted as a total deterrent to the effort for an abolition amendment, since all such movements face the same kind of entrenched opposition initially. Many of the so-called antislavery people kept (mistakenly) expecting support from the nonslaveholding elements in the South, once the latter had recognized their "true interest," and with this support a constitutional amendment would have been a real possibility.

11. Bernard De Voto, "The Essence of Our Tragedy," in *ibid.,* p. 112.

12. In his attempt to answer this question, Martin Duberman emphasizes northern fear of disunion. See "The Northern Response to Slavery," in Martin Duberman (ed.), *The Antislavery Vanguard: New Essays on the Abolitionists* (Princeton: Princeton University Press, 1965), pp. 395-402. One answer not discussed by Duberman was fear of emigration to the North by emancipated Negroes. See Williston H. Lofton, "Abolition and Labor," *The Journal of Negro History,* XXXIII (July, 1948), 274-76; Williston H. Lofton, "Northern Labor and the Negro during the Civil War," *ibid.,* XXXIV (July, 1949), 251-62.

13. One qualification of this treatment should perhaps be pointed out in advance. Because both of the groups whose interpretations are emphasized were Democratic, their arguments tend to be circumscribed by traditional Democratic dogma and to appeal more directly to Democratic than to Whig voters. Therefore, any generalizations on the basis of these arguments would

probably have a greater validity for the Democratic rather than the non-Democratic voting public. At the same time, however, both groups were trying to appeal to non-Democratic as well as to Democratic voters in their respective sections, much more so even than party politicians ordinarily do.

14. There is a widely accepted theorem of sociology which states: "If men define situations as real, they are real in their consequences." Robert K. Merton, *Social Theory and Social Structure* (Glencoe, Illinois: The Free Press, 1949), p. 179.

15. See above, n. 3. Alexander H. Stephens, who later admitted that he thought the Wilmot Proviso a *"humbug,"* in 1848 denounced the Clayton Compromise, which left the question of slavery in the territories to be ultimately decided by the predominantly southern Supreme Court, as a surrender of the sacred right of slaveowners to take their slaves into the territories. See Alexander H. Stephens to the Editor of the *Federal Union,* August 30, 1848, in Phillips (ed.), "Toombs, Stephens, Cobb Correspondence," pp. 117-24; Alexander H. Stephens to Linton Stephens, January 15, 1850, quoted in Johnston and Browne, *Alexander Stephens,* p. 245. Political considerations might well have induced Stephens to oppose the Clayton Compromise, since he was a Whig and it was a Democratic measure, but the point is that he based his opposition on the strict maintenance of a right which he elsewhere described as of no practical importance. Notwithstanding his later words, his action assumes that the issue was of practical importance.

16. "Remarks of Gen. W. Thompson," in the Washington *National Intelligencer,* October 21, 1847.

17. *Congressional Globe,* 29 Cong., 2 Sess., Appendix, p. 316. Cf. the speeches of Jacob Brinkerhoff and Samuel Gordon in *ibid.,* pp. 379, 390. Some southerners also claimed that slaves would be taken into the territories in large numbers. See *ibid.,* p. 291. They later blamed the antislavery agitation for this not having been done. See *ibid.,* 31 Cong., 1 Sess., p. 202, Appendix, p. 510.

18. The census listed no slaves in the New Mexico Territory and only twenty-six in the Utah Territory, presumed to be on their way to California with their masters. See *The Seventh Census of the United States* (Washington: Robert Armstrong, 1853), pp. 972, 998. The representative of the New Mexico Territory in Congress, who maintained that the region was unsuitable for slave labor, estimated that there were six slaves in New Mexico in 1850. See R. H. Weightman to H. S. Foote, December 16, 1851, in the *Congressional Globe,* 32 Cong., 1 Sess., Appendix, p. 35. The Mormon Church in Utah approved of Negro slavery and there were apparently some slaves residing in Utah in 1850. See James B. Christensen, "Negro Slavery in the Utah Territory," *The Phylon Quarterly,* XVIII (October, 1957), 299-301. The 1860 census listed twenty-nine slaves residing in Utah; there were none in New Mexico. See *The Population of the United States in 1860; Compiled from the Original Returns of the Eighth Census* (Washington: Government Printing Office, 1864), p. 575.

19. *Congressional Globe,* 29 Cong., 2 Sess., p. 454. Calhoun incorporated this idea into his "Address to the Southern People" for which he finally got enough southern congressional support to issue early in 1849. In the address he contends that there would be "one certain way to accomplish their [the abolitionists'] object, if the determination avowed by the North to monopolize all the territories should be carried into effect. That of itself would, at no distant day, add to the North a sufficient number of States to give her three

fourths of the whole; when, under the cover of an amendment of the Constitution, she would emancipate our slaves. . . ." Crallé (ed.), *Works of Calhoun,* VI, 308-9.

20. Calhoun later applied his doctrine of concurrent majorities to the problem and proposed a plural executive as a solution. See *ibid.,* I, 390-95.

21. This idea was expressed at the time in James Russell Lowell's tremendously popular antislavery poems, *The Biglow Papers:*

> They jest want this Californy
> So's to lug new slave-states in
> To abuse ye, an to scorn ye,
> An to plunder ye like sin.

James Russell Lowell, *The Biglow Papers* (Boston and New York: Houghton Mifflin Company, 1848), pp. 46-47. The first edition of fifteen hundred copies of *The Biglow Papers* sold out within a week. See Lorenzo Dow Turner, "Antislavery Sentiment in Literature Prior to 1865," *The Journal of Negro History,* XIV (October, 1929), 434, n. 43.

22. *Congressional Globe,* 29 Cong., 2 Sess., p. 365.

23. *Ibid.,* Appendix, p. 180.

24. Gardiner, *The Great Issue,* p. 108. The convention itself took this view, maintaining that "our wishes in this regard are strengthened immeasurably when we contemplate the evils which may result to the country and to the world by the further extension of the slave power in America." *Ibid.,* p. 135. Cf. "The Plan and the Object," in the Washington *National Era,* February 22, 1849. One careful historian of party politics in Ohio during this period concludes that the antislavery movement in the state was, in effect, primarily "a protest movement by leaders of both parties against political domination of the national government by the unified South." Holt, "Party Politics in Ohio," p. 391. Most of the major literary figures in the North publicly expressed this fear of slaveholder dominance. See Howard R. Floan, *The South in Northern Eyes, 1831 to 1861* (Austin: The University of Texas Press, 1958). Russell B. Nye has discussed the tremendous contribution of the northern belief in a great "slave power conspiracy" in "The Slave Power Conspiracy, 1830-1860," *Science and Society,* X (Summer, 1946), 262-74. For a refutation of the myth of a slave power conspiracy, see Chauncey S. Boucher, "*In Re* That Aggressive Slavocracy," *The Mississippi Valley Historical Review,* VIII (June-September, 1921), 13-79.

25. See the speeches of Preston King, Timothy Jenkins, Robert McClelland, and John A. Dix in the *Congressional Globe,* 29 Cong., 2 Sess., pp. 114, 420, 543, Appendix, p. 392.

26. "What Shall Be Done for the White Men" in the *New York Weekly Evening Post,* April 27, 1848. Cf. the "Address of the Democratic Members of the Legislature of the State of New York" in John Bigelow (ed.), *The Writings and Speeches of Samuel J. Tilden* (2 vols.; New York: Harper and Brothers, 1885), II, 569. The Barnburners' Utica convention of February, 1848, gave the idea a peculiar twist in an attempt to appeal more strongly to northern workers. The address of the convention reads: "[if foreign emigrants] be excluded by the presence of slave labor, from any part of Oregon, New Mexico, or California, it will seat itself in the free states and free territories there to compete with free labor, to the injury of itself, as well as to them." Gardiner, *The Great Issue,* p. 134.

27. *Congressional Globe,* 29 Cong., 2 Sess., Appendix, p. 180.

28. See, for example, the speech of James Dixon of Connecticut in *ibid.*, Appendix, p. 335.

29. "The Deception" in the Washington *National Era*, August 26, 1847. For claims by other free-soil journals that the slaveholders did not speak for the entire South, see "Voice from the South" in the *New York Weekly Evening Post*, May 4, 1848; "Present Aspects of Slavery" in the *New York Weekly Tribune*, October 20, 1847.

30. A northern writer articulated the common opinion in his diary on June 11, 1848: "[Southern slaveholder] domination is opposed to all the principles and opinions of the country, expressed by none more strongly than themselves. They are essentially an aristocracy, a collection of landed proprietors surrounded by serfs; their property in slaves is represented [as] the only property that gives political power, and they are a small minority in population of the whole country." [Nicholas B. Wainwright and Lois V. Given, (eds.)], "The Diaries of Sydney George Fisher, 1844-1849," *The Pennsylvania Magazine of History and Biography*, LXXXVI (January, 1962), 81. The image of the South as an aristocratic society was not limited to northerners. William R. Taylor writes: "By 1860 most Americans had come to look upon their society and culture as divided between a North and a South, a democratic commercial civilization and an aristocratic agrarian one." *Cavalier and Yankee* (New York: Braziller, 1961), p. 15. For a refutation of the view that the ante-bellum South was less democratic politically than the North, see Fletcher M. Green, "Democracy in the Old South," *The Journal of Southern History*, XII (February, 1946), 3-23.

31. "The Barnburners' Demonstration" in the *New York Weekly Tribune*, June 10, 1848.

32. The significance of the southern yeomanry is emphasized in Frank Lawrence Owsley, *Plain Folk of the Old South* (Baton Rouge: Louisiana State University Press).

33. Whitman, *Gathering of the Forces*, I, 209. That Whitman should make this statement is particularly significant since he was one of the northern writers least susceptible to a stereotyped picture of the South. See Floan, *South in Northern Eyes*, pp. 164-86.

34. On the eve of the Proviso struggle, one of Calhoun's followers in Georgia warned him: "That portion of the southern population who own no slaves generally feel very different on the subject than the slaveholders." Wilson Lumpkin to John C. Calhoun, January 6, 1847, in Jameson (ed.), "Calhoun Correspondence," p. 1103. While this supposed difference in feeling never manifested itself politically, it remained a potent source of fear for the slaveholders.

35. See, for example, the speeches of Paul Dillingham, Jr., Robert Mc-Clelland, James Dixon, William Upham, David Wilmot, and Bradford R. Wood in the *Congressional Globe*, 29 Cong., 2 Sess., pp. 355, 402, 548, Appendix, pp. 318, 334, 345, 392.

36. *Ibid.*, p. 420, Appendix, p. 334.

37. Dated April 12, 1848, in Martin Van Buren Papers, reprinted in Bigelow (ed.), *Writings of Tilden*, II, 569. The anticapitalist bent of the Barnburner attack upon slavery in the territories is emphasized in Arthur M. Schlesinger, Jr., *The Age of Jackson* (Boston: Little, Brown and Company, 1945), pp. 450-68.

38. Gardiner, *The Great Issue*, p. 119.

39. See the speech of Bradford R. Wood in the *Congressional Globe*, 29

Cong., 2 Sess., Appendix, p. 345. Cf. Paul Dillingham's statement, "the institution of slavery is gnawing at the vitals of your prosperity," in *ibid.*, p. 402.

40. See the speeches of Preston King, Martin Grover, James Rathbun, Paul Dillingham, and David Wilmot, in *ibid.*, pp. 115, 137, 363, 402, Appendix, 317. Cf. "What Shall Be Done for the White Men," in the *New York Weekly Evening Post*, April 27, 1848; Whitman, *Gathering of the Forces*, I, 202. A few free-soilers accepted abolition as an alternate goal, however. See Samuel Gordon's speech in the *Congressional Globe*, 29 Cong., 2 Sess., p. 390.

41. "It was with those states where slavery was," said Paul Dillingham, "to find a remedy." *Congressional Globe*, 29 Cong., 2 Sess., p. 402.

42. "The Wilmot Proviso Question" in the Washington *Daily Union*, August 26, 1847. The quotation is a composite of two separate nonconsecutive sentences.

43. Peter V. Daniel to Martin Van Buren, in Martin Van Buren Papers. Cf. John Tyler's statement: "The Wilmot Proviso is at this moment nothing less than a gratuitous insult on the slave-States. It seeks to stamp upon the records of the country an anathema and an edict that is unnecessary and wanton." John Tyler to the Portsmouth *Pilot*, undated (c. 1850), quoted in Tyler, *Tylers Letters*, II, 478. Late in 1848, Senator Robert M. T. Hunter, one of Calhoun's Virginia followers, told President Polk that he was "very desirous to settle the [territorial] question in any way to avoid the degradation of the South, by getting clear of the Wilmot Proviso." See Quaife (ed.), *Polk Diary*, IV, 238. Van Buren, who was familiar with southern politics, recognized that this was the most important basis of southern opposition to the Proviso. In his letter of acceptance to the nomination of the Buffalo Convention he wrote: "But it is insisted that the prohibition carries with it a reproach to the slaveholding States, and that submission to it would degrade them. This is obviously the principal if not the material ground of opposition to the measure. . . ." Gardiner, *The Great Issue*, p. 146.

44. Quoted in Denman, *Secession Movement in Alabama*, p. 3. One southerner remarked that "we ought not to have territory at all if the mad fanaticism of the North is resolved to make it the basis of agitation and the pretext to perpetuate cold and wanton insult upon us by denying our equality in the Union and excluding us from benefits to accrue." Francis Wilkinson Pickens to James Buchanan, June 4, 1847, in James Buchanan Papers, Historical Society of Pennsylvania. Cf. the speeches of Howell Cobb, Andrew P. Butler, Walter Colquitt, and Arthur P. Bagby in the *Congressional Globe*, 29 Cong., 2 Sess., pp. 360, 544, 554, Appendix, p. 399.

45. Calhoun's original production of the constitutional argument is illuminating in this respect. Three days before he had Burt present the constitutional argument for the first time in Congress, he wrote to the governor of South Carolina: "Both parties at the North seem resolved that we shall be excluded from whatever territory may be acquired. It seems to be their policy to let us spill our blood and expend our treasury, not to acquire additional territory for the common benefit, but to be used as an instrument to destroy us. Nothing but the united and determined resistance of the South can prevent the success of this base and dangerous plot against our power and safety." John C. Calhoun to David Johnson, January 13, 1847, in John C. Calhoun Papers. Neither in this letter, nor in one written the day after Burt's speech, nor in one written the day he himself stated the southern constitutional position, did he mention the "fact" that the northern position

violated the Constitution. John C. Calhoun to Henry W. Conner, January 17, 1847 [misdated 1846], John C. Calhoun to ——— [February 19, 1847], in Henry W. Conner Papers. Cf. John C. Calhoun to Mrs. Thomas G. Clemson, December 27, 1846, in Jameson (ed.), "Calhoun Correspondence," pp. 715-16. Calhoun had raised no constitutional objections to the Proviso in his conversation with Polk on December 21. See Quaife (ed.), *Polk Diary*, II, 283-84.

46. Southern politicians were *almost unanimous* in claiming that the Wilmot Proviso was unconstitutional even in spite of the fact that the validation of this claim would make the extension of the Missouri Compromise line, the most desirable solution from the southern standpoint, illegal constitutionally.

47. Jesse T. Carpenter, *The South as a Conscious Minority, 1789-1861* (New York: The New York University Press, 1930), p. 154.

48. See the Calhoun resolutions quoted on pp. 34-35. Cf. the resolutions of the Virginia legislature, known as the "Platform of the South," reprinted in Herman V. Ames (ed.), *State Documents on Federal Relations: The States and the United States* (Philadelphia: The Department of History of the University of Pennsylvania, 1906), p. 206.

49. Quoted in Dunbar Rowland, *History of Mississippi* (2 vols.; Chicago and Jackson: The S. J. Clarke Publishing Company, 1925), I, 698.

50. Quoted in Denman, *The Secession Movement in Alabama*, p. 160.

51. Phillips, *Course of the South to Secession*, p. 152.

52. William Hope Hull to Howell Cobb, January 26, 1849, in Phillips (ed.), "Toombs, Stephens, Cobb Correspondence," p. 142. In 1856, Robert J. Walker of Mississippi wrote: "In all the slave States there is a large majority of voters who are non-slaveholders; but they are devoted to the institutions of the South—they would defend them with their lives—and on this question the South are [sic] a united people." Quoted in Phillips, *Course of the South to Secession*, p. 155. Cf. the excerpt from a speech by Robert Toombs on the occasion of John Brown's raid, quoted in D. Y. Thomas, "Southern Non-Slaveholders in the Election of 1860," *Political Science Quarterly*, XXVI (March, 1911), 236.

53. Frederick Law Olmsted, *A Journey Through the Slave States with Remarks on their Economy* (New York: Dix and Edwards, 1856), p. 573.

54. "Popular prejudice if not popular instinct points to a separation of black from white as a condition of the abolition of slavery." Frederick Law Olmsted, *A Journey in the Back Country* (New York: Mason Brothers, 1860), p. 4.

55. "The Wilmot Proviso," in the *Charleston Mercury*, August 13, 1847.

56. "The Wilmot Proviso—The Ruin and Injustice of Its Operation," in *ibid.*, August 14, 1847.

57. *Ibid.*, August 16, 1847.

58. *Ibid.*

59. "The Wilmot Proviso—The Insincerity of Its Advocates," in *ibid.*, August 21, 1847.

60. "The Ruin of the Slaveholder and the Slave," in *ibid.*, August 23, 1847.

61. *Ibid.*, August 25, 1847.

62. *Ibid.*

63. In 1847, notwithstanding the virtually unanimous southern opposition to the Wilmot Proviso, there was a movement to abolish slavery in western Virginia, where there were few Negroes. The platform of the movement called for the removal of the black population from the area. See William Gleason Bean, "The Ruffner Pamphlet of 1847: An Antislavery Aspect of

Virginia Sectionalism," *The Virginia Magazine of History and Biography,*
LXI (July, 1953), 272-74. The same year a Kentucky emancipationist wrote:
"There seems to be an increase of disposition to emancipation [in Kentucky]
on the ground of the superiority of free labor . . . but there is also an increased
hostility and more wide as well to the *continuance of blacks among us if
freed.* I do not meet one in 20 of them who sincerely are in favor of emancipation but would condition it on expatriation. . . . Such is the common sentiment that no politician dares advocate the propriety or right of the negro to
remain here except in servitude." John C. Young to James G. Birney, May
29, 1847, in Dwight Lowell Dumond (ed.), *Letters of James Gillespie Birney,
1831-1857* (2 vols.; New York: D. Appleton-Century Company, Inc., 1938),
II, 1076. The mere existence of these southern emancipation movements in
the midst of the virtually unanimous sentiment against the Proviso is eloquent
testimony that white supremacy, rather than the slaveholding system as such,
was the paramount concern in the South.

64. Phillips, *Course of the South to Secession,* p. 126.

65. "The Mass Meeting at Herkimer" in the *New York Weekly Evening
Post,* October 21, 1847. The "racist" aspects of the Republican antislavery
movement are underlined in Robert F. Durden, "Ambiguities in the Antislavery Crusade of the Republican Party," in Duberman (ed.), *Antislavery
Vanguard,* pp. 362-94. Richard Hofstadter has called attention to this aspect
of Lincoln's thought in *The American Political Tradition and the Men Who
Made It* (New York: Vintage Books, 1948), pp. 110-20.

66. Lowell, *Biglow Papers,* pp. 26-31. For the popularity of the *Biglow
Papers* see above, n. 21.

67. Gardiner, *The Great Issue,* p. 134; Francis P. Blair to Martin Van
Buren, June 26, 1848, in Martin Van Buren Papers.

68. *Congressional Globe,* 29 Cong., 2 Sess., p. 365. Another free-soil
congressman referred to the Negroes as the "sable pall." See *ibid.,* p. 181.
In the local movement to make western Virginia free-soil they were called
"black vomit." See Bean, "Ruffner Pamphlet," p. 272. Cf. Wilmot's remark:
"By God sir, men born and nursed of white women are not going to be
ruled by men who were brought up on the milk of some damn negro wench."
Quoted in Going, *David Wilmot,* p. 175, n. 9.

69. *Congressional Globe,* 29 Cong., 2 Sess., p. 365. When asked by a
southerner what the South was to do with its Negroes, one northwesterner
Democratic adherent of the Proviso replied that this was the South's problem:
"Take care of them in your own States; keep them out of mine." *Ibid.,* p. 181.

70. Holt, "Party Politics in Ohio," pp. 129-31. In the Ohio state election
of 1846, the Whig candidate for governor who was identified with the repeal
of the Black Laws had felt it necessary himself to propose the prohibition
of Negro immigration. See Salmon P. Chase to Joshua R. Giddings, October
20, 1846, in Edward G. Bourne, *et al.,* (eds.), "Diary and Correspondence
of Salmon P. Chase," in Volume II of the *Annual Report of the American
Historical Association for the Year 1902* (Washington: Government Printing
Office, 1903), pp. 110-11. The Ohio constitutional convention of 1850-51
received eight petitions to exclude, and five petitions to remove, the Negroes
from the state. See Frank U. Quillan, *The Color Line in Ohio* (Ann Arbor:
George Wahr, 1913), p. 61.

71. *Congressional Globe,* 29 Cong., 2 Sess., p. 427. When an effort was
made to settle the freed slaves of John Randolph in Sawyer's district, "his
friends and neighbors had mustered the blacks out of the county." See *ibid.,*

p. 91. One public meeting in Ohio resolved to "resist the settlement of blacks and mulattoes in this country to the full extent of our means, the bayonet not excepted," and to remove the Negroes already living in the county "peacefully if we can, forcibly if we must." [Longstreet], *A Voice from the South,* pp. 34-35.

72. When Governor Smith renewed his emigration proposal the following year, emphasizing again Virginia's problem with the freed Negroes and the need for a territorial outlet for her surplus black population, the New York *Evening Post,* the most prominent of the Barnburner journals, reprinted Smith's speech as an argument *for* the Wilmot Proviso, to show its readers "what sort of destiny is contemplated for California and to what consequences the peculiar institution of the South leads." "Governor Smith on the New Territory Question" in the *New York Weekly Evening Post,* December 16, 1847.

73. See, for example, the summary of Ohio's "Black Laws" in Quillan, *Color Line in Ohio,* pp. 21-24. The laws were partially repealed in 1849 as a result of a political bargain, but civil discrimination persisted. See *ibid.,* pp. 38-40, 76, 82, 86. For an account of northern efforts to exclude the Negro as well as of northern civil discrimination against him, see Leon F. Litwack, *North of Slavery, The Negro in the Free States, 1790-1860* (Chicago: The University of Chicago Press, 1961), pp. 64-97.

74. The circumstances attending the ratification of the state constitution in Oregon suggest that northern settlers in the territories were more anxious to exclude the Negro than the institution of slavery. The popular vote ratifying the constitutional clause prohibiting Negro immigration was 8640 to 1081, as compared with a vote of 7727 to 2645 on the clause prohibiting slavery. See D. G. Hill, "The Negro as a Political and Social Issue in the Oregon Territory," *The Journal of Negro History,* XXIII (April, 1948), 140-41.

75. Lewis Henry Morgan to John C. Calhoun, June 30, 1848, in Boucher and Brooks (eds.), "Correspondence Addressed to Calhoun," pp. 445-46. In 1860, one of the most popular writers in the leading Republican journal put forward the same idea. James S. Pike wrote in the New York *Tribune:* "The slaveholder is claiming to spread the Negro everywhere, and the Popular Sovereignty man stands cooly by and says 'Let him do it wherever he can.' We say the Free States should say, confine the negro to the smallest possible area. Hem him in. Coop him up. Slough him off. Preserve just so much of North America as is possible to the white man and to free institutions." Quoted in Robert F. Durden, *James Shepherd Pike: Republicanism and the American Negro, 1850-1882* (Durham: Duke University Press, 1957), p. 33.

76. Gardiner, *The Great Issue,* p. 162.

77. *Ibid.,* p. 161.

78. *Ibid.,* p. 163.

79. Jacob Brinkerhoff to Salmon P. Chase, November 22, 1847, in Salmon P. Chase Papers, Historical Society of Pennsylvania.

CHAPTER V

1. "Silas Wright and the Wilmot Proviso," in the *New York Weekly Evening Post,* April 15, 1847; F. W. Byrdsall to John C. Calhoun, June 6, 1847, in John C. Calhoun Papers; James H. Titus to Silas Wright, April 10, 1847, in the *New York Weekly Evening Post,* October 14, 1847.

2. Silas Wright to James H. Titus, April 15, 1847, in *New York Weekly Evening Post,* October 14, 1847.

3. Fitzwilliam Byrdsall to John C. Calhoun, July 19, 1847, in Jameson (ed.), "Calhoun Correspondence," p. 1125.

4. "Col. Benton's Reply, May, 1847," in *Niles' Register,* LXXII (June 12, 1847), 225; [Thomas Hart Benton] to Azariah C. Flagg, August 22, 1847, in Azariah C. Flagg Papers, New York Public Library.

5. *New York Weekly Evening Post,* June 10, July 1, 1847. Not only was it bad politics to press Wright's claims in public too early but the Barnburners also had to reckon with Wright's reluctance to become a candidate. He objected to the public use of his name. See the quotation from a letter of his in John S. Jenkins, *The Life of Silas Wright* (Auburn: Alden Beardsley and Company, 1852), pp. 240-41.

6. Quaife (ed.), *Polk Diary,* II, 458.

7. The Democrats of Preston King's home county twice expressed their support for the Wilmot Proviso. See the Washington *National Era,* July 8, September 30, 1847. The only other sign of an effort by a Barnburner politician to arouse the public on the Proviso question reported by this antislavery journal deeply interested in such matters was James Rathbun's "Manifesto" in *ibid.,* May 27, 1847. For the Barnburners' determination to press the Proviso question, see the letter dated July 10, 1847, from the Washington correspondent "Luther Martin," in the Montgomery *Tri-Weekly Flag and Advertiser,* July 17, 1847; Elwood Fisher to John C. Calhoun, August 22, 1847, in Boucher and Brooks (eds.), "Correspondence Addressed to Calhoun," p. 394.

8. Report of the Washington correspondent "Luther Martin," dated July 10, in the Montgomery *Tri-Weekly Flag and Advertiser,* July 17, 1847; "The Respect for the Union," in the *New York Herald,* July 11, 1847.

9. "Speech of the President at Augusta, Me.," in the Concord *New Hampshire Patriot and State Gazette,* July 15, 1847.

10. James Buchanan to Charles Kessler *et al.,* August 25, 1847, in Moore (ed.), *Works of Buchanan,* VII, 385.

11. David Wilmot to Preston King, September 25, 1847, in Martin Van Buren Papers.

12. *Ibid.*

13. Silas Wright to A. C. Flagg, August 22, 1847, in A. C. Flagg Papers, New York Public Library; Silas Wright to Thomas M. Burt, August 22, 1847, in Gillet, *Silas Wright,* II, 1925.

14. A. E. Burr to Gideon Welles, August 31, 1847, in Gideon Welles Papers.

15. "The Game of Disorganization" in the *Albany Evening Atlas,* September 27, 1847; "Democratic State Convention" in *ibid.,* October 2, 1847.

16. Washington *National Era,* September 23, 1847. Cf. the St. Louis *Daily Union,* September 23, 1847.

17. "Mr. Wright on the Wilmot Proviso" in the *New York Weekly Evening Post,* September 16, 1847.

18. Preston King to Azariah C. Flagg, September 24, 1847, in the Azariah C. Flagg Papers, New York Public Library.

19. Azariah C. Flagg to Martin Van Buren, September 6, 1847, in the Martin Van Buren Papers; Preston King to Azariah C. Flagg, September 24, 1847, in the Azariah C. Flagg Papers, New York Public Library.

20. Preston King to Azariah C. Flagg, September 14, 1847, in *ibid.* Martin Van Buren later justified the concession on the grounds that it disposed of the charges that the Barnburners were insisting upon an unnecessary abstrac-

tion in order to defeat annexation. See "Address to the Democratic Members of the Legislature in New York" in Bigelow (ed.), *Writings and Speeches of Tilden,* II, 545-46.

21. "Democratic State Convention," in the *Albany Evening Atlas,* October 2, 1847.

22. Except where noted the story of the events of the fourth day of the convention including direct quotations is taken from the detailed account in the *Atlas.* See "Syracuse Democratic State Convention" in the *Albany Evening Atlas,* October 18, 1847. Cf. "Democratic State Convention" in the *Albany Daily Argus,* October 18, 1847. There is a very thorough analysis of the events of the entire convention in Walter L. Ferree, "The New York Democracy—Division and Reunion, 1847-1852" (Unpublished doctoral dissertation, University of Pennsylvania, 1953), pp. 71-86.

23. "The Democratic State Convention" in the *New York Herald,* October 6, 1847.

24. Preston King to Azariah C. Flagg, October 15, 1847, in Azariah C. Flagg Papers, Columbia University; Preston King to Azariah C. Flagg, October 8, 1847, in Azariah C. Flagg Papers, New York Public Library; John Van Buren to James S. Wadsworth, October 22, 1847, in James S. Wadsworth Papers, Library of Congress.

25. *Albany Evening Atlas,* October 6, 1847.

26. John Van Buren to James S. Wadsworth, October 24, 1847, in James S. Wadsworth Papers. Cf. the account of Cambreleng's activities in the Baltimore Convention, where he served as the Barnburners' leader, in the "Proceedings of the Democratic National Convention," in the Baltimore *Sun,* May 23-27, 1848.

27. See the letter from the correspondent at Utica, dated February 18, in the *New York Weekly Tribune,* February 26, 1848.

28. "John Van Buren" in George W. Bungay, *Off-Hand Takings; Or Crayon Sketches of the Notable Men of Our Age* (New York: DeWitt and Davenport, 1854), 127-31; John Bigelow, *Retrospections of an Active Life* (3 vols.; New York: The Baker and Taylor Company, 1909), I, 86-87.

29. John Van Buren to Martin Van Buren, April 30, 1848, in Martin Van Buren Papers. After he had left the free-soil movement, the younger Van Buren liked to explain his motive for avowing free soil in terms of a story of a boy frantically pitching hay who, when asked why he was working so hard, replied: "Stranger, dad's under there." See Donovan, *Barnburners,* p. 112. What he seems to have meant by the story was not that his father led him into the movement, as some historians have suggested, but that he wanted to punish his father's (and incidentally his own) enemies.

30. In six extant letters written by John Van Buren to a close political associate between the time of the introduction of the Wilmot Proviso and the Syracuse Convention there is no mention of the Proviso, in spite of the fact that the letters are primarily concerned with political affairs and particularly the strategy of the Barnburners. See the James S. Wadsworth Papers, Library of Congress. After the convention Van Buren mentions that he had prepared resolutions endorsing the Proviso to be presented at Syracuse, but it seems clear they were primarily intended to discomfit the Hunkers. See John Van Buren to James S. Wadsworth, October 22, 1847, in *ibid.*

31. See the report of the correspondent from Albany, dated October 9, in the *New York Herald,* October 12, 1847.

32. Azariah C. Flagg to Martin Van Buren, October 13, 1847, in Martin Van Buren Papers.

33. *Albany Evening Atlas,* October 5, 1847 ff.

34. *Ibid.;* Azariah C. Flagg to Martin Van Buren, October 13, 1847, in Martin Van Buren Papers. The *Atlas* placed the Syracuse ticket on its masthead.

35. Ferree, "New York Democracy," pp. 88-89.

36. "A Mass Meeting of the Democracy of the Whole State" in the *Albany Evening Atlas,* October 9, 1847.

37. Martin Van Buren to Azariah C. Flagg, October 12, 1847, in Martin Van Buren Papers.

38. Azariah C. Flagg to Martin Van Buren, October 13, 1847, in *ibid.;* John Van Buren to James S. Wadsworth, November 8, 1847, in James S. Wadsworth Papers. The Whigs adopted the rejected Field resolution at their own state convention. See "Whig State Convention," in the *New York Weekly Tribune,* October 13, 1847; "The Wilmot Proviso Resolution," in the *Daily Albany Argus,* October 11, 1847.

39. "The Mass Meeting at Herkimer" in the *Albany Evening Atlas,* October 16, 1847; "Mass Meeting of the Democracy," in *ibid.,* October 18, 1847.

40. David Wilmot to Martin Van Buren, October 6, 1847, Martin Van Buren to David Wilmot, October 22, 1847, in Martin Van Buren Papers; Martin Van Buren to the editor of the Wilkesbarre *Republican Farmer,* October 20, 1847, in *Niles' Register,* LXXIII (November 13, 1847), 172.

41. Washington *Daily Union,* October 18, 22, 1847; John Van Buren to James S. Wadsworth, October 22, 1847, in James S. Wadsworth Papers; John Van Buren to Martin Van Buren, November 13, 1847, in Martin Van Buren Papers.

42. A full account of the meeting including the speeches is given in Gardiner, *The Great Issue,* pp. 50-57.

43. "Mass Meeting of the Democracy of New York," in the *Albany Evening Atlas,* October 27, 1847.

44. *Ibid.;* "Speech of John Van Buren" in *The Great Issue,* p. 71; "New York," in *Niles' Register,* LXXIII (October 30, 1847), 144.

45. Preston King to John A. Dix, November 13, 1847, in John A. Dix Papers.

46. John Van Buren to James S. Wadsworth, November 8, 1847, in James S. Wadsworth Papers; John Van Buren to Martin Van Buren, November 13, 1847, in Martin Van Buren Papers; Azariah C. Flagg to John A. Dix, November 13, 1847, in John A. Dix Papers; A. Whitney to Levi Woodbury, March 8, 1848, in Levi Woodbury Papers, Library of Congress.

47. John Van Buren to James S. Wadsworth, November 8, 1847, in James S. Wadsworth Papers. Cf. Albert Lester to James S. Wadsworth, December 27, 1847, Isaac Sherman to James S. Wadsworth, January 3, 1848, in *ibid.* At the Baltimore Convention, one of the Barnburner delegates selected to present the faction's case repudiated the Herkimer convention. See below, p. 134.

48. A. E. Burr to Gideon Welles, November 5, 1847, in Gideon Welles Papers; Concord *New Hampshire Patriot and State Gazette,* October 21, 1847; Cleveland *Plain Dealer,* February 9, 1848; *Hartford Times,* quoted in the Washington *Daily Union,* November 4, 1847.

49. "The Disorganizers in New York," in the *Daily Richmond Enquirer,* October 25, 1847. On the eve of the national convention there were almost

no delegates willing to advocate the exclusive admission of the Barnburners. See "Correspondence of the Nashville Union," dated May 18, in the *Tri-Weekly Nashville Union,* May 27, 1848.

50. F. W. Byrdsall to John C. Calhoun, November 12, 1847, in Boucher and Brooks (eds.), "Correspondence Addressed to Calhoun," p. 410.

51. See the report of the Washington correspondent "Ion," dated January 7, in the Baltimore *Sun,* January 8, 1848.

52. "Speech of Mr. Clay" in *Niles' Register,* LXXIII (November 27, 1847), 197-200.

53. "Mr. Clay's Resolutions" in *ibid.,* p. 190. Clay wrote to Horace Greely seeking his and Seward's support for the presidency on the basis of the resolutions. See Glyndon G. Van Deusen, *The Life of Henry Clay* (Boston: Little, Brown and Company, 1937), pp. 388-89.

54. W. W. Holden to Sandy Harris, November 13, 1847, Owen Conally to James Buchanan, December 23, 1847, in James Buchanan Papers, Historical Society of Pennsylvania; Andrew Johnson to B. McDaniel, March 24, 1848, in Andrew Johnson Papers.

55. John Douglas Pitts Fuller, *The Movement for the Acquisition of All Mexico* (Baltimore: The Johns Hopkins Press, 1936), pp. 79-136.

56. One antislavery Democratic journal, which later acquiesced in Cass's popular sovereignty platform, declared: "We are glad to see the [northern] Democratic papers generally taking exception to Secretary Buchanan's letter on the Wilmot Proviso." "The Wilmot Proviso" in the *Cleveland Plain Dealer,* September 29, 1847.

57. I. M. Storms to James Buchanan, December 12, 1847, in James Buchanan Papers, Pennsylvania Historical Society. Buchanan himself admitted it would "require great effort to render it palatable at the North." James Buchanan to [William F. Ritchie], October 31, 1847, in *ibid.*

58. "Harrisburg Convention" in the Washington *Daily Union,* March 9, 1848. Cf. "Mr. Buchanan," in the *New York Weekly Evening Post,* February 17, 1848.

59. C. A. Bradford, J. C. Bowyer, John A. Parker to James Buchanan, September 27, November 23, 1847, January 5, 1848, in James Buchanan Papers, Historical Society of Pennsylvania; "The Buchanan Movement" in the Washington *National Era,* September 23, 1847. Even Calhoun's followers remained favorably disposed toward this solution and their organ, like the rest of the southern press, responded to Buchanan's letter with approval. See "Mr. Buchanan's Letter" in the *Charleston Mercury,* September 4, 1847.

60. "Dallas' Speech in Pittsburg, September 18, 1847" in the Philadelphia *Pennsylvanian,* September 27, 1847.

61. Dallas' position was generally interpreted in the South as indistinguishable from Calhoun's. See "Mr. Dallas and the Whig" in the *Daily Richmond Enquirer,* September 29, 1847; W. W. Holden to Sandy Harris, November 13, 1847, in James Buchanan Papers, Historical Society of Pennsylvania.

62. The antislavery Chicago *Democrat* endorsed Dallas' speech as free-soil. See Joseph G. Rayback, "Presidential Politics, 1845-1848" (Unpublished doctoral dissertation, Western Reserve University, 1939), p. 178. According to one antislavery Democrat, Wilmot himself reached the same conclusion. See James Taylor to John Van Buren, April 18, 1848, in Martin Van Buren Papers.

63. "Vice-President Dallas and the Missouri Compromise" in the *Albany Evening Atlas,* September 29, 1847; "Mr. Dallas on the Slavery Question," in the *New York Weekly Evening Post,* November 18, 1847.

64. Dallas' friends distributed two to three hundred thousand copies of his Pittsburgh speech in pamphlet form. See John Van Dyke to James Buchanan, December 2, 1847, in James Buchanan Papers, Historical Society of Pennsylvania.

65. Henry Stuart Foote, *War of the Rebellion* (New York: Harper and Brothers, 1866), p. 72.

66. *Congressional Globe,* 30 Cong., 1 Sess., p. 21.

67. John C. Calhoun to Henry W. Conner, December 16, 1847, in Henry W. Conner Papers.

68. Foote, *War of the Rebellion,* p. 73.

69. *Ibid.,* p. 74.

70. John C. Calhoun to Henry W. Conner, December 16, 1847, in Henry W. Conner Papers.

71. *Charleston Mercury,* December 30, 1847; *Albany Evening Atlas,* December 23, 1847; *New York Weekly Evening Post,* December 23, 30, 1847; John M. Niles to Martin Van Buren, December 16, 1847, in Martin Van Buren Papers.

72. John C. Calhoun to Henry W. Conner, December 16, 1847, in Henry W. Conner Papers.

73. John C. Calhoun to Franklin H. Elmore, December 22, 1847, in John C. Calhoun Papers.

74. Holsey Hopkins to Howell Cobb, December 31, 1847, Henry L. Benning to Howell Cobb, February 23, 1848, in Phillips (ed.), "Toombs, Stephens, Cobb Correspondence," pp. 92, 97; Milledgeville *Federal Union,* December 21, 1847; Tallahassee *Floridian,* December 25, 1847; Mobile *Register and Journal,* January 6, 1848.

75. "Democratic Meeting" in the *Daily Richmond Enquirer,* January 7, 1848.

76. See the report of the Washington correspondent "Luther Martin," dated November 9, in the Montgomery *Tri-Weekly Flag and Advertiser,* November 16, 1848. Before Congress met, Cass had been determined not to make a public statement. See Lewis Cass to Henry Hubard, September 30, 1847, in Lewis Cass Papers, University of Michigan. Cf. a letter from Cass written in late October quoted in Philip Shriver Klein, *President James Buchanan, A Biography* (University Park: The Pennsylvania State University Press, 1962), p. 202.

77. See the report of the Washington correspondent "X," dated December 20, in the Baltimore *Sun,* December 21, 1847; Jefferson Davis to Stephen Cocke, November 30, 1847, in Dunbar Rowland (ed.), *Jefferson Davis, Constitutionalist* (10 vols.; Jackson: Mississippi Department of Archives and History, 1923), I, 180-81.

78. See Cass's speech in the Senate on February 20, 1850, in the *Congressional Globe,* 31 Cong., 1 Sess., p. 398.

79. "Communication: Has Congress Power to Institute Slavery" in the Washington *National Intelligencer,* December 22, 1847; John McLean to Salmon P. Chase, December 22, 1847, in Salmon P. Chase Papers, Historical Society of Pennsylvania.

80. *Congressional Globe,* 31 Cong., 1 Sess., p. 398.

81. Foote, *War of the Rebellion,* pp. 74-75.

82. Lewis Cass to A. O. P. Nicholson, December 24, 1847, in the Washington *Daily Union,* December 30, 1847.

83. *Ibid.*

84. *Ibid.*

85. See "Editorial Correspondence," Washington, December 17, in the *Cleveland Plain Dealer,* December 20, 1847.

86. Washington *National Era,* September 23, 1847; Springfield *Illinois State Register,* November 26, 1847; Concord *New Hampshire Patriot and State Gazette,* December 16, 1847; Columbus *Daily Ohio Statesman,* January 5, 1848; New York *Daily Globe,* January 19, 1848; *Cleveland Plain Dealer,* February 16, 1848.

87. John McLean to Salmon P. Chase, December 22, 1847, February 8, 1848, in Salmon P. Chase Papers, Historical Society of Pennsylvania.

88. Lewis Cass to A. O. P. Nicholson, December 24, 1847, in the Washington *Daily Union,* December 30, 1847.

89. For the southern Democratic interpretation of the Nicholson letter, see "Gen. Cass's Nicholson Letter," in the Washington *Daily Union,* March 17, 1852. For the northern Democratic interpretation, see Chapter VIII, n. 82.

90. John C. Calhoun to Henry Gourdin, January 8, 1848, in John C. Calhoun Papers; *Charleston Mercury,* January 6, 17, 1848; *Albany Evening Atlas,* January 2, 1848; *New York Weekly Evening Post,* January 6, 1848; Milledgeville *Federal Union,* January 11, 1848; Mobile *Register and Journal,* January 6, 1848; Tallahassee *Floridian,* January 15, 1848; *Tri-Weekly Nashville Union,* January 21, 1848; Jackson *Mississippian,* January 11, 1848; Springfield *Illinois State Journal,* January 21, February 4, 25, 1848; Detroit *Daily Free Press,* January 12, 17, 21, 1848; *Cleveland Plain Dealer,* January 20, 21, 1848; *Albany Daily Argus,* January 4, 1848.

91. See the reports of the Washington correspondents in the Baltimore *Sun,* January 11, 1848, the New York *Journal of Commerce,* January 27, 1848, and the *Cleveland Plain Dealer,* February 16, 1848. Cf. "The Presidential Canvas in Congress" in the Baltimore *Sun,* January 2, 1848. Before the Nicholson letter appeared, John Tyler wrote that Buchanan appeared to be the obvious favorite for the nomination. See John Tyler to Caleb Cushing, November 1, 1847, in Tyler (ed.), *Tylers Letters,* II, 460. This was because of southern distrust on the Proviso question. One prominent southern journal, after arguing that the South had many friends in the North, linked Cass with John Van Buren, Preston King, David Wilmot, and other enemies of "southern rights." See "Who Are the Friends of the South?" in the Montgomery *Tri-Weekly Flag and Advertiser,* October 30, 1847.

CHAPTER VI

1. "Mass Meeting of the Democracy of New York" in the *Albany Evening Atlas,* October 27, 1847. Full accounts of the Barnburners' meetings at Herkimer and Utica, including resolutions, addresses, and many of the speeches, are given in Gardiner, *The Great Issue,* pp. 50 ff.

2. John Van Buren to James S. Wadsworth, November 8, 1847, in James S. Wadsworth Papers.

3. "Democratic Caucus" in the *Albany Evening Atlas,* November 17, 1847.

4. "Legislative Caucus—State Representation" in *ibid.,* November 19, 1847.

5. "The Last Bolt—Formal Secession of the Conservative Party" in *ibid.,* December 18, 1847.

6. Ferree, "New York Democracy," pp. 115-16.

7. *New York Herald,* January 17, 26, 1848; J. O. Barnes to Levi Woodbury, May 18, 1848, in Levi Woodbury Papers, Library of Congress.

8. "New York State Democratic Convention" in the Washington *Daily Union,* February 14, 1848.

9. "Can Slavery Exist in Mexico—Common Ground on which the Democracy Can Unite," in the New York *Daily Globe,* January 19, 1848. The letter attracted a great deal of attention outside New York. See the letters of the Washington correspondents in the Louisville *Daily Democrat,* January 28, 1848, and the Jackson *Mississippian,* March 10, 1848.

10. "New York State Democratic Convention" in the Washington *Daily Union,* February 14, 1848.

11. Charles Sumner to Joshua R. Giddings, December 1, 1847, quoted in George W. Julian, *Life of Joshua R. Giddings* (Chicago: A. C. McClurg and Company, 1892), p. 214; David Wilmot to Henry W. Simpson, December 26, 1847, in Simon Gratz Papers, Historical Society of Pennsylvania; Francis P. Blair to Martin Van Buren, February 29, 1848, Martin Van Buren to John Van Buren, May 3, 1848, in Martin Van Buren Papers. Van Buren moved to New York early in January and remained there until early in April. See Martin Van Buren to Gorham A. Worth, January 2, 1848, Martin Van Buren to A. W. Bradford, April 7, 1848, in Martin Van Buren Papers.

12. John Van Buren to Francis P. Blair, February 22, 1848, in Francis P. Blair Papers, Princeton University.

13. "Democratic State Convention" in the *Albany Evening Atlas,* February 27, 1848.

14. *Ibid.*

15. One correspondent reported on February 16 that he had definite information that Taylor would be nominated at Utica. See the *New York Herald,* February 17, 1848. Cf. the report of another correspondent at the Utica Convention, dated February 18, in the *New York Weekly Tribune,* February 26, 1848. Some of the Barnburners' friends in New England were shocked at their interest in Taylor. See William Pettit to Gideon Welles, February 22, 1848, A. E. Burr to Gideon Welles, February 23, 1848, in Gideon Welles Papers.

16. *Niles' Register,* LXXIII (July 10, 1847), 295.

17. Zachary Taylor to James W. Taylor, May 18, 1847, in *ibid.,* LXXIII (July 3, 1847), 288.

18. James W. Taylor to John Van Buren, November 2, 1847, in Martin Van Buren Papers. News of the Van Burens' interest in Taylor spread quickly. Early in 1848, the journalist, Henry J. Raymond, reported rumors that the Van Burens intended to support Taylor for the presidency. See Henry W. Raymond (ed.), "Extracts from the Journal of Henry J. Raymond," *Scribners' Monthly,* XIX (November, 1879), 60. By February, Stephen A. Douglas was writing that "John Van Buren is known to be a Taylor man against all the world." Stephen A. Douglas to Samuel Treat, February 19, 1848, in Robert W. Johannsen (ed.), *The Letters of Stephen A. Douglas* (Urbana: University of Illinois Press, 1961), p. 157.

19. Ellwood Fisher to John C. Calhoun, February 26, 1848, in John C. Calhoun Papers.

20. "Democratic State Convention" in the *Albany Evening Atlas,* February 27, 1848.

21. Francis P. Blair to Martin Van Buren, February 29, 1848, in Martin Van Buren Papers; James R. Doolittle to Zachary Taylor, February 22, 1848, in "Negro Question: Slavery and Reconstruction—Doolittle Correspondence,"

Publications of the Southern Historical Association, XI (January, 1907), 94-95.

22. "Democratic State Convention," in the *Albany Evening Atlas,* February 27, 1848. One reason for this decision was the freedom of action and flexibility it left to the national delegation. See Azariah C. Flagg to Gideon Welles, February 17, 1848, in Gideon Welles Papers.

23. "Levi Woodbury" in the Washington *National Era,* August 19, 1847.

24. Luke Woodbury to Levi Woodbury, October 16, 1847, in Levi Woodbury Papers.

25. Luke Woodbury to Levi Woodbury, October 28, 1847, Nehemiah Moses to Levi Woodbury, March 28, 1848, in *ibid.;* report of the correspondent, "Luther Martin," dated November 2, 1847, in the Montgomery *Tri-Weekly Flag and Advertiser,* November 9, 1847.

26. *Ibid.;* N. E. Upham to Levi Woodbury, March 5, 12, 1848, in Levi Woodbury Papers.

27. The official state Democratic journal claimed that, in contrast with the state election the previous summer, the Whigs had failed in their effort to distract the people from the true issues by their antislavery appeal. See "The Election—Its Results and Its Teachings," in the Concord *New Hampshire Patriot and State Gazette,* March 23, 1848. The Democrats had emphasized their commitment to the Wilmot Proviso much more strongly in the state election the previous summer. Cf. Nehemiah Moses to Levi Woodbury, March 23, 1848, in Levi Woodbury Papers.

28. "A Granite State Democrat" in the Washington *Daily Union,* March 25, 1848.

29. John D. Kellogg, A. Whitney, R. Ela, Lathrop Eddy, to Levi Woodbury, February 9, March 8, April 4, May 10, 1848, in Levi Woodbury Papers.

30. John D. Kellogg, George Bleeker, A. Whitney, Richard Jenness to Levi Woodbury, February 9, March 18, May 13, May 15, 1848, in *ibid.*

31. John M. Niles to Martin Van Buren, April 18, 1848, in Martin Van Buren Papers; Levi Woodbury to Samuel Treat, March 17, 1848, in Samuel Treat Papers.

32. See the report of the Washington correspondent, dated May 12, in the Baltimore *Sun,* May 13, 1848.

33. "Hon. Levi Woodbury," in the Concord *New Hampshire Patriot and State Gazette,* March 16, 1848.

34. "The Presidency" in *ibid.,* April 6, 1848; A. H. H. Clapp to Levi Woodbury, May 17, 18, 19, 1848, Richard Jenness to Levi Woodbury, May 19, 1848, in Levi Woodbury Papers. Cf. the report of the Boston correspondent in the *New York Herald,* May 22, 1848.

35. Charles McCool Snyder, *The Jacksonian Heritage, Pennsylvania Politics, 1833-1848* (Harrisburg: The Pennsylvania Historical and Museum Commission, 1958), pp. 188-92, 207.

36. John Coyle, Alfred Gilmore, Robert Tyler to James Buchanan, November 30, December 1, December 7, 1847, in James Buchanan Papers, Historical Society of Pennsylvania; George Plitt to James Buchanan, December 27, 1847, in James Buchanan Papers, Library of Congress.

37. E. W. Hutter to James Buchanan, March 2, 1848, in James Buchanan Papers, Historical Society of Pennsylvania. The vote in the convention for Buchanan was more than twice that of his opponents. See "Pennsylvania Democratic State Convention" in the Washington *Daily Union,* March 6, 1848.

38. George Plitt to James Buchanan, March 4, 1848, in James Buchanan Papers, Library of Congress; "Pennsylvania Democratic State Convention" in the Washington *Daily Union,* March 6, 1848.

39. John B. Sterigere to James Buchanan, March 11, 1848, John W. Forney to James Buchanan, March 12, 1848, in James Buchanan Papers, Historical Society of Pennsylvania.

40. John B. Sterigere to James Buchanan, March 11, 1848, in *ibid.*; "Pennsylvania State Convention" in the Washington *Daily Union,* March 9, 1848.

41. *Congressional Globe,* 30 Cong., 1 Sess., p. 306.

42. Going, *David Wilmot,* pp. 305-8.

43. *Ibid.*; John W. Forney to James Buchanan, March 7, 1848, in James Buchanan Papers, Historical Society of Pennsylvania.

44. *Ibid.* Even Buchanan misunderstood the resolution. See John B. Sterigere to James Buchanan, April 21, 1848, in *ibid.*

45. Detroit *Daily Free Press,* March 20, 1848; Springfield *Illinois State Register,* March 24, 1848; Jackson *Mississippian,* March 24, 1848; Edmund Burke to Levi Woodbury, April 24, 1848, in Levi Woodbury Papers; John B. Sterigere to John Van Buren, April 22, 1848, in Martin Van Buren Papers.

46. E. W. Hutter to James Buchanan, April 5, 1848, in James Buchanan Papers, Historical Society of Pennsylvania.

47. John W. Forney to James Buchanan, March 12, 1848, John B. Sterigere to James Buchanan, April 21, 1848, in *ibid.*

48. John M. Reed to James Buchanan, March 6, 15, 1848, in *ibid.*

49. Daniel T. Jenks to James Buchanan, March 24, 1848, John M. Reed to James Buchanan, April 12, May 12, 1848, in *ibid.*

50. John W. Forney to James Buchanan, May 11, 1848, John M. Reed to James Buchanan, May 12, 1848, in *ibid.*; Philadelphia *Pennsylvanian,* May 12, 1848.

51. A. H. H. Clapp to Levi Woodbury, May 10, 1848, in Levi Woodbury Papers.

52. Benjamin F. Butler to Martin Van Buren, May 31, 1844, in Martin Van Buren Papers; Holt, "Party Politics in Ohio," p. 89, n. 178.

53. Holt, "Party Politics in Ohio," p. 174; Samuel Medary to Martin Van Buren, December 27, 1847, in Martin Van Buren Papers; Elwood Fisher to John C. Calhoun, December 2, 1846, in Jameson (ed.), "Calhoun Correspondence," p. 1098; Elwood Fisher to John C. Calhoun, December 4, 1847, in John C. Calhoun Papers.

54. Samuel Medary to Martin Van Buren, December 27, 1847, in Martin Van Buren Papers.

55. Holt, "Party Politics in Ohio," pp. 152-53.

56. Samuel Medary to Martin Van Buren, May 5, 1848, in Martin Van Buren Papers.

57. Holt, "Party Politics in Ohio," pp. 108, 116, 174; Samuel Medary to Martin Van Buren, May 5, 1848, in Martin Van Buren Papers.

58. C. P. Wolcott to Edwin M. Stanton, December 7, 1848, quoted in Phila Stanton Wolcott to Editor of the *Sun,* in the New York *Sun,* March 9, 1872.

59. John R. John to John P. Hale, December 25, 1847, in John P. Hale Papers, New Hampshire Historical Society; C. P. Wolcott to Edwin M. Stanton, December 12, 1847, quoted in Phila Stanton Wolcott to Editor of the *Sun,* in the New York *Sun,* March 9, 1872; Salmon P. Chase to Edwin M. Stanton, January 9, 1848, in Edwin M. Stanton Papers, Library of Congress;

D. Radebaugh and William Neede to Martin Van Buren, December 6, 1847, in Martin Van Buren Papers.

60. See the correspondent's report dated January 8 in the Columbus *Ohio State Journal,* January 10, 1848; Salmon P. Chase to Edwin M. Stanton, January 9, 1848, in Edwin M. Stanton Papers.

61. "Columbus Correspondence," January 8 in the *Cleveland Plain Dealer,* January 8, 1848; Salmon P. Chase to Edwin M. Stanton, January 9, 1848, in Edwin M. Stanton Papers.

62. "Democratic State Convention Resolutions" in the Columbus *Daily Ohio Statesman,* January 11, 1848.

63. One of the members of the platform committee later admitted that the resolutions were intended to satisfy both adherents and opponents of the Wilmot Proviso. See Robert B. Warden, *An Account of the Private Life and Public Services of Salmon Portland Chase* (Cincinnati: Wilstoch, Baldwin and Company, 1874), p. 317. Stanton found them particularly objectionable for that very reason, but both Tappan and Brinkerhoff accepted them as satisfactory. See Edwin M. Stanton to Salmon P. Chase, February 16, 1848, in Salmon P. Chase Papers, Historical Society of Pennsylvania.

64. See the correspondent's report dated January 8, in the Columbus *Ohio State Journal,* January 10, 1848; Samuel Medary to Martin Van Buren, May 5, 1848, James W. Taylor to John Van Buren, April 18, 1848, in Martin Van Buren Papers.

65. "Democratic State Convention Resolutions" in the Columbus *Daily Ohio Statesman,* January 11, 1848.

66. "Ohio Nomination" in *Niles' Register,* LXXIII (January 15, 1848), 320.

67. "General Cass in Ohio" in the *New York Weekly Evening Post,* January 28, 1848.

68. [J. O. Barnes] to Levi Woodbury, February 7, 1848, in Levi Woodbury Papers; Francis P. Blair to Martin Van Buren, January 23, 1848 [misdated 1847], in Martin Van Buren Papers.

69. Salmon P. Chase to Edwin M. Stanton, January 9, 1848, in Edwin M. Stanton Papers; Edwin M. Stanton to Salmon P. Chase, February 16, 1848, Jacob Brinkerhoff to Salmon P. Chase, February 2, March 28, 1848, in Salmon P. Chase Papers, Historical Society of Pennsylvania; James Taylor to John Van Buren, April 18, 1848, in Martin Van Buren Papers.

70. Jeff G. Thurber to Alpheus Felch, April 15, 1848, E. Ransom to Alpheus Felch, June 10, 1848, in Alpheus Felch Papers.

71. "Michigan—Gen. Cass," in the Charleston *Mercury,* February 21, 1848; Theodore Clark Smith, *The Liberty and Free Soil Parties in the Northwest* (New York: Longmans, Green and Company, 1897), p. 122. The freesoil resolution was killed in the state senate. See Floyd Benjamin Streeter, *Political Parties in Michigan, 1837-1860* (Lansing: Michigan Historical Commission, 1918), p. 96.

72. [Charles A.] Loomis to his father, March 8, 1848, quoted in William L. Jenks, "Senator Charles A. Loomis," *Michigan History Magazine,* X (April, 1926), 217-18.

73. "Nomination of Gen. Cass" in *Niles' Register,* LXXIII (February 19, 1848), 393.

74. *Albany Evening Atlas,* May 11, 1848.

75. "Indiana Democratic State Convention" in the Washington *Daily Union,* January 22, 1848.

76. "Indiana" in *Niles' Register,* LXXIII (January 29, 1848), 339; [J. O. Barnes] to Levi Woodbury, February 7, 1848, in Levi Woodbury Papers.

77. Francis P. Blair to Martin Van Buren, January 23, 1848 [misdated 1847], in Martin Van Buren Papers; Elwood Fisher to John C. Calhoun, January 17, 1848, in Boucher and Brooks (eds.), "Correspondence Addressed to Calhoun," p. 423.

78. Springfield *Illinois State Register,* January-April, 1848.

79. "Democratic State Convention" in *ibid.,* April 28, 1848.

80. Samuel Treat to A. H. H. Clapp, April 25, 1848, A. H. H. Clapp to Levi Woodbury, April 10, 1848, J. O. Dow to Levi Woodbury, May 16, 1848, in Levi Woodbury Papers.

81. Samuel Treat to A. H. H. Clapp, April 25, 1848, in *ibid.;* "Democratic State Convention" in the Springfield *Illinois State Register,* April 28, 1848.

82. Samuel Treat to A. H. H. Clapp, April 25, 1848, J. M. Brodhead to Levi Woodbury, May 13, 1848, Edmund Burke to Levi Woodbury, May 17, 1848, in Levi Woodbury Papers.

83. J. P. Bartlett to John P. Hale, November 27, 1847, in John P. Hale Papers. It seemed that Wentworth might waver for a time after the Baltimore Convention, but this was apparently to insure renomination in his district, which was strongly free-soil. See *ibid.* After his renomination he expressed surprise that there was any doubt about his regularity. See his letter of June 23, in the Springfield *Illinois State Register,* July 7, 1848.

84. "Proceedings of the Democratic Convention" in the Jackson *Mississippian,* January 14, 1848.

85. See the report of the correspondent "Oliver" in the *New York Weekly Evening Post,* January 28, 1848; "Mississippi" in the *New York Weekly Tribune,* February 5, 1848.

86. "Arkansas" in the Washington *Daily Union,* January 24, 1848.

87. "Texas" in the *Daily Richmond Enquirer,* March 18, 1848.

88. "Louisiana Democratic State Convention" in the Washington *Daily Union,* March 27, 1848.

89. "State Convention" in the *Tri-Weekly Nashville Union,* January 15, 1848.

90. "Presidential Signs" in *ibid.,* March 18, 1848; Francis P. Blair to Martin Van Buren, January 23, 1848 [misdated 1847], in Martin Van Buren Papers.

91. S. E. Benson to A. O. P. Nicholson, April 17, 1848, in Miscellaneous Papers (S. E. Benson), New York Historical Society; John M. Niles to Martin Van Buren, April 18, 1848, in Martin Van Buren Papers; Alfred Balch to James Buchanan, May 5, 1848, in James Buchanan Papers, Historical Society of Pennsylvania; Henry W. Conner to John C. Calhoun, May 24, 1848, in John C. Calhoun Papers.

92. "Democratic County Meeting" in the St. Louis *Daily Union,* January 10, 1848; Francis P. Blair to Martin Van Buren, February 2, 1848, in Martin Van Buren Papers.

93. Lewis Cass to Aaron Hobart, December 3, 1847, in Lewis Cass Papers, University of Michigan.

94. "Address of the Democratic State Convention of Missouri" in the *Jefferson Inquirer,* April 15, 1848; Frank P. Blair, Jr. to Francis P. Blair, April 22, 1848, Francis P. Blair to Martin Van Buren, May 2, 1848, in Martin Van Buren Papers; A. H. H. Clapp to Levi Woodbury, April 3, 1848,

Samuel Treat to A. H. H. Clapp, April 25, 1848, Allen M. Lane to Levi Woodbury, April 30, 1848, in Levi Woodbury Papers.

95. See Chapter VII, n. 93.

96. Robert B. McAtee to James Buchanan, March 15, 1848, in James Buchanan Papers, Historical Society of Pennsylvania; Richard M. Johnson to Lewis Cass, April 6, 1848, in Lewis Cass Papers, University of Michigan; J. Knox Walker to James K. Polk, May 22, 24, 1848, in James K. Polk Papers.

97. "Proceedings of the Democratic Convention" in the Milledgeville *Federal Union,* December 28, 1847.

98. E. S. Barclay to Howell Cobb, December 24, 1847, in Robert P. Brooks (ed.), "Howell Cobb Papers," *The Georgia Historical Quarterly,* V (June, 1951), 31. Cf. Holsey Hopkins to Howell Cobb, December 31, 1847, in Phillips (ed.), "Toombs, Stephens, Cobb Correspondence," p. 92. Cobb was one of the strong supporters of Cass who requested publication of the Nicholson letter. See the report of the Washington correspondent "Ion," dated December 31, in the Baltimore *Sun,* January 1, 1848.

99. *Huntsville Democrat,* August 25, 1847.

100. Dixon H. Lewis to the Editors of the *State Guard,* October 6, 1847, in the Montgomery *Tri-Weekly Flag and Advertiser,* October 16, 1847.

101. James E. Saunders to George S. Houston, December 3, 1847, in George S. Houston Papers.

102. *Ibid.;* "United States Senator" in the Montgomery *Tri-Weekly Flag and Advertiser,* October 28, 1847.

103. William Fleming *et al.* to William R. King, December 10, 1847, in the Montgomery *Tri-Weekly Flag and Advertiser,* January 15, 1848; James E. Saunders to George S. Houston, January 16, 1848, F. G. Norman to George S. Houston, January 23, 1848, in George S. Houston Papers. Norman, one of the signers of the questionnaire, admitted the hostile intention toward Lewis.

104. John A. Campbell to John C. Calhoun, November 20, 1847, in Jameson (ed.), "Calhoun Correspondence," p. 1144; Charles Woodbury, William L. Yancey, Dixon H. Lewis to Levi Woodbury, January 28, March 10, March 28, 1848, in Levi Woodbury Papers.

105. Dixon H. Lewis to William Fleming *et al.,* December 12, 1847, in the Montgomery *Tri-Weekly Flag and Advertiser,* January 15, 1848.

106. J. A. Campbell to John C. Calhoun, December 20, 1847, in Jameson (ed.), "Calhoun Correspondence," p. 1152. One Democratic journal claimed that Lewis' commitment made his election a victory for the regular faction. See "The Late Senatorial Election," in the Mobile *Register and Journal,* January 19, 1848. The correspondence was widely reprinted, including in the Washington *Daily Union,* January 22, 1848.

107. John C. Calhoun to Joseph W. Lesesne, February 11, 1848, in Joseph W. Lesesne Papers, The University of North Carolina. Cf. Henry W. Conner to Armistead Burt, February 11, 1848, in Armistead Burt Papers, Duke University.

108. McMillan, "Taylor's Presidential Campaign in Alabama," p. 89. In late January, Woodbury's son still thought Yancey was probably "in the Taylor movement." Charles Woodbury to Levi Woodbury, January 28, 1848, in Levi Woodbury Papers.

109. W. L. Yancey to Wm. P. Browne, January 31, 1848, in the Montgomery *Tri-Weekly Flag and Advertiser,* February 8, 1848.

110. "The Democratic Meeting on Monday Night" in *ibid.,* January 6, 1848.

111. *Ibid.*; "Democratic Meeting" in *ibid.*

112. "Democratic Meeting" in *ibid.*

113. *Ibid.*

114. See "The Taylor Meeting at the Capitol," in *ibid.*, January 11, 1848.

115. "Democratic Meeting" in *ibid.*, January 20, 1848.

116. "The Prospect Before Us," in *ibid.*, February 5, 1848; F. J. Lindsay to John C. Calhoun, February 9, 1848, in John C. Calhoun Papers.

117. See the article signed "PW" in the Montgomery *Tri-Weekly Flag and Advertiser,* February 12, 1848.

118. See the article signed "PW" in *ibid.*, February 15, 1848.

119. *New York Herald,* January 17, 26, 1848.

120. William L. Yancey to Levi Woodbury, March 10, 1848, in Levi Woodbury Papers; J. J. Lockhart to George S. Houston, January 7, February 29, 1848, James E. Saunders to George S. Houston, January 15, February 26, 1848, in George S. Houston Papers.

121. James E. Saunders to George S. Houston, January 15, 1848, Edward A. O'Neal to George S. Houston, February 6, 1848, in George S. Houston Papers; William L. Yancey to Levi Woodbury, March 10, 1848, in Levi Woodbury Papers.

122. James E. Saunders to George S. Houston, February 26, 1848, in George S. Houston Papers.

123. *Congressional Globe,* 30 Cong., 1 Sess., pp. 241, 261.

124. "Democratic Convention" in the Montgomery *Tri-Weekly Flag and Advertiser,* February 12, 1848.

125. "Journal of the Democratic Convention" in *ibid.*, February 17, 1848.

126. *Ibid.*; John A. Campbell to John C. Calhoun, March 1, 1848, in Boucher and Brooks (eds.), "Correspondence Addressed to Calhoun," p. 431; William L. Yancey to the Editor of the *State Gazette,* in the Montgomery *Tri-Weekly Flag and Advertiser,* April 18, 1848.

127. "Journal of the Democratic Convention" in the Montgomery *Tri-Weekly Flag and Advertiser,* February 17, 1848.

128. William L. Yancey to Levi Woodbury, March 10, 1848, in Levi Woodbury Papers; R. Norman to George S. Houston, April 13, 1848, in George S. Houston Papers.

129. "Journal of the Democratic Convention" in the Montgomery *Tri-Weekly Flag and Advertiser,* February 17, 1848.

130. William L. Yancey to the Editor of the *State Gazette,* April 14, 1848, in *ibid.*, April 18, 1848; William L. Yancey to Levi Woodbury, March 10, 1848, in Levi Woodbury Papers; George W. Gayle to James Buchanan, February 16, 1848, in James Buchanan Papers, Historical Society of Pennsylvania; report of the correspondent "Jefferson," dated May 15, in the *New York Herald,* May 16, 1848.

131. "The Monitor" in the Montgomery *State Gazette,* July 11, 1848; William L. Yancey to Levi Woodbury, March 10, 1848, in Levi Woodbury Papers.

132. George W. Gayle to James Buchanan, February 16, 1848, in James Buchanan Papers, Historical Society of Pennsylvania; James E. Saunders to George S. Houston, April 3, 1848, in George S. Houston Papers. In his original report of the convention, Saunders had not thought Yancey's resolutions important enough to mention. See James E. Saunders to George S. Houston, February 26, 1848, in George S. Houston Papers.

133. George W. Gayle to James Buchanan, March 9, 1848, in James Buchanan Papers, Historical Society of Pennsylvania.

134. "Journal of the Democratic Convention" in the Montgomery *Tri-Weekly Flag and Advertiser,* February 17, 1848; *ibid.,* April 13, 1848.

135. *Ibid.,* March 7, 18, 1848; William Lowndes Yancey, *An Address to the People of Alabama* (Montgomery: Office of the Flag and Advertiser, 1848), pp. 23-27.

136. Montgomery *Tri-Weekly Flag and Advertiser,* April 13, 1848.

137. George W. Gayle to James Buchanan, March 9, 1848, in James Buchanan Papers, Historical Society of Pennsylvania; William L. Yancey to Levi Woodbury, March 10, 1848, in Levi Woodbury Papers.

138. William L. Yancey to Levi Woodbury, March 10, 1848, in Levi Woodbury Papers.

139. Dixon H. Lewis to Levi Woodbury, March 24, 1848, in *ibid.*

140. "Democratic State Convention" in the Tallahassee *Floridian,* March 25, 1848. On the day of the convention the Calhounite organ in Tallahassee had reprinted the Alabama Platform. See "Alabama State Democratic Convention" in the Tallahassee *Southern Journal,* March 20, 1848.

141. "Virginia Democratic Convention Resolutions" in the *Daily Richmond Enquirer,* March 6, 1848; John C. Calhoun to Henry W. Conner, April 20, 1848, in Henry W. Conner Papers.

142. "The Virginia Doctrine" in the *New York Weekly Evening Post,* March 16, 1848; Montgomery *Tri-Weekly Flag and Advertiser,* April 13, 1848; John A. Parker to James Buchanan, May 8, 1848, in James Buchanan Papers, Historical Society of Pennsylvania.

143. John A. Parker to James Buchanan, May 8, June 9, 1848, in James Buchanan Papers, Historical Society of Pennsylvania.

144. J. D. Wescott to Joel R. Poinsett, November 24, 1847, in Joel R. Poinsett Papers, Historical Society of Pennsylvania; James Buchanan to Robert Tyler, July 13, 1848, in Tyler, *Tylers Letters,* II, 460; *Daily Richmond Enquirer,* June 30, 1848; R. M. T. Hunter to John Randolph Tucker, May 28, 1848, in Tucker Family Papers, The University of North Carolina.

145. John A. Parker, J. C. Bowyer, Richard Pollard to James Buchanan, May 3, 11, 21, 1848, in James Buchanan Papers, Historical Society of Pennsylvania.

146. *Daily Richmond Enquirer,* March 3, 6, 1848.

147. W. W. Holden to Sandy Harris, November 13, 1847, Sandy Harris to James Buchanan, November 15, December 3, 1847, in James Buchanan Papers, Historical Society of Pennsylvania.

148. Raleigh *North Carolina Standard,* April 19, 1848.

149. See the report of the Washington correspondent dated May 22, in the *New York Weekly Tribune,* May 27, 1848.

150. Henry W. Conner to John C. Calhoun, April 13, 1848, in Jameson (ed.), "Calhoun Correspondence," pp. 1166-67.

151. "The Meeting at Georgetown" in the *Charleston Mercury,* May 5, 1848.

152. John C. Calhoun to Henry W. Conner, April 4, 28, 1848, in Henry W. Conner Papers.

153. Armistead Burt to Henry W. Conner, May 21, 1848, in *ibid.*

154. John C. Calhoun to Henry W. Conner, April 20, 1848, in *ibid.* The Calhounites did not have much confidence that Woodbury could be elected even if he got the nomination. See John A. Campbell to John C. Calhoun,

November 20, 1847, in Jameson (ed.), "Calhoun Correspondence," p. 1144; Henry W. Conner to Armistead Burt, February 11, 1848, in Armistead Burt Papers.

155. Armistead Burt to Henry W. Conner, May 28, 1848, in Henry W. Conner Papers. Cf. Henry W. Conner to Armistead Burt, January 26, May 25, 1848, in Armistead Burt Papers; John C. Calhoun to Joseph W. Lesesne, February 11, 1848, in Joseph W. Lesesne Papers.

CHAPTER VII

1. "Mr. Rathbun's Speech to the Utica Convention" in Gardiner, *The Great Issue,* p. 94.

2. "George Rathbun's Attack on Gen. Cass" in the Detroit *Daily Free Press,* March 13, 1848. The full text of the letter, which was dated September 30, 1846, was reprinted one month later under the title "George Rathbun— His Inconsistency Proved," in *ibid.,* April 13, 1848.

3. "Hon. George Rathbun" in the *New York Weekly Tribune,* May 6, 1848. Two clauses have been transposed in the statement as reported (without changing its meaning) in order to make it read more clearly.

4. James Buchanan to John Meredith Read, January 18, 1848, in James Buchanan Papers, Historical Society of Pennsylvania; R. Ela to Levi Woodbury, April 4, 1848, in Levi Woodbury Papers. Dallas' supporters also hoped to capitalize on the Barnburners' antagonism. See J. I. Albert to Lewis Coryell, April 12, 1848, in Lewis Coryell Papers, Historical Society of Pennsylvania.

5. John W. Forney to James Buchanan, April 7, 1848, in James Buchanan Papers, Historical Society of Pennsylvania.

6. John B. Sterigere to John Van Buren, April 22, 1848, John Van Buren to Martin Van Buren, April 30, 1848, in Martin Van Buren Papers; John B. Sterigere to James Buchanan, May 4, 1848, in James Buchanan Papers, Historical Society of Pennsylvania.

7. John Van Buren to John B. Sterigere, May 1, 1848, J. Porter Brawley to James Buchanan, May 13, 1848, John B. Sterigere to James Buchanan, May 14, 16, 1848, in James Buchanan Papers, Historical Society of Pennsylvania.

8. R. Ela to Levi Woodbury, April 4, 1848, in Levi Woodbury Papers.

9. John Van Buren to Martin Van Buren, April 30, 1848, in Martin Van Buren Papers; N. G. Upham to Levi Woodbury, March 16, 1848, Fernando Wood to J. O. Barnes, May 9, 1848, Richard Jenness to Levi Woodbury, May 15, 1848, in Levi Woodbury Papers.

10. R. Ela to Levi Woodbury, April 4, 1848, Lathrop F. Eddy to Levi Woodbury, May 10, 1848, in Levi Woodbury Papers; Albert Lester to Charles S. Benson, April 26, 1848, in Samuel J. Tilden Papers, New York Public Library.

11. Fernando Wood to J. O. Barnes, May 9, 1848, Lathrop F. Eddy to Levi Woodbury, May 10, 1848, in Levi Woodbury Papers.

12. Levi Woodbury to Samuel Treat, April 18, 1848, in Samuel Treat Papers; Lathrop F. Eddy to Levi Woodbury, May 10, 1848, in Levi Woodbury Papers.

13. John D. Kellogg to Levi Woodbury, May 11, 1848, Fernando Wood to J. O. Barnes, May 11, 1848, J. O. Barnes to Levi Woodbury, May 18 (morning), 1848, in Levi Woodbury Papers.

14. Lathrop F. Eddy to Levi Woodbury, May 10, 1848, in *ibid.*

15. *Ibid.*; A. Whitney to Levi Woodbury, May 13, 1848, in *ibid.*

16. Lathrop F. Eddy, Edmund Burke, A. H. H. Clapp, J. O. Barnes to Levi Woodbury, May 10, 17, 18 (morning), 1848, in *ibid.*

17. A. Whitney to Levi Woodbury, May 13, 1848, in *ibid.*

18. John Van Buren to Martin Van Buren, April 30, 1848, in Martin Van Buren Papers; John Van Buren to John B. Sterigere, May 1, 1848, in James Buchanan Papers, Historical Society of Pennsylvania.

19. John B. Sterigere to James Buchanan, May 4, 1848, John B. Sterigere to John Van Buren, May 9, 1848, in James Buchanan Papers, Historical Society of Pennsylvania.

20. "The Alabama Resolutions—Extract of a Letter from Yancey to *Alabama State Gazette*" in the Washington *Daily Union,* May 14, 1848; A. H. H. Clapp to Levi Woodbury, May 18, 1848, in Levi Woodbury Papers.

21. "Mr. Woodbury's Opinions" in the *New York Weekly Evening Post,* May 25, 1848; Ben ——— to Levi Woodbury, May 17, 1848, in Levi Woodbury Papers.

22. Richard Jenness, A. H. H. Clapp, J. O. Barnes, Henry Hibbard to Levi Woodbury, May 15, 18, 18 (afternoon), 19, 1848, in Levi Woodbury Papers.

23. J. M. Brodhead to Levi Woodbury, May 13, 1848, in *ibid.*

24. William L. Yancey to James Buchanan, May 3, 1848, in James Buchanan Papers, Historical Society of Pennsylvania.

25. Levi Woodbury to William L. Yancey, May 15, 1848, Richard Jenness to Levi Woodbury, May 17, 1848, in Levi Woodbury Papers.

26. A. H. H. Clapp to Levi Woodbury, May 18, 1848, in Levi Woodbury Papers; Yancey, *Address to the People of Alabama,* p. 53.

27. A. H. H. Clapp to Levi Woodbury, May 19, 1848, in Levi Woodbury Papers.

28. Benjamin F. Butler to R. H. Gillet, May 8, 1848 (copy) in Martin Van Buren Papers; J. O. Barnes to Levi Woodbury, May 18 (morning), 1848, in Levi Woodbury Papers.

29. Preston King to Gideon Welles, March 18, May 1, 1848, in Gideon Welles Papers; Martin Van Buren to John Van Buren, May 3, 1848, in Martin Van Buren Papers.

30. F. W. Byrdsall to John C. Calhoun, April 9, 13, 1848, in John C. Calhoun Papers. Cf. the reports of the New York correspondent dated March 30 and April 21, in the Washington *Daily Union,* April 2, 22, 1848.

31. "Address of the Democratic Members of the Legislature of New York" in Bigelow (ed.), *Writings and Speeches of Tilden,* II, 535-36. The address was published in the leading Barnburner journals. See the *New York Weekly Evening Post,* April 20, 1848, *Albany Evening Atlas,* April 14, 1848.

32. "Address of the Democratic Members of the Legislature of New York" in Bigelow (ed.), *Writings and Speeches of Tilden,* II, 546.

33. *Ibid.,* pp. 547-60.

34. *Ibid.,* p. 564.

35. *Ibid.,* pp. 565-66.

36. *Ibid.,* p. 573.

37. *Ibid.,* p. 574.

38. Jared Willson to Samuel J. Tilden, April 15, 1848, Charles S. Benson to Samuel J. Tilden, May 1, 1848, in Samuel J. Tilden Papers; Martin Van Buren to John Van Buren, May 3, 1848, in Martin Van Buren Papers. Some of the Barnburners' evidence is presented in their "Address to the Democratic

Electors of the State of New York," reprinted in Bigelow (ed.), *Writings and Speeches of Tilden,* I, 235.

39. Preston King to Gideon Welles, March 18, May 1, 1848, in Gideon Welles Papers; Lathrop F. Eddy to Levi Woodbury, May 10, 1848, in Levi Woodbury Papers.

40. John Van Buren to Martin Van Buren, April 30, 1848, in Martin Van Buren Papers.

41. Martin Van Buren to John Van Buren, May 3, 1848, in *ibid.*

42. "Suggestions for the Conduct of the Utica Delegation at the Baltimore Convention," in Martin Van Buren Papers. The dictates of the memorandum closely follow the advice offered in the letter. The compiler of the calendar to the Van Buren papers dates it some time between May 3, when Van Buren wrote his son, and May 17, the day before the Barnburner caucus in New York. See West (comp.), *Calendar of Van Buren Papers,* p. 582.

43. *Ibid.*

44. Martin Van Buren to John Van Buren, May 3, 1848, in *ibid.*

45. "Suggestions for the Baltimore Convention," in *ibid.*

46. *Ibid.* Unlike his letter to his son, the memorandum left the delegation the option of withdrawing from the convention although it advised against it.

47. Jared Willson to Martin Van Buren, May 9, 1848, Martin Van Buren to Jared Willson, May 15, 1848, in *ibid.*

48. John La Porte to Samuel J. Tilden, May 12, 18, 1848, in Samuel J. Tilden Papers.

49. J. O. Barnes to Levi Woodbury, May 18, 1848, in Levi Woodbury Papers.

50. John Van Buren to Martin Van Buren, April 30, 1848, in Martin Van Buren Papers.

51. "The Next President" in the *New York Weekly Evening Post,* April 20, 1848; "The Vote of New York" in *ibid.,* May 18, 1848.

52. "We Can Elect Our President Without New York" in the Detroit *Daily Free Press,* April 29, 1848. The editorial quoted the correspondent of another western journal as saying that Democrats in Washington were "heartily tired" of the New York dispute.

53. *Congressional Globe,* 30 Cong., 1 Sess., Appendix, p. 578.

54. A copy of the pamphlet is in the Mason Family Papers, University of Virginia. Bayly's argument was used by many of the southern Democratic journals to justify their support of Cass.

55. "Correspondence of the Nashville *Union,*" Washington, May 18, in the *Tri-Weekly Nashville Union,* May 25, 1848. The correspondent was the editor, who was a strong supporter of Cass. See "The Baltimore Convention" in *ibid.,* June 3, 1848; Pearson Cogswell to Levi Woodbury, May 11, 1848, in Levi Woodbury Papers.

56. "Correspondence of the Nashville *Union,*" Washington, May 18, in the *Tri-Weekly Nashville Union,* May 25, 1848.

57. "Proceedings of the Democratic National Convention," May 22, in the Baltimore *Sun,* May 23, 1848. The account of the convention is taken from the "Proceedings" of three newspapers, the Baltimore *Sun,* the Washington *Union,* and the New York *Herald.* The *Sun's* proceedings seem to be the most accurate, though not necessarily the most complete, and are generally used as a reference for resolutions, parliamentary maneuvers, comments, and so forth. The *Union's* proceedings give a much fuller account of many of

the speeches, while the *Herald* admirably conveys the atmosphere as well as much of the byplay of the convention.

58. *Ibid.*

59. *Ibid.*

60. "Proceedings of the Democratic National Convention," May 22, in the Washington *Daily Union,* May 23, 1848.

61. "Proceedings," May 22, in the Baltimore *Sun,* May 23, 1848.

62. *Ibid.*; report of the correspondent "W," dated May 23, in the *New York Herald,* May 25, 1848.

63. "Proceedings of the Democratic National Convention," May 22, in the *New York Herald,* May 24, 1848.

64. "Proceedings," May 23, in *ibid.,* May 25, 1848.

65. See the report of the correspondent, dated May 22, in the Mobile *Register and Journal,* May 31, 1848. Cass's western supporters were said to have agreed to the two-thirds rule before the convention opened. See the report of the correspondent, dated May 20, in the *Charleston Courier,* May 26, 1848.

66. See the report of the correspondent "W," dated May 23, in the *New York Herald,* May 25, 1848.

67. Richard C. Bain, *Convention Decisions and Voting Records* (Washington: The Brookings Institute, 1960), Appendix D; D. D. Wagener to James Buchanan, May 22, 1848, in James Buchanan Papers, Historical Society of Pennsylvania.

68. John W. Forney to James Buchanan, May 23, 1848, in James Buchanan Papers, Historical Society of Pennsylvania.

69. See the report of the correspondent "W," dated May 23, in the *New York Herald,* May 25, 1848. An incident which occurred during the debate forcibly reminded the delegates of the action taken four years before and helped make the vote a test of the earlier decision. See J. Knox Walker to James K. Polk, May 24, 1848, in James K. Polk Papers.

70. "Proceedings," May 23, in the Washington *Daily Union,* May 25, 1848. It was rumored on the first day of the convention that the Barnburners were so strong for Woodbury that they were prepared to nominate him as an independent candidate if they were excluded from the convention. See the report of the correspondent "X," dated May 22, in the Baltimore *Sun,* May 23, 1848.

71. "Proceedings," May 23, in the Baltimore *Sun,* May 24, 1848.

72. *Ibid.*

73. See the report of the correspondent "W," dated May 24, and of the Washington correspondent "Galviensis," dated May 23, in the *New York Herald,* May 25, 1848. Yancey wrote to Dixon H. Lewis that Cass was "dead." See R. Beale to Levi Woodbury, May 24, 1848, in Levi Woodbury Papers.

74. See Allen's statement, in an interview given in 1879, quoted in Reginald Charles McGrane, *William Allen, A Study in Western Democracy* (Columbus: The Ohio State Archeological and Historical Society, 1925), p. 129; Francis P. Blair to Martin Van Buren, June 26, 1848, in Martin Van Buren Papers.

75. J. Knox Walker to James K. Polk, May 22, 24, 1848, in James K. Polk Papers.

76. "Proceedings," May 24, in the Washington *Daily Union,* May 25, 26, 1848.

77. See the report of the correspondent "H," dated May 21, in the Baltimore *Sun,* May 22, 1848.

78. "Proceedings," May 24, in the Washington *Daily Union,* May 25, 26, 1848.

79. Preston King to Gideon Welles, May 1, 1848, in Gideon Welles Papers. The Utica delegation had disclaimed any desire to agitate the slavery question, and King later felt compelled to deny the accusation that it was he who had introduced the subject into the convention. See "Proceedings," May 24, in the Washington *Daily Union,* May 27, 1848. The delegation had been warned by a Barnburner representative in Congress of the danger of having their case prejudiced by radical spokesmen like King. See Ransom H. Gillet to Benjamin F. Butler, May 11, 1848, in Benjamin F. Butler Papers.

80. "Proceedings," May 24, in the Washington *Daily Union,* May 26, 1848.

81. *Ibid.*

82. One of the delegates wrote to Buchanan: "At one time today the Barnburners had all on their side and would doubtless have been admitted but for an abolition speech of Mr. King which has prostrated them forever." Jonathan Foltz to James Buchanan, May 24, 1848, in James Buchanan Papers, Historical Society of Pennsylvania. Cf. the report of the correspondent, dated May 25, in the Portland *Age,* May 30, 1848. From King's point of view, the danger of being compromised was obviously great, since the delegation was prepared not only to forego agitation of the territorial issue but also to acquiesce in the nomination of candidates who had met the southern test. See the report of the correspondent "H," dated May 21, in the Baltimore *Sun,* May 22, 1848; report of the correspondent "X," dated May 24, in *ibid.,* May 25, 1848; "Suggestions for the Baltimore Convention," in Martin Van Buren Papers.

83. "Proceedings," May 24, in the *New York Herald,* May 26, 1848.

84. *Ibid.*

85. *Ibid.*

86. *Ibid.*

87. The two southerners who spoke on the New York question both rejected Yancey's reasons for excluding the Barnburners. See "Proceedings," May 24, in the Washington *Daily Union,* May 27, 1848.

88. "Proceedings of the Committee on Credentials," May 23, in the *New York Herald,* May 24, 1848. For the effort to get the convention to unite on Polk's renomination, see J. Knox Walker to James K. Polk, May 22, 24, 1848, A. W. Venable to James K. Polk, May 24, 1848, in James K. Polk Papers.

89. "Proceedings," May 24, in the Washington *Daily Union,* May 27, 1848.

90. For an analysis of the vote, see the report of the correspondent "The Doctor," dated May 24, in the *New York Herald,* May 26, 1848.

91. See the report of a correspondent from Albany, dated May 26, in the *New York Herald,* May 29, 1848; William A. Butler to George Bancroft, June 10, 1848, reprinted as "Letter of William A. Butler, 1848," *Proceedings of the Massachusetts Historical Society,* LX (January, 1927), 119.

92. See the correspondent's report from Washington dated May 25 in the *New York Weekly Tribune,* June 3, 1848. When Senator Dickinson later told the convention that the Hunkers favored Cass and would have voted for him if given exclusive seats, the reporter for the *Herald* commented that that accounted for the Barnburners remaining in the convention until after the nomination. See "Proceedings," May 26, in the *New York Herald,* May 30, 1848.

93. L. Hoyt to Samuel J. Tilden, May 25, 1848, in Samuel J. Tilden Papers; report of the correspondent "X," dated May 24, in the Baltimore *Sun,* May 25, 1848. One of the Barnburners tried unsuccessfully to help one of the Missouri delegates, bound by the unit rule, to record his vote against Cass during the balloting the next day. See the report of the correspondent "Halifax," dated May 25, in the Raleigh *North Carolina Standard,* May 31, 1848.

94. A majority of the Ohio and Indiana delegates voted for the compromise in spite of the fact that both delegations were firmly committed to Cass's nomination. See the report of the correspondent "The Doctor," dated May 24, in the *New York Herald,* May 26, 1848. One correspondent pointed out that some of the Cass men sympathized with the Barnburners. See the report of the correspondent "X," dated May 25, in the Baltimore *Sun,* May 26, 1848. For the attitude of one such politician, see Samuel Medary to Martin Van Buren, May 5, 1848, in Martin Van Buren Papers.

95. Two of Buchanan's supporters argued that the exclusion of the Barnburners would not help Cass. One of them maintained that he could not be elected if nominated by Hunker votes and the other that the Hunker votes would not be sufficient to nominate him. See E. W. Hutter to James Buchanan, May 25, 1848, James Thompson to James Buchanan, May 25, 1848, in James Buchanan Papers, Historical Society of Pennsylvania. The *Sun* correspondent "X," also questioned whether Cass could be nominated if the Barnburners were excluded. See the Baltimore *Sun,* May 25, 1848.

96. See the report of the correspondent of the Seneca *Observer,* quoted in "The Address of the Barnburner Delegation" in the Washington *Daily Union,* June 7, 1848; report of the correspondent "X," dated May 25, in the Baltimore *Sun,* May 26, 1848.

97. *Ibid.* The *Herald* correspondent "Waterloo" commented, after the nominations, that the ticket seemed to be "expressly constructed to secure all the West and Southwest to make up the deficit of New York." See the *New York Herald,* May 27, 1848.

98. See the correspondent's report from Washington dated May 25, in the *New York Weekly Tribune,* June 3, 1848. On May 22, the correspondent "X," had written: "Without New York or Ohio being secured to the Democratic party, all idea of success seems to be hopeless." See the Baltimore *Sun,* May 23, 1848.

99. Richard Pollard to James Buchanan, May 25, 1848, in James Buchanan Papers, Historical Society of Pennsylvania.

100. John A. Parker to James Buchanan, June 9, 1848, in *ibid.* Cf. the report of the correspondent, dated May 24, in the *Charleston Courier,* May 29, 1848.

101. George Plitt to James Buchanan, May 27, 1848, in James Buchanan Papers, Library of Congress; John W. Forney to James Buchanan, May 21, 23, 1848, Simon Cameron to James Buchanan, May 22, 23, 1848, in James Buchanan Papers, Historical Society of Pennsylvania. One of Buchanan's supporters wrote that he feared that the members of the state administration had "turned the Virginia Delegates." See Robert Tyler to James Buchanan, May 22, 1848, in *ibid.*

102. George Plitt to James Buchanan, May 12, 1848, in James Buchanan Papers, Library of Congress; report of the correspondent "X," dated May 23, in the Baltimore *Sun,* May 24, 1848.

103. J[ohn] A. P[arker] to James Buchanan, May 24, 1848, in James Buchanan Papers, Historical Society of Pennsylvania.

104. Richard Pollard, John A. Parker, John Sterigere, to James Buchanan, May 25, June 7, June 9, 1848, in *ibid.*

105. "Proceedings," May 25, in the *New York Herald,* May 27, 1848.

106. The editor of the *North Carolina Standard,* who was originally one of Buchanan's warmest friends in the delegation, made a point of emphasizing that Ohio would vote for Cass after the nomination was made. See his report dated May 25, in the Raleigh *North Carolina Standard,* May 31, 1848.

107. "Proceedings," May 25, in the Baltimore *Sun,* May 26, 1848.

108. *Ibid.*

109. Jonathan Foltz to James Buchanan, May 24, 1848, in James Buchanan Papers.

110. The Barnburners were pleased with Butler's nomination and considered supporting him for the vice-presidency. See the report of the correspondent "R," dated May 26, in the *New York Weekly Tribune,* June 3, 1848; Benjamin F. Butler to Martin Van Buren, June 1, 1848, in Martin Van Buren Papers.

111. Yancey, *Address to the People of Alabama,* pp. 48, 58.

112. *Ibid.*

113. The Barnburners had been willing to accept this resolution and later adopted it at one of their meetings, as Yancey was to point out. See "Suggestions for the Baltimore Convention," in Martin Van Buren Papers; "Editorial Correspondence" in the *New York Daily Globe,* May 23, 1848; Yancey, *Address to the People of Alabama,* pp. 57-58.

114. Yancey, *Address to the People of Alabama,* p. 48.

115. Yancey seems to have recognized this. See *ibid.,* pp. 50-51.

116. *Ibid.,* p. 49.

117. *Ibid.*

118. "Proceedings," May 26, in the Baltimore *Sun,* May 27, 1848.

119. "Proceedings," May 26, in the Washington *Daily Union,* May 28, 1848.

120. "Proceedings," May 26, in the Baltimore *Sun,* May 27, 1848.

121. *Ibid.*

122. "Proceedings," May 26, in the *New York Herald,* May 30, 1848.

123. *Ibid.* The Democratic organ in Virginia, whose editor was a delegate, made the same defense of Virginia's vote. See "The National Convention and Its Nominations" in the *Daily Richmond Enquirer,* June 2, 1848.

124. See the report of the correspondent "X," dated May 26, in the Baltimore *Sun,* May 28, 1848; James C. Dobbin to Howell Cobb, June 15, 1848, Henry H. Jackson to Howell Cobb, June 21, 1848, in Phillips (ed.), "Toombs, Stephens, Cobb Correspondence," pp. 108, 110-11. Nine of the thirty-six votes were cast by South Carolina's single delegate. The "Proceedings" of the *Herald* clearly indicate the initial hesitancy of many of the southern delegations to oppose Yancey's amendment.

CHAPTER VIII

1. See the report of the correspondent "The Doctor," dated May 28, in the *New York Herald,* May 30, 1848.

2. See Senator Dickinson's speech to the convention in "Proceedings," May 25, in the Washington *Daily Union,* May 27, 1848. According to one

observer, on the last day "the Hunkers hung around all day long to get someone to offer a resolution endorsing them as delegates, but the feeling was so strong against it that no one would do it." Matthias Martin to Samuel J. Tilden, May 26, 1848, in Samuel J. Tilden Papers.

3. See the report of the correspondent "R," dated May 26, in the *New York Weekly Tribune,* June 3, 1848.

4. Azariah C. Flagg to Martin Van Buren, June 19, 1848, in Martin Van Buren Papers; John A. Dix to Azariah C. Flagg, June 5, 1848, in Azariah C. Flagg Papers, Columbia University.

5. "Democratic State Convention" in the *Albany Evening Atlas,* May 29, 1848.

6. New York *Daily Globe,* June 1, 1848; *New York Weekly Evening Post,* June 8, 1848.

7. Benjamin F. Butler to Martin Van Buren, May 29, 30, 31, June 1, 1848, in Martin Van Buren Papers.

8. Holman Hamilton, *Zachary Taylor, Soldier in the White House* (Indianapolis and New York: The Bobbs-Merrill Company, Inc., 1951), pp. 79-83. (The Allison letter is reprinted in full.)

9. J. L. White to Henry Clay, May 26, 1848, in Henry Clay Papers, Library of Congress; J. B. Mower to John McLean, June 5, 1848, in John McLean Papers, Library of Congress; L. Hoyt to Samuel J. Tilden, May 25, 1848, in Samuel J. Tilden Papers; report of the correspondent, dated May 27, in the *New York Herald,* May 28, 1848.

10. John Van Buren to Martin Van Buren, April 22, 1848, in Martin Van Buren Papers; "Movements of the Barnburners," in the *New York Herald,* June 13, 1848. For the importance which the Barnburners attached to winning the state election in order to provide themselves a future political base of operations, see Martin Van Buren to John Van Buren, May 3, 1848, in Martin Van Buren Papers; John A. Dix to Azariah C. Flagg, June 5, 1848, in Azariah C. Flagg Papers, Columbia University; Martin Van Buren to John A. Dix, October 2, 1848, in John A. Dix Papers.

11. "The Barnburners and the Presidency" in the *New York Herald,* June 3, 1848; Oliver Dyer, *Great Senators of the United States Forty Years Ago* (New York: Robert Bonner's Sons, 1889), pp. 62-65. Dyer, who seems to have been as poor in deduction as he was keen in observation, concluded that Weed was trying to *help* Taylor at Clay's expense. A southern delegate at the Philadelphia Convention wrote that the New York politicians "were greatly intent on getting [sic] some one a little more odorous on the negro question than Cass," and that Taylor did not fulfill the requirement. He also claimed that they thought that the Barnburner revolt would render the state safe for Clay, "and they did not care about shuffling the cards or trying any other experiments." See Joseph G. Baldwin to George Saunders, June 12, 1848, reprinted in Malcolm C. McMillan, "Joseph Glover Baldwin Reports on the Whig National Convention of 1848," *The Journal of Southern History,* XXV (August, 1959), 375-76. Taylor's biographer, Holman Hamilton, has concluded after an examination of the fragmentary evidence that Weed was actually working for the nomination of John M. Clayton of Delaware. See *Zachary Taylor,* pp. 74-75, 88.

12. "Great Meeting of the Old Guard Democracy of New York, Alias the Barnburners" in the *New York Herald,* June 7, 1848.

13. John Van Buren to Salmon P. Chase, June 7, 1848, in Salmon P. Chase Papers, Historical Society of Pennsylvania.

14. Francis P. Blair to Martin Van Buren, June 26, 1848, in Martin Van Buren Papers.

15. Thomas H. Benton to Martin Van Buren, May 29, 1848, in Martin Van Buren Papers.

16. See the telegram quoted in Godwin, *William Cullen Bryant,* II, 43.

17. John A. Dix to Azariah C. Flagg, June 5, 1848, in Azariah C. Flagg Papers, Columbia University; S. E. Benson to A. O. P. Nicholson, June 7, 1848, in Miscellaneous Papers (S. E. Benson), New York Historical Society. On May 30, the correspondent "Galviensis" reported that Benton was to arrange a bargain between the Barnburners and the Hunkers whereby the latter were to support Dix for governor in return for Barnburner support for the national ticket; this would give the Barnburners the state offices and patronage and leave the federal "spoils" for the Hunkers. See the *New York Herald,* June 1, 1848. Some of the Barnburner leaders were evidently prepared to go along with Benton. See Thomas H. Benton to Lewis Cass (received June 20, 1848), in Lewis Cass Papers, University of Michigan; speech of Samuel J. Tilden in "Barnburners' Convention," in the *New York Herald,* June 25, 1848.

18. Thomas H. Benton to Lewis Cass (received June 20, 1848), in Lewis Cass Papers, University of Michigan; S. E. Benson to A. O. P. Nicholson, June 20, 1848, in Miscellaneous Papers (S. E. Benson), New York Historical Society. Benson told Nicholson that Senator Bright of Indiana had a letter from Van Buren in which the former President said that he supported the Baltimore nominees and would publicly announce his support at the first opportunity. Whatever commitment of this sort Van Buren may have made was undoubtedly hedged about with his usual qualifications which the party leaders evidently ignored. Van Buren's letter to Benton was so qualified. See Martin Van Buren to John A. Dix, June 20, 1848, in John A. Dix Papers.

19. Martin Van Buren to John A. Dix, June 20, 1848, in John A. Dix Papers.

20. Martin Van Buren to Benjamin F. Butler, June 20, 1848, in Benjamin F. Butler Papers.

21. *Ibid.;* Martin Van Buren to John A. Dix, June 20, 1848, in John A. Dix Papers.

22. Addison Gardiner to John Van Buren, June 24, 1848, Nelson J. Waterbury to John Van Buren, June 21, 1848, in Martin Van Buren Papers.

23. Isaac Butts to John A. Dix, July 7, 1848, in John A. Dix Papers. In addition, Dix was extremely anxious to avoid being nominated and made these sentiments known to the delegates. See John A. Dix to Benjamin F. Butler, June 19, 1848, in Benjamin F. Butler Papers.

24. Martin Van Buren to Samuel Waterbury *et al.,* June 20, 1848, in "Barnburners' Convention," in the *New York Herald,* June 25, 1848; Charles S. Benton to Henry Dodge, June 27, 1848, quoted in Ernest Paul Muller, "Preston King: A Political Biography" (Unpublished doctoral dissertation, Columbia University, 1957), p. 440. The Liberty Party people in New York were urging the Barnburners "to bring out such candidates at Utica as all the friends of free soil can rally on." See H. B. Stanton to Salmon P. Chase, June 6, 1848, in Salmon P. Chase Papers, Library of Congress. The issuance of his letter made Van Buren far and away the best candidate from this point of view. If they had nominated a lesser person, he would probably have been superseded at Buffalo, which would have ruined their plans with regard to New York.

25. See the speech of B. Bailey in "Barnburners' Convention" in the *New York Herald,* June 25, 1848.

26. See the correspondent's report from Utica dated June 23, in the *New York Weekly Tribune,* July 1, 1848.

27. John Van Buren to Martin Van Buren, June 26, 1848, in Martin Van Buren Papers. One delegate claimed that Van Buren's nomination was "strongly resisted by those more intimately connected with him." See Charles S. Benton to Henry Dodge, June 27, 1848, quoted in Muller, "Preston King," p. 440. Flagg called the nomination the result of "spontaneous combustion." See Azariah C. Flagg to John A. Dix, July 20, 1848, in John A. Dix Papers. John Van Buren told one associate that he did not know what his father's response would be to the nomination. See Ferree, "New York Democracy," p. 209.

28. "Barnburners' Convention" in the *New York Herald,* June 25, 1848; "Address of the Democratic State Convention" in the *Albany Evening Atlas,* July 3, 1848.

29. Lewis Cass to Samuel Treat, July 3, 1848, in Samuel Treat Papers; Lewis Cass to Henry Hubbard, July 29, 1848, in Miscellaneous Papers (Henry Hubbard), New York Historical Society; Thomas H. Benton to Lewis Cass, July 10, 1848, Simon Cameron to Lewis Cass, July 12, 1848, in Lewis Cass Papers, University of Michigan; James Buchanan to Robert Tyler, July 13, 1848, in Tyler, *Tylers Letters,* II, 451.

30. Hamilton, *Zachary Taylor,* p. 95.

31. Stanley Mathews to Salmon P. Chase, June 12, 1848, in Salmon P. Chase Papers, Library of Congress; Henry Wilson, *History of the Rise and Fall of the Slave Power in America* (2 vols.; Boston: Houghton Mifflin and Company, 1874), II, 142-44.

32. Salmon P. Chase to [Adam Jewett], August 15, 1846, Salmon P. Chase to [R. Errett], September 4, 1846, Charles Sumner to Salmon P. Chase, December 4, 1846, in Salmon P. Chase Papers, Library of Congress. Chase had plans for the meeting as early as February of 1848. See Salmon P. Chase to Charles Sumner, February 19, 1848, in Edward G. Bourne *et al.* (eds.), "Diary and Correspondence of Salmon P. Chase," Volume II of the *Annual Report of the American Historical Association for the Year 1902,* pp. 129-30.

33. Salmon P. Chase to John P. Hale, June 15, 1848, in Bourne *et al.* (eds.), "Chase Diary and Correspondence," p. 136.

34. Salmon P. Chase to Charles Sumner, May 25, June 5, June 20, 1848, in *ibid.,* pp. 132, 133, 137; "Politics," in the Washington *National Era,* May 4, 1848; "Autobiographical Sketch," in Warden, *Life of Chase,* p. 318.

35. Salmon P. Chase to John P. Hale, June 15, 1848, in Bourne *et al.* (eds.), "Chase Diary and Correspondence," p. 136.

36. "Elements of a New Coalition" in the Washington *Daily Union,* June 30, 1848.

37. "The Free Territory Convention in Ohio" in the Washington *National Era,* June 29, 1848; "The Ohio Free Territory Convention" in *ibid.,* July 6, 1848.

38. "Ohio State Liberty Convention" in *ibid.,* July 6, 1848; Liberty Party Meeting to Columbus Convention, June 17, 1848, in Salmon P. Chase Papers, Library of Congress.

39. M. Sturges to Salmon P. Chase, July 27, 1848, in Salmon P. Chase Papers, Library of Congress.

40. "A General Review—The Position of the Liberty Party Union" in the

Washington *National Era,* July 6, 1848; "Mr. Hale and the Buffalo Convention" in *ibid.,* July 13, 1848.

41. Edward Pierce, *Memoir and Letters of Charles Sumner* (4 vols.; Boston: Roberts Brothers, 1894), III, 165, 167; Charles Sumner to Salmon P. Chase, June 12, 1848, in Salmon P. Chase Papers, Library of Congress; letter from Charles Sumner quoted in Julian, *Life of Giddings,* p. 247.

42. "Free Soil Convention in Massachusetts" in the *New York Weekly Tribune,* July 8, 1848; "Elements of a New Coalition" in the Washington *Daily Union,* June 30, 1848.

43. John Van Buren to Salmon P. Chase, June 7, 1848, in Salmon P. Chase Papers, Historical Society of Pennsylvania; Salmon P. Chase to John Van Buren, June 19, 1848, in Bigelow (ed.), *Tilden Letters,* I, 51-52. In spite of its date, the Chase letter was not completed and sent until after June 22. The correct date might be July 19.

44. "Barnburners' Convention," in the *New York Herald,* June 25, 1848. This had been done at John Van Buren's suggestion. John Van Buren to Benjamin F. Butler, June 16, 1848, in Benjamin F. Butler Papers.

45. "Important Political Movement—The Barnburners in Motion," in the *New York Herald,* May 29, 1848; J. B. Mower to John McLean, June 5, 1848, in John McLean Papers; John Van Buren to Benjamin F. Butler, June 16, 1848, in Benjamin F. Butler Papers; Preston King to Martin Van Buren, July 12, 1848, in Martin Van Buren Papers.

46. L. E. Chittenden, *Personal Reminiscences, 1840-1890* (New York: Richmond Croscup and Company, 1893), pp. 12-16.

47. Samuel J. Tilden to Salmon P. Chase, July 29, 1848, in Bourne *et al.* (eds.), "Chase Diary and Correspondence," p. 469.

48. "The Buffalo Convention" in the *New York Weekly Evening Post,* August 10, 1848.

49. Charles Sumner to Salmon P. Chase, July 7, 1848, in Salmon P. Chase Papers, Historical Society of Pennsylvania; Charles Sumner to John G. Whittier, July 12, 1848, quoted in Pierce, *Memoir of Sumner,* III, 161; M. Sturges to Salmon P. Chase, July 27, 1848, in Salmon P. Chase Papers, Library of Congress; Salmon P. Chase to John McLean, August 2, 1848, in John McLean Papers.

50. Richard Henry Dana, Jr., to Jared Willson, July 26, 1848, in Richard Henry Dana, Jr., Papers, Massachusetts Historical Society.

51. Charles Sumner to Salmon P. Chase, July 7, 1848, in Salmon P. Chase Papers, Library of Congress.

52. Preston King to Martin Van Buren, July 12, 1848, Charles Francis Adams to Martin Van Buren, July 16, 1848, in Martin Van Buren Papers.

53. "Union of the Friends of Freedom—The Obstacle," in Washington *National Era,* July 13, 1848; Henry Van Dyke to Martin Van Buren, July 17, 1848, in Martin Van Buren Papers. On the eve of the Buffalo Convention, one of the leading Barnburner journals suggested that the faction support a bill abolishing slavery in the District of Columbia and ventured to predict that Van Buren would not veto such a bill. See "The Buffalo Convention" in the Washington *Daily Union,* August 8, 1848.

54. Martin Van Buren to Charles Francis Adams, July 24, 1848, in Martin Van Buren Papers; Charles Francis Adams Diary, July 28, 1848, in Charles Francis Adams Papers, Massachusetts Historical Society; Richard Henry Dana, Jr., to Jared Willson, July 26, 1848, in Richard Henry Dana,

Jr., Papers. Cf. Martin Van Buren to James S. Wadsworth, August 7, 1848, in James S. Wadsworth Papers.

55. Salmon P. Chase to Charles Sumner, June 20, 1848, in Bourne *et al.* (eds.), "Chase Diary and Correspondence," p. 137.

56. Salmon P. Chase to John McLean, August 2, 1848, in John McLean Papers.

57. Bradford R. Wood, Charles Sumner, James W. Taylor to John McLean, July 3, July 31, August 3, 1848, in *ibid.*

58. John McLean to Salmon P. Chase, August 2, 4, 1848, in Salmon P. Chase Papers, Historical Society of Pennsylvania.

59. Salmon P. Chase to John McLean, August 4, 12, 1848; E. S. Hamlin to John McLean, August 17, 1848, in John McLean Papers.

60. Salmon P. Chase to James W. Taylor, August 15, 1848, in Salmon P. Chase Papers, Historical Society of Pennsylvania.

61. *Ibid.*; Charles Francis Adams Diary, August 8, 1848, in Charles Francis Adams Papers; letter from Salmon P. Chase, dated March 21, quoted in Warden, *Life of Chase,* p. 318; remarks of Preston King in Oliver Dyer, *Phonographic Report of the Proceedings of the Free Soil Convention at Buffalo, N.Y.* (Buffalo: G. H. Derby and Company, 1848), p. 5.

62. Dyer, *Phonographic Report,* p. 5.

63. *Ibid.,* p. 10; report of the correspondent "Cyclops" from Buffalo, dated August 10, in the *New York Herald,* August 11, 1848.

64. Dyer, *Phonographic Report,* p. 8; Richard Henry Dana, Jr., Journal, August 9, 10, 1848, in Richard Henry Dana, Jr., Papers.

65. See the report of the correspondent "Cyclops" from Buffalo, dated August 8, in the *New York Herald,* August 11, 1848; Salmon P. Chase to John McLean, August 12, 1848, E. S. Hamlin to John McLean, August 17, 1848, in John McLean Papers. Adams became skeptical of McLean when he saw the letters and telegrams the judge had written to Chase, but he did not give him up entirely as a candidate until he received the final word on the 10th that "McLean would not consent to stand." See Charles Francis Adams Diary, August 9, 10, 1848, in Charles Francis Adams Papers.

66. Charles Francis Adams Diary, August 10, 1848, in Charles Francis Adams Papers; Richard Henry Dana, Jr., Journal, August 10, 1848, in Richard Henry Dana, Jr., Papers.

67. Dyer, *Great Senators,* p. 101.

68. Stanton, *Random Recollections,* pp. 163-64. Dyer evidently got a second-hand account of the incident which he published in *Great Senators,* p. 101.

69. Richard Henry Dana, Jr., Journal, August 10, 1848, in Richard Henry Dana, Jr., Papers; Salmon P. Chase to John McLean, August 12, 1848, in John McLean Papers. Contrary to the positive statements by Dana and Chase and to his own later account of the speech in *Great Senators* (p. 101), Dyer in a postscript to the *Phonographic Report* (p. 32) claimed that a delegate told him that "Mr. Butler would not place Mr. Van Buren on the platform any further than his letter would warrant, urging that his nomination would be a sufficient guarantee of his approval of the platform." It seems evident, however, that Butler was able to satisfy the delegates with respect to Van Buren's position. One Massachusetts Whig reported in the Liberty Party organ that "Butler's statement of Mr. Van Buren's position was perfectly satisfactory to every delegate." See "The Buffalo Convention" in the Washington *National Era,* September 7, 1848. After the convention Butler, at Chase's sug-

gestion, persuaded Van Buren to endorse the entire platform including abolition in the District of Columbia. See Salmon P. Chase to Benjamin F. Butler, August 12, 1848, in Benjamin F. Butler Papers; Benjamin F. Butler to Salmon P. Chase, August 17, 1848, Martin Van Buren to Salmon P. Chase, August 29, 1848, in Salmon P. Chase Papers, Historical Society of Pennsylvania.

70. Richard Henry Dana, Jr., Journal, August 10, 1848, in Richard Henry Dana, Jr., Papers.

71. *Ibid.* Adams had already decided that there was "no alternative but Mr. Van Buren" before the meeting, when he heard of McLean's final decision not to be a candidate, but he himself voted for Giddings in order to avoid the appearance of bargaining for the vice-presidency for which he had been mentioned. A recent biographer of Dana has claimed that Adams advised Dana to vote for Van Buren with the idea of himself becoming the vice-presidential nominee and eventual leader of the movement. See Samuel Shapiro, *Richard Henry Dana, Jr., 1815-1882* (Lansing; Michigan State University Press, 1962), p. 37. But in the August 10 entry of Dana's journal which Shapiro uses as his primary source for the claim, there is no mention of this, nor does it fit with what Dana does say about the nominations in his journal.

72. Richard Henry Dana, Jr., Journal, August 10, 1848, in Richard Henry Dana, Jr., Papers.

73. "Address of Hon. Milton M. Fisher of Medway" in *Reunion of the Free-Soilers of 1848 at Downer's Landing, Higham, Massachusetts, August 9, 1877* (Boston: Albert J. Wright, 1877), p. 59.

74. Richard Henry Dana, Jr., Journal, August 10, 1848, in Richard Henry Dana, Jr., Papers; Charles Francis Adams Diary, August 10, 1848, in Charles Francis Adams Papers; Salmon P. Chase to James W. Taylor, August 15, 1848, in Salmon P. Chase Papers, Historical Society of Pennsylvania.

75. Dyer, *Phonographic Report*, pp. 28, 31.

76. Henry W. Conner to John C. Calhoun, September 28, 1848, in Jameson (ed.), "Calhoun Correspondence," p. 1183. Cf. Fitzwilliam Byrdsall to John C. Calhoun, July 31, 1848, in *ibid.*, p. 1181; Fitzwilliam Byrdsall to John C. Calhoun, June 25, 1848, in Boucher and Brooks (eds.), "Correspondence Addressed to Calhoun," p. 444; Smith, *Liberty and Free Soil Parties*, p. 148.

77. *General Taylor and the Wilmot Proviso* (Boston: Wilson and Darnorell, 1848), p. 21; Salmon P. Chase to Charles Sumner, November 27, 1848, in Bourne *et al.* (eds.), "Chase Diary and Correspondence," p. 142; Washington *Daily Union*, September 1, October 4, 27, 1848.

78. Salmon P. Chase to John Van Buren, June 19, 1848, in Bigelow (ed.), *Tilden Letters*, I, 53; Hannibal Hamlin to George F. Emory, 1851, quoted in Charles Eugene Hamlin, *The Life and Times of Hannibal Hamlin* (Cambridge: Riverside Press, 1899), p. 181. Congressman John Wentworth's Chicago *Journal* made the same claim. See Bessie Louise Pierce, *A History of Chicago* (3 vols.; New York and London: Alfred A. Knopf, 1937), I, 398-99.

79. "General Cass and the Proviso—Our Position" in the *Cleveland Plain Dealer,* June 7, 1848.

80. "Reflections on the Defeat of Lewis Cass," November, 1848, in Henry Garnett Learned (ed.), Papers Related to Gideon Welles, Library of Congress.

81. "General Cass and the Proviso—Our Position" in the *Cleveland Plain Dealer,* June 7, 1848. Cf. "Free Soil in New Hampshire" in the Concord *New Hampshire Patriot and State Gazette,* August 10, 1848.

82. "Shall We Have a Slavemonger for President?" in the Augusta *Age,* July 28, 1848. Cf. "Gen. Taylor and the Southern Slaveholders" in the Detroit *Daily Free Press,* September 20, 1848.

83. James K. Polk to Lewis Cass, August 24, 1848, Lewis Cass to Samuel Beardsley, October 6, 1848, in Lewis Cass Papers, University of Michigan; J. Gould to James K. Polk, August 12, 1848, in James K. Polk Papers; "The Buffalo Convention" in the Washington *Daily Union,* August 12, 1848.

84. Lewis Cass to A. O. P. Nicholson, August 5, 1848, in Lewis Cass Papers, Detroit Public Library; J. Gould to James K. Polk, August 12, 1848, in James K. Polk Papers; George Fries to Howell Cobb, September 4, 1848, George S. Houston to Howell Cobb, September 25, 1848, in Phillips (ed.), "Toombs, Stephens, Cobb Correspondence," pp. 124-25. Although there is some dispute among historians whether the Free Soil Party helped the Democrats throughout the entire Northwest, W. Dean Durham, after a county by county analysis of the returns in the region, concludes that "a majority of the Free Soil strength was drawn from the Whig Party." "It would seem probable," he continues, "that had no such party run in 1848 the Whigs would have carried at least Illinois, Indiana, and Ohio." *Presidential Ballots, 1836-1892* (Baltimore: The Johns Hopkins Press, 1955), pp. 155-56.

85. William Allen to Lewis Cass, September 9, 1848, in Lewis Cass Papers, University of Michigan.

86. Wilmot admitted that there was not much interest in free soil in Pennsylvania, outside his own district. See David Wilmot to Salmon P. Chase, May 29, 1848, in Salmon P. Chase Papers, Historical Society of Pennsylvania.

87. Malcolm Rogers Eiselin, *The Rise of Protectionism in Pennsylvania* (Published doctoral dissertation, The University of Pennsylvania, 1932), pp. 205-14.

88. James Buchanan to Robert Tyler, July 13, 1848, in Tyler, *Tylers Letters,* II, 461; Simon Cameron to Lewis Cass, July 12, 1848, James K. Polk to Lewis Cass, August 24, 1848, in Lewis Cass Papers, University of Michigan; Simon Cameron to James Buchanan, September 17, 1848, in James Buchanan Papers, Library of Congress.

89. James Buchanan to Robert Tyler, July 13, 1848, in Tyler, *Tylers Letters,* II, 461.

90. Armistead Burt to Henry W. Conner, May 28, 1848, in Henry W. Conner Papers; H. Bailey to John C. Calhoun, June 2, 1848, in Boucher and Brooks (eds.), "Correspondence Addressed to Calhoun," p. 438.

91. Armistead Burt to Henry W. Conner, June 3, 1848, in Henry W. Conner Papers.

92. "Remarks of Mr. Yancey" in the *Charleston Mercury,* June 12, 1848.

93. "Democratic Meeting" in *ibid.,* June 7, 1848.

94. William L. Yancey to John C. Calhoun, June 14, 1848, in Boucher and Brooks (eds.), "Correspondence Addressed to Calhoun," p. 441.

95. *Ibid.*

96. Montgomery *State Gazette,* June 20, 1848.

97. Quoted in DuBose, *Life of Yancey,* p. 224.

98. Montgomery *State Gazette,* June 20, 1848.

99. "Democratic Ratification Meetings" in the Montgomery *Tri-Weekly Flag and Advertiser,* June 22, 1848.

100. *Ibid.*

101. *Ibid.*

102. *Ibid.*

103. "Ratification Meeting at Wetumpka" in *ibid.,* June 27, 1848.
104. William L. Yancey to John C. Calhoun, June 21, 1848, in Jameson (ed.), "Calhoun Correspondence," p. 1144; Dixon H. Lewis to William L. Yancey, June 29, 1848, in William L. Yancey Papers, Alabama State Department of Archives and History.
105. Stephen A. Douglas to Lewis Cass, June 13, 1848, in Johannsen (ed.), *Douglas Letters,* p. 161; Thomas H. Benton to Lewis Cass, July 10, 1848, in Lewis Cass Papers, University of Michigan; James Kimmins Greer, "Louisiana Politics, 1845-1848," *The Louisiana Historical Quarterly,* XII (October, 1929), 559-60.
106. "Democratic Meeting in Richmond" in the *Daily Richmond Enquirer,* June 2, 1848; Robert M. T. Hunter to John Randolph Tucker, May 28, 1848, in Tucker Family Papers; James A. Seddon to Robert M. T. Hunter, June 16, 1848, in Charles Henry Ambler (ed.), "Correspondence of R. M. T. Hunter, 1826-1876," Volume II of the *Annual Report of the American Historical Association for the Year 1916* (Washington: Government Printing Office, 1918), pp. 90-91.
107. *Daily Richmond Enquirer,* June 2, 6, 15, September 21, 1848.
108. James C. Dobbin to Howell Cobb, June 15, 1848, in Phillips (ed.), "Toombs, Stephens, Cobb Correspondence," p. 108; W. B. Gulick to David S. Reid, May 30, 1848, James C. Dobbin to David S. Reid, June 16, 1848, in David S. Reid Papers, North Carolina State Department of Archives and History; "Democratic National Convention" in the Raleigh *North Carolina Standard,* June 7, 1848.
109. Henry R. Jackson to Howell Cobb, June 21, 1848, in Phillips (ed.), "Toombs, Stephens, Cobb Correspondence," p. 110.
110. *Ibid.*; James Jackson to Howell Cobb, July 9, 1848, in *ibid.,* p. 115; "Objections to General Cass" in the Mobile *Register and Journal,* June 14, 1848.
111. "Democratic Convention" in the Milledgeville *Federal Union,* June 27, 1848.
112. "Resolutions Unanimously Adopted by the Florida State Central Committee" in the Tallahassee *Floridian,* June 17, 1848.
113. Tallahassee *Southern Journal,* June 19, July 10, July 17, 1848; Tallahassee *Floridian,* June 17, August 5, 1848. One of the delegates to the Baltimore convention who had co-operated with Yancey publicly took this position. See Lawrence O'Brien Branch to the Democratic Party in Florida, June 27, 1848, in the Tallahassee *Floridian,* September 16, 1848. By September, even Senator David Yulee, Calhoun's closest political associate outside of South Carolina, had announced his support for Cass. See David Yulee to J. G. Readon and W. J. Spann, September 23, 1848, in *ibid.,* October 7, 1848.
114. Montgomery *Tri-Weekly Flag and Advertiser,* June 15, 24, 1848; Mobile *Register and Journal,* June 14, August 16, 1848; Yancey, *Address to the People of Alabama,* p. 73.
115. M. C. Galloway to George S. Houston, June 25, 1848, in George S. Houston Papers; M. C. Galloway and John S. Kennedy to Dixon H. Lewis, June 24, 1848, in the Montgomery *State Gazette,* July 24, 1848.
116. Dixon H. Lewis to William L. Yancey, June 27, 1848, in William L. Yancey Papers.
117. Dixon H. Lewis to M. C. Galloway and John S. Kennedy, July 2, 1848, in the Montgomery *State Gazette,* July 24, 1848.
118. *Ibid.,* June 26, 28, July 1, 7, 1848.

119. Cf. *ibid.,* June 24, 1848. Every one of Alabama's thirteen Democratic journals supported the regular nominees. See the Montgomery *Tri-Weekly Flag and Advertiser,* June 24, 1848.

120. Montgomery *State Gazette,* August 12, 1848.

121. Yancey, *Address to the People of Alabama,* pp. 66-74, 76.

122. *Ibid.,* pp. 76-77.

123. Montgomery *State Gazette,* June 22, July 12, September 8, 1848.

124. John C. Calhoun to Henry W. Conner, October 18, 1848, in Henry W. Conner Papers; John C. Calhoun to a Gentleman in Georgia, October 16, 1848, in David Rankin Barbee (ed.), "A Sheaf of Old Letters," *Tyler's Quarterly Historical and Genealogical Magazine,* XXXII (October, 1950), 90.

125. While Congress was considering a bill for the government of the Oregon territory, Calhoun sent the following message, via Waddy Thompson, to Thomas L. Clingman, a Whig congressman from North Carolina: "If you and Toombs, and Stephens and Preston (of Virginia) will unite with him [Calhoun] and his friends, in an address to the people of the South, asking them to join, without distinction of party, in holding a convention, to insist on a proper recognition of their rights, he will, this morning, in the Senate, take ground against the Clayton Compromise and defeat it, for he is satisfied that it does not do justice to the South." Quoted in Thomas L. Clingman (ed.), *Selections from the Speeches and Writings of Thomas L. Clingman* (Raleigh: John Nichols, 1877), p. 229.

126. See the report of Calhoun's speech to a public meeting in Charleston in the *Charleston Mercury,* August 21, 1848. Cf. John C. Calhoun to Henry W. Conner, July 9, 1848, in Henry W. Conner Papers.

127. John C. Calhoun to the Editor of the *Charleston Mercury,* September 1, 1848, in the *Charleston Mercury,* September 5, 1848.

128. James K. Polk to Lewis Cass, August 24, 1848, in Lewis Cass Papers, University of Michigan.

129. Quaife (ed.), *Polk Diary,* III, 502; John A. Wentworth to Edmund S. Kimberly, June 26, 1848, quoted in Pierce, *History of Chicago,* I, 399, n. 210; John Woodward Crisfield to Mrs. Mary Handy Crisfield, June 25, 1848, in John Woodward Crisfield Papers, Maryland Historical Society; Robert Tyler to James Buchanan, July 8, 1848, in James Buchanan Papers, Historical Society of Pennsylvania; Lewis Cass to Alpheus Felch, July 17, 1848, in Alpheus Felch Papers.

130. Quaife (ed.), *Polk Diary,* III, 503-4; *Congressional Globe,* 30 Cong., 1 Sess., p. 875.

131. Calhoun took credit for blocking this and every other settlement of the territorial question. See John Calhoun to Thomas G. Clemson, July 23, 1848, in Jameson (ed.), "Calhoun Correspondence," p. 760.

132. "Correspondence of the Mercury" in the *Charleston Mercury,* July 17, 1848; *Congressional Globe,* 30 Cong., 1 Sess., p. 927.

133. The bill is reprinted in full in *ibid.,* pp. 1002-5. Polk recorded Calhoun's summary of its essential features. See Quaife (ed.), *Polk Diary,* IV, 20, 22. The *Mercury* correspondent, who strongly favored the bill, mentioned that it was Dickinson's idea. See the *Charleston Mercury,* July 22, 1848.

134. Quaife (ed.), *Polk Diary,* IV, 21.

135. See above, n. 125.

136. *Congressional Globe,* 30 Cong., 1 Sess., p. 1002.

137. "From Washington" in the *Charleston Mercury,* July 28, 1848; Henry D. Gilpin to Martin Van Buren, July 28, 1848, in Martin Van Buren Papers;

Clingman, *Speeches and Writings,* p. 230; Thomas Corwin to James A. Pearce, July 14, 1848, in James A. Pearce Papers, Maryland Historical Society.

138. *Congressional Globe,* 30 Cong., 1 Sess., p. 1007.

139. *Ibid.*

140. *Ibid.,* p. 1027. The bill is reprinted in full in *ibid.,* pp. 1078-81.

141. *Ibid.,* p. 1061.

142. *Ibid.,* p. 1078.

143. Quaife (ed.), *Polk Diary,* IV, 60, 67-68.

144. James K. Polk to George Bancroft, September 15, 1848, in "Bancroft Papers," p. 105. Cf. John Catron to James K. Polk, July 12, 1848, in James K. Polk Papers.

145. Quaife (ed.), *Polk Diary,* IV, 61-62, 70-71, 75.

146. "Correspondence of the Mercury" in the *Charleston Mercury,* August 8, 1848; "The Compromise Bill in the House" in *ibid.,* August 2, 1848.

147. "From Washington" in *ibid.,* July 28, 1848. The similarity of the views expressed by Rhett and those expressed in the *Mercury*'s correspondence suggest that Rhett was the correspondent. For Rhett's views, see Henry D. Gilpin to Martin Van Buren, July 28, 1848, in Martin Van Buren Papers. Rhett was reported to have decided to support Cass shortly after Van Buren's nomination at Utica. See Dixon H. Lewis to William L. Yancey, June 27, 1848, in William L. Yancey Papers. He may have decided that the Barnburners' defection provided him an opportunity to play a significant role in the Cass administration, as well as precluding an independent movement in the South and, encouraged by Cass's friends in Congress, made the southern Whigs' opposition to the Clayton Compromise the pretext for announcing his support. This is hinted at in Gideon Welles' contemporary writings. See the quotation from his diary in Hamilton, *Zachary Taylor,* p. 107; "The Slave Power and the Cass Campaign of 1848," October 21, 1848, in Learned (ed.), Papers Relating to Gideon Welles. Cf. S. E. Benson to A. O. P. Nicholson, June 12, 1848, in Miscellaneous Papers (S. E. Benson), New York Historical Society; William R. King to James Buchanan, June 28, 1848, in James Buchanan Papers, Historical Society of Pennsylvania.

148. "Resolutions" in the *Charleston Mercury,* August 21, 1848.

149. "Democratic Meeting" in *ibid.,* August 22, 1848; James Henry Hammond to William Gilmore Simms, September 7, 1848, William Gilmore Simms to James Henry Hammond, August 29, 1848, in James Henry Hammond Papers. Rhett's speech to the meeting is reprinted in the Tallahassee *Floridian,* October 1, 1848.

150. "The Presidency—Our Position" in the *Charleston Mercury,* August 21, 1848.

151. "Politics and Business" in *ibid.,* August 22, 1848; James Henry Hammond to William Gilmore Simms, September 7, 1848, in James Henry Hammond Papers; Robert Toombs to John J. Crittenden, September 27, 1848, in Phillips (ed.), "Toombs, Stephens, Cobb Correspondence," pp. 128-29.

152. James K. Polk to Lewis Cass, August 28, 1848, in Lewis Cass Papers. Gideon Welles, a free-soiler in Washington, confessed that the move reinvigorated the party "through the whole South" and created a "probability that Cass will succeed, which until these indications seemed an . . . impossibility." Quoted in Hamilton, *Zachary Taylor,* p. 107.

153. John C. Calhoun to Thomas G. Clemson, August 11, 1848, in Jameson (ed.), "Calhoun Correspondence," p. 761.

154. David Wilmot to Salmon P. Chase, May 29, 1848, in Salmon P. Chase Papers, Historical Society of Pennsylvania.
155. William J. Brown to Lewis Cass, September 25, 1848, in Lewis Cass Papers, University of Michigan.
156. Robert Tyler to James Buchanan, July 8, 1848, in James Buchanan Papers, Historical Society of Pennsylvania; Simon Cameron to Lewis Cass, July 12, 1848, in Lewis Cass Papers, University of Michigan; Eiselin, *Rise of Protectionism in Pennsylvania*, pp. 212-13. One significant factor in the revival of the tariff issue was the drop in the price of iron.
157. Simon Cameron to James Buchanan, July 7, 1848, in James Buchanan Papers, Library of Congress. Cf. George Plitt to James Buchanan, July 11, 1848, in *ibid.*
158. Klein, *James Buchanan,* p. 205.
159. George M. Dallas to Lewis Cass, October 21, 1848, in Lewis Cass Papers, University of Michigan; Simon Cameron to Jeremiah S. Black, October 23, 1848, in Jeremiah S. Black Papers, Library of Congress.
160. William L. Marcy to P. W. Wetmore, October 11, 1848, in William L. Marcy Papers, Library of Congress. Cf. C. P. Dorman to James P. Davidson, October 15, 1848, in James P. Davidson Papers, Duke University.
161. Quaife (ed.), *Polk Diary,* IV, 166; John Addison Thomas to James K. Polk, November 2, 1848, in James K. Polk Papers; Going, *David Wilmot,* pp. 325-27.
162. James K. Polk to George M. Dallas, October 14, 1848, James K. Polk to Lewis Cass, November 4, 1848, in James K. Polk Letterbook, Library of Congress; George M. Dallas to Lewis Cass, October 21, 1848, James K. Polk to Lewis Cass, November 14, 1848, in Lewis Cass Papers, University of Michigan; William L. Marcy to P. W. Wetmore, November 1, 1848, in William L. Marcy Papers.
163. George S. Houston to Howell Cobb, October 23, 1848, in Phillips (ed.), "Toombs, Stephens, Cobb Correspondence," pp. 131-32.
164. Washington *Daily Union,* October 14, 1848; Jackson *Mississippian,* September 22, 1848; William J. Brown to Lewis Cass, September 25, 1848, John Young Mason to Lewis Cass, September 25, 1848, in Lewis Cass Papers, University of Michigan; John H. Lumpkin, James F. Cooper, George S. Houston, Thomas D. Harris to Howell Cobb, August 22, October 20, 23, 29, 1848, in Phillips (ed.), "Toombs, Stephens, Cobb Correspondence," pp. 116-17, 131, 132, 133.
165. Dixon H. Lewis to William L. Yancey, June 27, 1848, in William L. Yancey Papers. The Washington *Union* reaffirmed the commitment on August 1. See "Michigan and General Cass" in the Washington *Daily Union,* August 1, 1848.
166. Washington *Daily Union,* June 18, July 14, August 22, October 4, 27, 1848; *Daily Richmond Enquirer,* September 13, 21, 1848; Milledgeville *Federal Union,* June 20, 27, 1848; Tallahassee *Floridian,* July 1, August 5, 1848.
167. See above, notes 107, 110, 113, 114; "Gen. Cass's Nicholson Letter" in the Washington *Daily Union,* March 17, 1852.
168. "Mr. Fillmore's Abolition Platform" in the Washington *Daily Union,* September 1, 1848. From September 5 until election day the Richmond *Enquirer* carried the abolitionist statement to which Fillmore had subscribed on its masthead outlined in black. Robert Toombs, the leading Whig campaigner in Georgia, wrote: "[Fillmore's letter] has fallen upon us like a wet

blanket and has very much injured us in the State." Robert Toombs to John J. Crittenden, September 27, 1848, in Phillips (ed.), "Toombs, Stephens, Cobb Correspondence," p. 128. Cf. [George Lewis Prentiss (ed.)], *Memoir of S. S. Prentiss* (2 vols.; New York: Charles Scribner's Sons, 1881), II, 456.

169. Charles N. Webb to John C. Calhoun, September 1, 1848, in Boucher and Brooks (eds.), "Correspondence Addressed to Calhoun," p. 472.

170. William Hope Hull to Howell Cobb, July 22, 1848, quoted in Arthur Charles Cole, *The Whig Party in the South* (Washington: American Historical Association, 1913), p. 132.

171. Sergeant S. Prentiss to George Lewis Prentiss, August 25, 1848, in [Prentiss (ed.)], *Memoir of S. S. Prentiss*, II, 457.

172. "The Oregon Bill" in the Washington *Daily Union,* September 6, 1848. Cf. "The Oregon Bill" in the *Tri-Weekly Nashville Union,* September 9, 1848.

173. Nashville *Republican Banner,* September 6, 1848, quoted in Rayback, "Presidential Politics," p. 374.

174. Dixon H. Lewis to William L. Yancey, June 27, 1848, in William L. Yancey Papers; William R. King to James Buchanan, June 28, 1848, in James Buchanan Papers, Historical Society of Pennsylvania; James Jackson to Howell Cobb, July 9, 1848, in Phillips (ed.), "Toombs, Stephens, Cobb Correspondence," p. 115; "Louisiana" in the Detroit *Daily Free Press,* September 11, 1848.

175. One regular southern Democrat wrote of Van Buren's nomination at Utica: "Where can we [now] find the men to elect Cass or any other Democrat? If the hostility to slavery has become so extended as to tempt Martin Van Buren to bow low and worship at its shrine for the highest office in the gift of the people, how long will it be before our own security will require that we withdraw from those who deem themselves contaminated by our touch?" W. C. Daniels to Howell Cobb, July 1, 1848, in Phillips (ed.), "Toombs, Stephens, Cobb Correspondence," p. 114. One of Calhoun's followers wrote him that "the defection of Van Buren has shaken men's confidence in the integrity of Northern aspirants for favor." Richard K. Crallé to John C. Calhoun, July 23, 1848, in Boucher and Brooks (eds.), "Correspondence Addressed to Calhoun," p. 460. Cf. Charles N. Webb to John C. Calhoun, September 1, 1848, in *ibid.,* p. 472.

176. William Hope Hull to Howell Cobb, July 22, 1848, quoted in Cole, *The Whig Party in the South,* p. 132; "Substance of Col. Davis' Speech at Jackson," in the Jackson *Mississippian,* October 20, 1848.

177. Yancey, *Address to the People of Alabama,* pp. 6-8, 67-73; "Election Scrapbook, 1848" in the Alexander R. Boteler Papers, Duke University. By September this criticism had so stung Cass that he wrote an explanation of his early position on the Wilmot Proviso to be inserted in the Washington *Union.* See Lewis Cass to William J. Brown, September 16, 1848, in Franklin H. Elmore Papers, Library of Congress; "General Cass and the Wilmot Proviso" in the Washington *Daily Union,* September 23, 1848. The *Union,* in fact, had already begun to explain Cass's position on its own. See "From Michigan" in *ibid.,* September 22, 1848.

178. John A. Calhoun to Joseph W. Lesesne, February 19, 1848, in Joseph W. Lesesne Papers.

179. Apalachicola *Advertiser,* August 19, 1848, quoted in the Tallahassee *Floridian,* August 26, 1848. Cf. "General Cass and Millard Fillmore" in the Milledgeville *Federal Union,* August 15, 1848; Cleo Hearon, "Mississippi and

the Compromise of 1850," *Publications of the Mississippi Historical Society,* XIV (1914), 31, n. 56.

180. William Rutherford to Howell Cobb, April 16, 1850, in Phillips (ed.), "Toombs, Stephens, Cobb Correspondence," p. 189; *General Taylor and the Wilmot Proviso,* pp. 19-23. The famous Whig orator, Sergeant S. Prentiss, asked a southern crowd: "Why can't the Democrats take Old Zach? If we can stand him without any pledges or platform why can't they?" Quoted in Dallas C. Dickey, *Sergeant S. Prentiss, Whig Orator of the Old South* (Baton Rouge: Louisiana State University Press, 1945), p. 330.

181. Jefferson Davis to Barksdale and Jones, December 27, 1851, in Rowland (ed.), *Jefferson Davis, Constitutionalist,* I, 113-14.

182. James F. Cooper to Howell Cobb, November 11, 1848, in Phillips (ed.), "Toombs, Stephens, Cobb Correspondence," p. 137. On October 11, Cooper had written to Cobb that "the vote of Georgia for Cass and Butler is as sure as any future event." See *ibid.,* p. 131. Cooper's analysis of the election seems to be an accurate representation of the situation throughout the South. There is no evidence of defection by any important Democratic leader other than Yancey.

183. Hamilton, *Zachary Taylor,* pp. 132-33. Taylor obtained more than 52 per cent of the votes in the slaveholding states. See Burnham, *Presidential Ballots,* pp. 252-54. The Democratic organization in Louisiana was likened to a "well-drilled regiment of regular soldiers." See Greer, "Louisiana Politics," p. 559.

184. Taylor carried Delaware, Maryland, Kentucky, Tennessee, North Carolina, Florida, Georgia, and Louisiana.

185. Salmon P. Chase to Charles Sumner, November 27, 1848, in Bourne *et al.* (eds.), "Chase Diary and Correspondence," p. 144; Holsey Hopkins to Howell Cobb, February 13, 1849, Henry L. Benning to Howell Cobb, July 1, 1849, in Phillips (ed.), "Toombs, Stephens, Cobb Correspondence," pp. 148-49, 169; R. I. Moses to John C. Calhoun, July 26, 1849, in Boucher and Brooks (eds.), "Correspondence Addressed to Calhoun," pp. 518-19.

186. See the statement quoted in Hamilton, *Zachary Taylor,* p. 232. Cf. Henry L. Benning to Howell Cobb, July 1, 1849, in Phillips (ed.), "Toombs, Stephens, Cobb Correspondence," p. 169. According to Theodore Clark Smith, "the anti-slavery men of 1849 almost uniformly looked for allies to the Democratic Party." See *The Liberty and Free Soil Parties,* pp. 222-23.

187. *Charleston Mercury,* December 19, 1848. Cf. Holsey Hopkins to Howell Cobb, February 13, 1849, in Phillips (ed.), "Toombs, Stephens, Cobb Correspondence," pp. 148-49; William O. Lynch, "Anti-Slavery Tendencies of the Democratic Party in the Northwest, 1848-1850," *The Mississippi Valley Historical Review,* XI (December, 1924), 319-31; Roger H. Van Bolt, "The Hoosiers and the Eternal Agitation, 1848-1850," *The Indiana Magazine of History,* XLVIII (December, 1952), 331-68.

188. Holsey Hopkins to Howell Cobb, January 29, February 13, 1849, George S. Houston to Howell Cobb, June 26, 1849, in Phillips (ed.), "Toombs, Stephens, Cobb Correspondence," pp. 142-45, 148-52, 166-67; John C. Calhoun to Mrs. T. G. Clemson, January 24, 1849, John C. Calhoun to Andrew Pickens Calhoun, January 12, 1850, in Jameson (ed.), "Calhoun Correspondence," pp. 762, 780.

189. Holman Hamilton, *Prologue to Conflict, The Crisis and Compromise of 1850* (Lexington: University of Kentucky Press, 1964), pp. 135-65. The clauses of the Compromise dealing with slavery in the territories are subjected

to a precise analysis by Robert R. Russel in "What Was the Compromise of 1850?" *The Journal of Southern History,* XXII (August, 1956), 492-509.

190. Roy F. Nichols, *The Disruption of American Democracy* (New York: The Macmillan Company, 1948), pp. 288-320. At the national convention in 1860, the southern Democrats were unwilling to accept even an explicit statement of the southern version of popular sovereignty, since that had been called into question by Douglas' advocacy of the Freeport Doctrine. They objected most strongly to Douglas himself, whose fight against the LeCompton Constitution had made him a symbol of the free-soil interpretation of popular sovereignty. What they demanded, therefore, was a platform incorporating a federal slave code for the territories, which represented a genuine repudiation of the spirit that underlay free-soil sentiment. For northern Democrats this was an impossible demand.

191. Don E. Fehrenbacher, *Prelude to Greatness, Lincoln in the 1850's* (Stanford: Stanford University Press, 1962), p. 142.

Index